First Released 2019

C000170633

This book is for informational purposes only. It is sold with the understanding that
no one associated with the production of this product, including but not limited to
the author, publisher and distributers may be held liable for the use or misuse of the
information contained herein.

This information has been channelled for learning purposes and giving information
for instruction.

Spacing in this book has been purposely done for greater understanding and
learning to help the mind comprehend the vast amount of learning within the
publication.

The author is not responsible for errors or omissions and does not claim to be
qualified to offer legal, professional or medical advice to readers.

Sovereign Lord Emmanuel The Great, Caeayaron (Kryon), the Archangels, Ascended
Masters, Galactic Federations of Light, Universal Bodies of Light and the Pleiadians
of Love have requested that people purchase, directly or indirectly, legitimate copies
from Caeayaron Ltd, as this book has been given to mankind to support peace and
love and the Great Divine Purpose.

They will give rays of healings and awakening to all those who are open to greater
love and understanding and who support the Great Divine Purpose. They cannot
support and give rays of love and awakening to anyone who has not received a
legitimate copy purchased, directly, or indirectly, from Caeayaron Ltd.

To contact Caeayaron Ltd: E-mail: caeayaron@gmail.com or info@caeayaron.com

Home page: www.caeayaron.com

Join Suzanna Maria Emmanuel today on Facebook & YouTube

ISBN 978-1-912214-03-7

The Living Words from

Sovereign Lord Emmanuel The Great

Walking the Pathway of Life

Volume 1

With Suzanna Maria Emmanuel

Divine Love Element, Universal Light Grid Programmer, Divine Ascension Channel, The Word & Author of Sovereign Lord Emmanuel The Great & Caeayaron, The Great Mountain of Light

Books by same author

Learning to Dance in Cosmic Love Spaces to Find Your Inner Power to Create Change, with Ammorah, Pleiadian High Priestess.

Your History Revealed, How You Are Involved, with Halisarius, Pleiadian Chief Commander, Chief Galactic Federation Leader.

The Living Words from Sovereign Lord Emmanuel the Great, Walking the Pathway of Life, Volume 1.

The Living Words from Sovereign Lord Emmanuel the Great, Walking the Pathway of Life, Volume 2.

Dedication

I dedicate this book to THE GREAT FATHER EMMANUEL and CAEAYARON who are here to guide us back to the Divine Realms of Eternal Love. I am forever grateful for their love, and forever grateful they allowed me, as their channel, to adjust to their high love frequencies with their patience and their great love.

I dedicate this book to all the Universal Love Beings who have worked hard to help create the Pathway of Life. Without their love and dedication to our greater path, neither SOVEREIGN LORD EMMANUEL THE GREAT, nor CAEAYARON could have guided us upwards, so I am eternally grateful to them.

I dedicate this book to all who become part of the highest realms of love by listening to Divine, at this time, and gaining their Codes of Life back with CAEAYARON. How long has our journey been to come here; to this time of the Great Alignment? Thank you Great Divine, for allowing us to return to the eternal love realms. Thank you for teaching us how to walk in the love as a Great Collective.

During this book I have needed to do much forgiveness for many memories were given back to me. Though painful they are, I am also eternally grateful for them. I am grateful for having the opportunity to return to be The Messenger for Divine Love and am looking forward to seeing our gifts increase as more become a part of the Great Collective, 'gathered' into 'The Mountain of Light.'

May we forever be grateful for this time as we now have an opportunity to truly be released from the denseness and grow into our star selves again, eternally becoming part of the highest love creation.

Suzanna Maria Emmanuel

Contents

Introduction by Suzanna Maria Emmanuel

Namaste, my name is Suzanna Maria Emmanuel, and I am so pleased you desired to read these words within these Divine pages of great love for you. May your life be forever blessed because of it.

The first part of this book, originally, came to me in 2014 but then it was not yet the time to become released, as I needed to grow so much more as a channel and so much knowledge needed to come to the earth before it could become released. All is in Divine Timing and I trust all ways of Divine Love.

In late 2018 I was asked by Divine to revisit this book once again. I was in awe of the knowledge from the original writings of 2014. Once I began to work on it with SOVEREIGN LORD EMMANUEL THE GREAT, much more information came through. I was truly amazed by the flows, direction and the perfection in which the words and guidance came through. So grateful I am to Divine for these pages to come into existence at this time of the Great Divine Calling.

I have been sent by Divine to help the people understand the greater ways of love and truth. When I was little, already Divine Angels approached me and spoke to me of the great work ahead. I promised to work with them and I dedicated my life to the Divine Work at a very young age.

In 2009 SOVEREIGN LORD EMMANUEL THE GREAT approached me and began to work with me. I did not have the great connection with the highest realms of love yet, as slowly I needed to 'reconnect' greater.

I began to understand certain things and that I was on an important mission, and that no one else could bring through the Divine Assignment other than myself, but I was unaware of my greater role as a Universal Light Grid

Programmer at that time. I did not know of my role in Lemuria as the Divine Love Element. I did not know of the Universal Game.

My gifts as a channel accelerated quickly and a few months later, after opening in October 2009, I was working in front of groups as a channel.

In 2010, SOVEREIGN LORD EMMANUEL THE GREAT came through as EMMANUEL THE GREAT, and then slowly HE began to introduce himself to the groups, during the channeled messages, as LORD EMMANUEL THE GREAT. Later HE began to describe to me who HE is and how important HE is.

At the end of April 2014, KRYON approached me and began to work with me. He desired to come through for the groups quite quickly, however, it took me until November 2014 to 'allow' KRYON to begin to work with me publicly, as I had great difficulty accepting the task to be the channel of KRYON. I knew deep within me the enormity of the work coming, though on the conscious level I did not understand why my resistance with KRYON was so great, and why my mind was in so much conflict regarding the work with KRYON.

In April 2015, Whakatane, New Zealand, I was greatly privileged to work with KRYON on the first Divine Pineal Gland Activations with a beautiful group of people. I saw their spiritual growth being accelerated and much healing happened. This was the first time I 'toned' with KRYON the 'light programmes' through, and to me it sounded like 'yodeling.' The toning of the 'light programmes' grew stronger with each Divine Activation.

During the teachings of KRYON, through myself as his channel (when he taught the people in the room and for the viewers on YouTube) he began to explain the greater universal story and what the 'Divine Love Element' was. I did not realize, until much later that KRYON, being the Divine Judge as CAEAYARON, was building a Divine Court Case. Slowly, he began to bring through his greater purpose, the Lemurian Consciousness Fall, the agreements between the Galactic Federations, the Universal Game, the role of the Light Grid Programmers, the importance of Jesus as the Divine Love Element, the purpose of the Divine Activations, and how CAEAYARON and SOVEREIGN LORD EMMANUEL THE GREAT are our Great Creators.

In 2016, KRYON began to reveal his true purpose and his true name as we knew it in Lemuria to be, 'CAEAYARON,' meaning BUILDER OF LIGHT FLOWS, or BUILDER OF LIGHT FREQUENCIES.

My Divine Guides taught me how to work as a channel, a healer and a spiritual workshop facilitator; as I learned from them how to work with Spirit on a higher level. They taught me how to bring readings to people to help them in their life and to bring healings through on a higher level.

When I first opened as a spiritual medium in 2009, I first needed to have a human medium teacher to teach me, and soon after that my Guide 'Ron,' who I now know to be 'CAEAYARON,' ushered me away from my 'human teachers' to become their greater student.

Upon beginning the readings with people, I began to understand how the Master Guides in the higher love dimensions desired readings to take place, and great gifts were given to all my clients as they helped me grow from strength to strength together with my very high and loving Spiritual Guides.

Not once have my loving Spiritual Guides let me down, though hard were the lessons at times. Not all information I understood but I kept going and persevering, always seeking greater answers and evidence to state all they said was true. Proof and explanations were always given to me to help me gain greater trust in Divine Love. My strength as a channel rose greater and greater.

At times I find it hard to hear CAEAYARON talk about me as his channel in public, on his videos for YouTube. I accept all things, however, and know that Divine Wisdom is far greater than my own wisdom, though I do not understand everything at the time the information comes through.

My life purpose is to help millions to become Activated into the Divine Love of the GREAT CAEAYARON so that they can become of love and become blessed eternally in the higher love dimensions with SOVEREIGN LORD EMMANUEL THE GREAT, who is the Great Divine Love Source of all of creation in all of existence.

I am truly grateful for all that is now being shown to us, and for the Divine Guidance, to move our consciousness forward, to understand our times we are living in, and the reason why we have suffered so much as mankind.

How grateful we can be to Divine for allowing our greater purpose to be shown to us if we are willing to accept Divine Guidance, which is always our own choice.

Continuously I stand humbly before the Divine Beings of Great Love and say to them, 'Please give me enough love, strength, and wisdom to bring through what I need to in this lifetime, to help many people see your Divine Truth and your Divine Ways of Love.

May I humbly work with you, Great Divine Love, so that the people feel the great love of your Divine Selves. May I grow much stronger as a channel of Divine Love in the many years to come and may your Divine Ways of Love shine through so that the people who desire the love, understand the higher way and may grow into eternal love, everlastingly.

May your Divine Name be praised eternally, in all corners of the earth. May the people come to the Great Love and be blessed with the eternal blessings and may this earth change to love.

May the people see Divine Truth and grow into love, and then be able to bring the great love to this planet that needs it so much. May the people learn the higher ways of Divine Love, and never suffer any longer after this lifetime.'

I want to thank Stephen, my partner in life, for proofreading, and also for creating the artwork of the cover of this book.

May all who read it become eternally blessed.

Namaste, and forever I send you my eternal love from the highest Divine Realms of Love,

Suzanna Maria Emmanuel

Divine Love Element, Universal Light Grid Programmer, Divine Ascension Channel, The Word & Author of SOVEREIGN LORD EMMANUEL THE GREAT & CAEAYARON, THE GREAT MOUNTAIN OF LIGHT.

I AM Sovereign Lord Emmanuel The Great

Part 1: Who I AM as SOVEREIGN LORD EMMANUEL THE GREAT

"Greetings, I AM SOVEREIGN LORD EMMANUEL THE GREAT. I AM the GREAT MASTER TEACHER. I AM the One who made all things possible to come into creation. I AM pure love. I AM pure love consciousness. I have prepared the way for you to come home and I AM preparing the greater way for you to come home.

I, SOVEREIGN LORD EMMANUEL THE GREAT, AM an ancient Being, without a beginning and without an end. I AM eternal force, eternal power, eternal existence. I AM life, love, and pure existence. Within me, the DIVINE FATHER lies eternally, as I AM part of all that is. I AM the DIVINE FATHER, THE GREAT DIVINE SOURCE.

In my full existence I was not able to create life as my life force power is too powerful to create within. All things that come into my thoughts of my Great Divine Power cannot live, as my Divine Power is greater than all force of creation in ALL OF EXISTENCE. However, all things live, as all things exist within the power of the Great Divine, for nothing can exist outside of the Great Power of Divine.

To allow life to exist in form, my Great Divine Being, The One I AM eternally in existence within, created a part of itself to allow life to come into harmony within itself, without it being destroyed because of the enormous life-force power held within it. That Being became separated from Eternal Power Force and it was birthed into a new creation. That Being was called 'EMMANUEL,' the 'LIFE FORCE GIVER OF ALL OF CREATION.'

I AM the GREAT ETERNAL EMMANUEL, from the Eternal Sovereign Universes. I, SOVEREIGN LORD EMMANUEL THE GREAT, AM eternal. I do not have a beginning, nor do I have an end. I AM life-force creation. I AM pure love life-force creation, and I, SOVEREIGN LORD EMMANUEL THE GREAT, only desire love to be within me.

I desired to create life so much, because of my eternal love for all of life, and therefore I, SOVEREIGN LORD EMMANUEL THE GREAT, separated a part of my being, to create the way for life to come into existence.

Happy are the ones who desire to learn the higher ways of love and desire to remember the higher path. They have been awaiting my Great Return, and for them it is truly the time of celebration.

Greetings, I AM SOVEREIGN LORD EMMANUEL THE GREAT. I AM Eternal Love for all of creation who desires to become more of love."

See the Great Lord returning,

With all His precious gifts,

To give to the children of the light,

Who have been searching for the gifts of life,

For them, the Great Lord states,

'Happy you are for awaiting the Promise,

Of my Great Return,

Open your hearts of love,

Learn to forgive all the old ways,

And come back into the ways of love.'

I AM Sovereign Lord Emmanuel The Great

Part 2: CAEAYARON and the Divine Love Element come into creation

"Greetings, I AM SOVEREIGN LORD EMMANUEL THE GREAT. My eternal power of love as THE GREAT EMMANUEL is great; too great to bring other creation into life. Therefore I, SOVEREIGN LORD EMMANUEL THE GREAT, needed to create another part from my Divine Being to bring life into existence; to allow consciousness to play in the higher love universes.

This part became THE GREAT CAEAYARON, who is the Great Frequency Creator and Magnetic Force to bring all into creation and structure for consciousness to exist within, to allow life to evolve and play within.

I, SOVEREIGN LORD EMMANUEL THE GREAT, have assigned THE GREAT CAEAYARON, who is a part of my Divine Self Being (as no separation can exist in the higher love realms), to help all align upwards to the higher universal love dimensions.

I, SOVEREIGN LORD EMMANUEL THE GREAT, together with the GREAT CAEAYARON, created a sacred pathway; 'The Gate of Life,' to reach all creation with.

This pathway was called 'The Way, The Road, and The Life.' This pathway was the Divine Love Element Archangel, the Feminine part of all of creation.

The Divine Love Element Archangel allowed creation, in the higher love realms, to feel the love of our Divine Beings as our power is too great to reach any of creation. If we as Divine Makers came too close to any of our creation, then nothing could exist. However, the Divine Love Element Gate of Life, through which all flows of life came into existence, was created as the pathway to all of creation, so that all creation could be blessed with our Divine Love. This is how all came into existence, and all existence, at the beginning of creation we saw as 'good,' as all lived in the great love, and only love existed within them.

I, SOVEREIGN LORD EMMANUEL THE GREAT, desire no one to worship us, as Divine Creators, as worship is not the way of the GREAT DIVINE LOVE. We desire all to come INTO the love within their heart, for it is the heart that will always guide all upwards into greater evolution.

All of creation was created with the pathway of the heart within them, as all are connected into the Sacred Collective Heart of the Universe; that being, the Divine Love Element Archangel, 'The Gateway of Life.'

The choice was given to all of creation; which way did they desire to grow with? Would they come to the Great Universal Creators with their hearts of love? Or would they not? Would they fight the Divine Love ways? Resisting the greater way upwards would mean fighting their own greater path of evolution, as all is part of the Great Divine Pathway and no true separation can exist within the universe. Separation is an illusion.

I, SOVEREIGN LORD EMMANUEL THE GREAT, bless all those on your earth who return to the higher ways of love through 'The Great Mountain of Light,' CAEAYARON, and the Divine Love Element, sent to your earth as Suzanna Maria Emmanuel, as this is the way upwards, and the road to eternal love.

I, SOVEREIGN LORD EMMANUEL THE GREAT, will only work with one channel, my Designated Channel whose name is Suzanna Maria Emmanuel. She is the one who was created for this Divine Assignment to bring the messages from Divine to the people and to bring the life-force energies to the people, so that they can return home, and I, SOVEREIGN LORD EMMANUEL THE GREAT, have prepared the way home for those who desire to listen.

I desired all of creation to understand the Divine Path so much that I, SOVEREIGN LORD EMMANUEL THE GREAT, together with CAEAYARON, created a pathway, The Word, to allow our thoughts to come to all of creation. All of creation who desired to understand our higher thoughts of love would then be able to become blessed greater, as our Divine ways are a great blessing to all lovers of love and truth.

Those ones will certainly celebrate all their love eternally. Do you desire to return to the great love dimensions where only peace and love exists? I, SOVEREIGN LORD EMMANUEL THE GREAT, invite you to read these pages to help you return to the eternal love dimensions.

Greetings, I AM SOVEREIGN LORD EMMANUEL THE GREAT. I AM here to bring the great light before you, to shine your path before you, to help you grow eternally on the road of love."

Happy are those who see these times and say,

'Great Lord, we have been waiting for you,

We desire to understand your ways of love,

Bless us so we understand your ways greater,

Bless us in all of eternity,

Guide us to the higher ways of love,

Shine a torch for us so that we may see,

Set us free eternally,

Great Father of the Great Love.'

I AM Sovereign Lord Emmanuel The Great

Part 3: The Great Purification Flames to help you come back home

"Greetings, I AM SOVEREIGN LORD EMMANUEL THE GREAT. Come all you people who desire to listen to the great ways of wisdom. Come all you who are thirsting for spiritual waters. Come all you who hunger for spiritual food. I, SOVEREIGN LORD EMMANUEL THE GREAT, have prepared a banquet for your feasting so you never need to spiritually hunger or thirst any longer.

The Great Purification Flames, the Flames of Life, from my Divine Being SOVEREIGN LORD EMMANUEL THE GREAT, arrived on your plane during the Divine Pineal Gland Activations of CAEAYARON and HIS Sacred Universal Light Grid Programmer, my Designated Channel, Suzanna Maria Emmanuel, in August 2017.

These Great Purification Flames, the Flames of Life, are the gateway to becoming released from your human state of consciousness to return to the greater dimensions of eternal love and freedom where no limitation exists within.

Whoever receives those flames are released home. The flames of my Sacred Spirit will choose as to which dimension the activated of CAEAYARON will go to, and thus the intensity of the flames will vary with all individuals. One cannot be released from your state of being, the human consciousness existence, without the Sacred Flames to purify you, to allow you to return to your true homes.

I, therefore, SOVEREIGN LORD EMMANUEL THE GREAT (in order for the higher realms of existence to allow your return to happen), gave the Great Code Carrier, who you know as the Universal Light Grid Programmer, Divine Love Element, to the Realms as it is only the Sacred Divine Love Element, Ascension Code Carrier, who is able to be used by the Great Aligner, CAEAYARON, to bring the flames and the codes of life to the people.

Hence, when the Sacred Light Code Carrier, Divine Love Element, Light Grid Programmer came to your earth as the man Jeshua or Jesus, Jesus was able to speak to the people about a time of release coming, a time when the Great Lord, my Being, 'EMMANUEL,' the one who carries the Great Light, would return to the people to give them the 'Sacred Flames of Life.'

The Great Purification Flames of Life are the greatest treasures one can have, as they mean their eternal soul path is then their great 'Mansion of the Great Love,' where they can exist eternally within. These Mansions are the Great Love Realms where no suffering can exist within. These treasures, or great gifts, to allow the Great Mansions to open, are gifted to the people by CAEAYARON through the Divine Love Element, as this is the Eternal Gateway of Life.

Rust cannot consume these treasures, nor can any man or other being take them away from the one who has received them. It is the great promise I, SOVEREIGN LORD EMMANUEL THE GREAT, made to the people 2,000 years ago, through Jesus, my Designated Channel, that the Light Way would open, and the people would be able to receive the Great Purification Flames of Life upon my Great Return.

Who would be ready to receive them when the Great Lord would return to the people? Who would be ready within their heart to feel the Great Presence, to recognize the Great Light, to recognize the Great Existence? It is only those who would feel the Great Lord who would be awake to the times of the Great Flames of Life Eternal Existence.

Are you awake to these times when I, SOVEREIGN LORD EMMANUEL THE GREAT, have returned to you? Do you recognize The Road and The Way to the eternal dimensions of love? Do you desire to understand these sacred messages?

In the times of Jesus, once his followers understood that a Time would come of my Great Return when the people would be able to come into the great freedom eternally, he stated: *'Go and search for the people who desire to understand these words. Go and search for the people who are open within their hearts. Let them come to me so that they too can hear THE GREAT FATHER speak to them. Let them come so that they too understand the Great Path to the Great Love.*

Go and spread the news to all you see. To those who do not desire to understand, do not be concerned about them. Let them go. Wipe your hands from them and leave. However, upon finding a person who does desire to listen, invite them to come and listen for this is where they will find spiritual nourishment eternally.'

Greetings, I AM SOVEREIGN LORD EMMANUEL THE GREAT. I have returned to search for those who desire the ways of love, truth and happiness eternally."

The Great Mountain of Light is here with you,

The Great Gathering of the people has begun,

For those who desire the ways of love,

Eternally,

Come quickly all who desire to be,

Eternally free,

Come all seekers of love and truth,

Come all,

Who have been praying for my Great Return,

Blessed are those,

Who have spiritual eyes to see,

Blessed are those,

Who desire to come to the Gateway of Life,

For they will be blessed eternally.

I AM Sovereign Lord Emmanuel The Great

Part 4: Your sacred mission

"Greetings, I AM SOVEREIGN LORD EMMANUEL THE GREAT. In 2009, I, SOVEREIGN LORD EMMANUEL THE GREAT, approached my Designated Channel, Suzanna Maria Emmanuel, whose life path it is to pass the Great Purification Flames of Life and of Light, to the people whosoever are ready to receive them and whosoever desires them within their heart, and whosoever listens to the Divine Calling.

When Jesus was called 2,000 years ago to his great path, he was young. He was told he was the one who was prophesied about and that he had a great mission on the earth. Because people supported that path of Jesus, he was greatly taught by great master teachers.

In this lifetime, Suzanna was also approached when she was young. She was also told of a Divine Mission ahead of her. She promised Divine to always be there when the calling was there. However, in this lifetime she was not supported in the way Jesus was. Hence, her awakening was more difficult.

When she awoke in 2009 to the Divine Calling, because she was not supported by others, it was more difficult for her to accept, or remember, the importance of her being in this world, upon your plane.

Very early on she understood that she had carried the sacred mission of SOVEREIGN LORD EMMANUEL THE GREAT before in a previous lifetime.

I, SOVEREIGN LORD EMMANUEL THE GREAT, approached my channel very gently, as I, DIVINE LOVE, know Suzanna very well. Because she is honest and pure within her heart, and the humblest person living upon your plane, I, SOVEREIGN LORD EMMANUEL THE GREAT, knew if I was to make known my existence, my great purpose to her, and my identity, very early on, she would refuse to carry on working with Divine.

We, her Divine Masters, taught her gently and steadily about her greater purpose. Step by step we moved her forward to help her understand the greater importance of her existence here upon your planet.

You also are taught gently, steadily and greatly about your purpose upon your planet, as each of you has a vital mission to complete. Whether you complete your vital mission is your choice.

Your mission you will not fully recognize in this life until you come to the Realms of Love with your 'Sacred Talents'; the greatest of which is the Holy Sacred Purification Flames of Love and Freedom.

These are given to you when you come to the Sacred Divine Activations with CAEAYARON, who activates your Sacred Codes to return to the Sacred Existence of Life in the greater love dimensions.

You are then seen as to be spiritually 'resurrected' in the higher existence, as the higher existence is the place where you originally come from. In the time of the Great Fall, you fell into a spiritual 'death.' A 'death' without the possibility of you ever returning to the greater states of life, unless a Gateway of Life was formed. Your spiritual death meant the loss of your Great Flames of Life and of possible existence in the higher love dimensions.

Therefore, the quest to receive back the Great Sacred Flames has been a great quest for you personally. The 'Way' was provided for you to gain back those Sacred Flames if you desired to awaken to the call of Divine Love in your timeline.

This would be the greatest gift for those who would awaken to the Divine Call; the gift to find the way back to your 'Home of Love.'

I, THE GREAT FATHER, say to everyone who receives the Divine Flames of Love from my Being, SOVEREIGN LORD EMMANUEL THE GREAT, 'Welcome to the times of learning. Welcome to the times of becoming present with who you are. Welcome to the times when you can truly understand your greater path.'

There is not a path that is greater than this one; the path of returning home. This path is the 'Home to the Heart,' for your Great Enlightened Heart is great. Your Great Enlightened Heart is where you exist in the greater dimensions.

Therefore, the Sacred Flames can also be called the 'Resurrection of Life Flames,' where you enter a sacred holy state between Great Divine and you. There you are in those spaces of eternal wisdom and love, constantly cared for by Great Divine Love.

Blessed are those who have received these writings, for in these writings, I, SOVEREIGN LORD EMMANUEL THE GREAT, have given gifts, so whoever reads these pages, and meditates upon the words, may open their heart to the greater road of love. Those ones who awaken to the Great Calling at this time, and act upon it, are truly blessed eternally.

These gifts are eternal gifts of love. I AM Divine Love, and I support all who desire to understand these ways of love. Always learn to trust in the highest Divine Ways of Love. Those who desire the highest Divine Love, will always find that all things are taken care of. They are truly blessed.

Begin to understand the power of trust in the Great Divine. Know your freedom is close when you desire to understand these words of love. The wise ones will not consider these words to be foolish. They will recognize these words are from the highest wisdom and love. The wise ones know these ways, for these ways, are within them. Unlike the foolish ones who will not desire these ways. They are unwise and will never come into love.

Do you desire the ways of love and peace? Do you desire to understand the higher flows of frequencies upon your earth now and those which are coming to your earth? Do you desire to understand why you are in the Age of Awakening?

Welcome home. Greetings, I AM SOVEREIGN LORD EMMANUEL THE GREAT. I AM here to help you find the way home to the love. I AM here to help you find your Sacred Talents to gain your place in the Divine Realms of Great Love."

It is within the heart you awaken,

To the precious love within you,

Awaken dear ones,

Hear the Divine Call happening,

Awaken to Divine Love,

Find the love within you,

Find the peace within you,

Come home to the love,

Become of love.

I AM Sovereign Lord Emmanuel The Great

Part 5: We come in love to you

"Greetings, I AM SOVEREIGN LORD EMMANUEL THE GREAT. I AM from Supreme Spaces of Divine Eternal Love and Divine Eternal Light. I AM here to guide you, and millions of people, to peace and love in their hearts. I AM here to help you have the great joy in your life and to find the great peace in your hearts.

Mankind has been on a quest for thousands of years of how to find peace back in the heart and how to return to true unity. Many leaders have come, and many leaders have gone, and yet no one has found the answer to the greatest question, which is, 'Who can bring peace?'

At this time, I would like to speak to your heart, to help you find the greatest truth within you. I would like to speak to your mind and to settle it down into peace, to help you understand it is recognized and we desire to help you find peace.

We come in love to you. We come with the greatest joy to you. We bring you the knowledge and the wisdom of the Ancients with us. We are Eternal Beings in the Greatest Light and we sing to you songs of Eternal Truth of Wisdom and of Love and Light.

For you, living upon your earth, you need direction and spiritual understanding. Many do not understand how strong their spiritual existence is, but all come from spirit, and thus all, upon your planet, need to understand true spiritual direction.

In all your lifetimes upon your planet, you searched for greater spiritual truth, and the great confusion upon your earth created many conflicts within you. Many of you fear to go deeper. Many people fear greater spiritual truth to discover another path. Many people fear not knowing what the future holds. Therefore, would you not consider it to be important to gain greater direction and understanding?

Do you have the courage to look within greater? Do you have the courage to see a higher path? Do you desire to find the higher path of love and truth?

Please join us through these pages to help you understand how to find peace in your life and to help you find the answers to the age-old question, 'How to find peace in a world troubled by pain.'

Greetings, I AM SOVEREIGN LORD EMMANUEL THE GREAT, Divine Universal Master of the Great Universe. I AM here to guide you home to the eternal love dimensions. All is your choice. Do you desire to learn how to come home?"

Finding peace within you,

Is what you always desired to find,

In your prayers you always asked:

'Great Lord, how can we find peace within?'

I, The Great Lord say in reply,

'Go within your heart of love,

Awaken your heart of love,

And you will find the answers within.'

I AM Sovereign Lord Emmanuel The Great

Part 6: The treasures within your heart

"Greetings, I AM SOVEREIGN MASTER, LORD EMMANUEL THE GREAT, and I speak to you now with my Great Love to your heart.

In your heart, you will find the grandest treasures of truth. Within your heart are many dimensions of play and within your heart are many answers to be found.

We ask you, when you read these pages of this book, to close your mind off from thinking and instead feel within your heart.

When your heart is open to the Great Light, that is found within these pages, it will awaken you, and the Great Light will reach within your heart to give you your truth. Then you will find greater peace within your life.

The joy that can be found in your life right now, in this very moment of your existence, can be yours to have. It can be found in every moment of your life. Not only in good times but also in the times when you experience trouble, sickness, and situations which are difficult for you to cope with.

The ones who find these treasures of peace and joy, are finding it within their heart as they reach within and find their peace, even though their lives may not always be of peace.

Therefore, we teach you to learn to be in your heart.

Learn to understand the depths within your being, for within the deepest parts is where your eternal truth is. This is where the higher connections exist within. You will begin to understand you are not only your human self, but you are connected to a Higher Existence.

Again, I, SOVEREIGN LORD EMMANUEL THE GREAT, ask you to listen with your heart, for with the heart you will understand these lessons. With the heart, you will hear us speaking to you.

Your mind may not comprehend these deeper levels of our Being. Your mind does not understand your Greater Light Existence. It understands your human existence and it is there to help you through your days. However, your heart is eternal, and it is there you will find your fountains of great wisdom.

Your mind understands your life you have now. It calculates decisions based on your experiences and the experiences of others. It does not understand deeper love. It does not understand greater things.

In the heart, you will find the deeper connections and the deeper flows. Therefore, it is so important to learn to be in the heart.

The deeper flows are the deeper existences. You are an exquisite being. You were created with the purpose of being in the Greatness of your Great Love and now you are able to return to your Greater Self. You are able to return to your greater existence.

In the Greater Realms of Light, I see you as already perfect. Hence, you can claim this perfection now as no sin exists in the eyes of Divine Love.

However, you fell away from the Great Love, but now you have the opportunity to come back to the Great Love of Divine. This is the gift I, SOVEREIGN LORD EMMANUEL THE GREAT, created for you. This is why I, SOVEREIGN LORD EMMANUEL THE GREAT, sent my Designated Divine Love Ascension Gateway to your plane, to help you understand how to come back.

Jesus stated to the people, *'I am perfect as my light is perfect. I am who I am. I stand in Union with THE GREAT FATHER who is perfect, and THE GREAT FATHER speaks truth. In all things, in the Greater Heavens, I am already perfect.'*

It is this knowledge that my Designated Channel, Jesus, spoke of to the people 2,000 years ago. *'I am perfect.'*

This was important knowledge for the people in those days as the people did not believe in eternal perfection, or that the people were blessed in the realms above. They believed in judgment greatly and walked in fear with their burdens on their shoulders.

Jesus showed the way to the 'New Path of Enlightenment.' He could speak like this to the people as he was the 'Bringer of Truth and of Light.' He spoke truth and he was the truth.

It is the same with my 'Designated Channel,' 'Designated Messenger,' 'Designated Word,' I bring to the earth in your time you are living in.

I promised to return did I not? I could only return in the same way I came in the first place; through my Designated Channel. This time it is not a man I speak through, but a beautiful woman.

Why is it that the people have forgotten how I, as THE GREAT SOVEREIGN LORD, work with the people? Because you have been filled with untruth. You have been kept asleep and confused and Jesus was made out to be the 'Holy One.' But he never claimed to be the 'Holy One.'

Jesus stated, *'I am a messenger of THE GREAT FATHER. It is HIS words you hear, not mine. I speak of no wisdom from my own self. The wisdom you hear is the Wisdom from Above, for all the Great Wisdom from THE GREAT FATHER EMMANUEL is eternal and perfect as HE is Everlasting and Eternal Wisdom. There is no greater wisdom than the wisdom from THE GREAT FATHER EMMANUEL, and we are part of that Great Wisdom.*

It is where we will all return to, for you also are part of that Great Wisdom. Learn to listen with your heart instead of your head and your fear. Go within and search deeper within and you too will find truth and peace. Go within.'

Greetings. I AM SOVEREIGN LORD EMMANUEL THE GREAT. I AM here to guide you to your greatest treasures, not of the earth, but from the greatest heavens. Happy are those who have prayed for this time to come and who are recognizing these times of awakening to the power of love."

The treasures within you,

Are found within your heart,

These treasures are worth more,

Than all the finest gems upon your earth.

These treasures are spiritual,

They will lead you to the greater treasures,

In the love of eternal freedom and happiness.

Will your heart awaken to the higher path?

Will you desire to open,

To your Divine treasures within?

I AM Sovereign Lord Emmanuel The Great

Part 7: Creation created with Divine Love

"Greetings, I AM SOVEREIGN LORD EMMANUEL THE GREAT. In this lesson, let us discover how each person upon your plane, and each being upon your plane, was created with the purest love; with intense Divine Love.

Divine Love creates. Divine Love is pure joy. Divine Love is pure bliss and it understands all levels of existence very well. Divine Love is intelligent, and when Divine Love is intense and divinely purposed, it becomes a creation within itself.

The human is not part of the animal world. You were created with far greater intelligence than the animal. However, the animals are part of you and they are here to teach you how to become more of love. They serve a greater reason than you are aware of.

Without the animal race, without the fish and life in the seas, without the insects, you would cease to exist. All life depends on each other. When all flows in harmony, all work in purpose together.

The animals upon your plane were created to help you return to your heart. The animal kingdom was created to help you remember the love you have within your heart.

Many people upon your plane believe you are part of the animal kingdom, and thus many believe you can behave the same as the animals in many ways.

We say you are not from the animal kingdom. You were created with intelligence, with desire, with great love, care, and a great deal of thought because you have a far greater purpose than the animals.

You were created with power and you have the power within you to go deeper. You will find this power only, however, when you choose to return to your spiritual heart.

Your spiritual heart has many dwellings within it. When you open one door to a dwelling, others will open. Each dwelling has higher gifts for you to discover. Therefore, it is now important to discover the heart of love for you are able to step into higher frequencies of Love and Greatness.

You are opening to higher learnings by opening your heart and entering within it.

Your quest to find peace has been long and it has always been within you to find it. Your quest, your greatest quest, is to return to the heart. Feel the heart and be in the heart and you will receive the peace and the joy you have been looking for.

The heart will awaken you to states of life and love. Love is the only way to live, as love brings eternal existence in the love foundations. When one learns to open the dimensions of the heart of love, one will find eternal joy and source of peace, for only love and peace exists in the heart of love when one can find the heart of love. It awakens and empowers life-force energies to create life with, for no life can exist without the heart of love. All carry the heart of love which gives life to you and which gives purpose to you.

To find the greater dimensions of love within the heart, is to go deeper within and find the expression of pure love. It is in that love all love is created and all peace can come within.

Greetings, I AM SOVEREIGN LORD EMMANUEL THE GREAT, the Great Divine Master of the Universal Love and Peace. I AM here to guide you to your greater wisdom, to your greater evolution for those who desire to grow within their higher thoughts of love."

When you ask my Divine Being,

'How is it that I can find the great peace,

Great Lord Emmanuel?'

I then answer you in this way,

'Keep praying that you awaken,

To the love within you,

Especially during these times,

Of the light rising upon your earth,

Have the courage to go within,

You will then find the doors of your heart,

Opening to your true self,

You will then find your greater truth.'

I AM Sovereign Lord Emmanuel The Great

Part 8: Why is it difficult to stay within your heart?

"Greetings, I AM SOVEREIGN LORD EMMANUEL THE GREAT. I have returned to your people. I use my Designated Channel, Suzanna Maria Emmanuel, who comes from Great Divine Spaces, to bring these Great Divine Messages to the people.

You are blessed when you are reading these words, for within the words, within these pages, you will be healed with Divine Love from my Great Being, SOVEREIGN LORD EMMANUEL THE GREAT. I AM the Great Divine Teacher. I AM the 'Way of Life, Freedom and Eternal Power.'

A long, long time ago, I promised I would return to help the people to find the 'Greater Road to Freedom.'

'When will this be?' the people asked.

I then spoke through my channel Jesus. I, SOVEREIGN LORD EMMANUEL THE GREAT, answered, *'I will return when the people are ready to find the Great Light and are ready to return to the Great Heart.'*

I, as a Great Divine Master of Great Love, ask you now, 'Are you ready to discover your greater depth? Are you ready to return to the love of your spiritual heart? Are you ready to return to the Great Heart of Life?'

Your heart to us is beautiful and precious, and your life is important to us. Each person is important, and each person carries greatness within.

The heart always has been the song of the human. Many have sung about the heart. Many have had broken hearts, and many have felt the intense yearnings of returning 'home.' Though, you may ask, 'Where is home?'

Many have desired to find love, but how does one find it? How does one begin to search for it?

These questions are not new, for these same questions the ancient people also asked.

Within your heart lies incredible power and wisdom. Can you imagine for a moment, if you learned to focus upon your heart in your daily life, how much could you learn as a human being?

Imagine, if you came together as a group to discuss your spiritual hearts, how you discovered yourself during the week and how you reached into the depths of your beings and found greater answers, if you could do this together, your wisdom would increase as you would discover greatness together.

We say to you as Loving Beings: 'Learn to look within yourselves. Learn not to look outside of yourselves. Learn not to turn to others for advice but instead learn to turn to your inner voice within your heart. Learn not to find information first from other people for your deepest questions, but first find the voice within your heart to find the answers deep within your heart.'

In your heart, you will find encouragement to move towards your higher dreams. Many people look to other people for encouragement and support. We say there is nothing wrong with looking to others for support. Having support is important. However, you must also learn to find the deep courage from within, for then you find your deeper power of courage.

The true encouragement you need for your dreams and your desires lie within your heart. It is you who powers up the dreams with your inner desire and your inner fire.

Many people desire to reach a dream but are easily put off by another's comment or thoughts.

When this happens, many forget to look within, and they give up on the dream. You could have reached the great dream had you stayed on the path of your heart.

Why is it so difficult for many to stay in their heart? Is this perhaps because many have forgotten how to be in the heart? Is it because many have paid great amounts of attention to the views and perspectives of others, that you forgot to look within, to find the encouragement within?

When one veers off the path of their heart, one will feel the pain and will become lost in the spaces of frustration and sadness.

It is far better to stay in your heart and to feel the warmth and determination of your fire within, and to keep following the deeper path, for then you will find what you have been seeking. Help is always given to those who truly desire the higher path of Great Love.

We desire to steer you and guide you to a higher path of love. We can only do this when you desire it, for when you desire our Great Love for you, your heart path opens, and we can then bless it greatly.

We are teaching you to play in the heart, for the heart gives you greater understanding you are eternal beings of Light. You are connected to the Great Light. The Great Light is within All because All is part of the All Great Love of the Great Divine.

Greetings, I AM SOVEREIGN LORD EMMANUEL THE GREAT. I speak to those who desire the love upon your plane to grow. I speak to those who remember the Greatness and the Love."

Look within your heart,

For comfort,

Strength and great direction,

Learn to turn inwards for higher guidance,

Do not constantly seek the guidance of others,

But learn to see,

All is found within your heart.

Discover the path of your heart,

Awaken to the power,

Within your heart of love.

I AM Sovereign Lord Emmanuel The Great

Part 9: Learning to be in the Being Space

"Greetings, I AM SOVEREIGN LORD EMMANUEL THE GREAT. I AM here because of my Great Divine Love for the people. When I say: 'For the people,' I love everyone individually as well as a collective race together.

You are blessed by reading these words. This is the first book I, SOVEREIGN LORD EMMANUEL THE GREAT, have given to my Designated Channel Suzanna Maria Emmanuel in this lifetime. The stronger she becomes as my Divine Word, the greater the flows of healing will be for the people.

You are in a time when you will see the Great Light expanding within the people who desire it. Blessed are those who are awake to these times and who rejoice about the Great Light returning within their hearts, for you are welcomed by us as Divine Beings. We enjoy teaching you. We enjoy guiding you to greatness and love.

Let us carry on to this lesson. I invite you to ponder upon the Being Space and what this means to you.

The Being Space is a space of being in the heart. Many people upon your plane call it 'the nothingness,' or a 'state of nothingness.'

We say it is far from 'nothing,' for this space is a state of learning to be with your deeper soul; the deeper part that flows eternally within you.

You are far from only human.

You exist on many levels. Your human level you can comprehend well. You look at your bodies and you see your physical self. You also live in many other dimensions and these dimensions are trying to reach you with their knowledge.

They cannot reach you until you open the deeper chambers within your spiritual heart.

You all carry enormous amounts of potential to reach all your dreams and your desires. Your higher selves and your dimensions on the higher levels constantly desire to feed you with light and information to heal your life.

However, you can only connect with this knowledge if you reach within the quiet of your heart and are willing to go deep within the heart.

It is in the heart you can connect to your Higher Self and your Higher Light Dimensions. It is within the heart your highest Spirit Guides, who are Beings of Great Love, can give you the wisdom and can give you a deeper understanding of your life. It is where you can find great strength. If you learned to do this, you would solve many of your issues on your plane and in your life.

The mind cannot comprehend these deeper levels without the heart understanding. Great numbers of your children are connected to their hearts and feel within their hearts. It is when they grow up, they begin to believe their minds hold more power than their hearts.

This is all an illusion, for within your heart you have the power and all the knowledge within you.

On your plane logic of the mind is more focused upon than reaching within intuitive wisdom. We say to you, it is the intuitive wisdom from your heart that can lead you to deeper joy in your life. It is the logical mind that throws the intuitive wisdom out of balance.

You were created with an incredible amount of intuition and logic. Both working together create an incredible partnership. Each contributes greatly to create a life filled with greatness and love. Each side has diverse views on life.

Over the course of your discoveries of life together you began to lose faith in the intuitive heart and began to believe in the logical mind more. This created a greater sense of separation, for you will find the deeper connection only in the deeper heart of your being. Hence, because of the deeper separation, you created realities together and you stepped deeper into the fear and the pain of the mind.

The heart does not carry the pain or fear. The heart carries love and truth. The mind is deceiving. You must learn to figure out which is more beneficial for you. This will require some deep thought.

There was a time, a long, long time ago, in ancient times, when you created with the hearts together on higher levels. You constantly asked for the Great Wisdom of the Great Knowing, the Great Divine, and hence your creation came from deeper levels of wisdom and love.

Now, many on your plane have forgotten to live from the intuitive heart. The mind has created more pain and fear than in all times of your history together.

It is now you must find the intuitive heart once again. This is where we are guiding you. Within your spiritual heart are the deeper places within yourself.

Are you ready to discover your true self? Are you ready to discover your wisdom within you?

We desire to guide you to your Greater Self. We ask you, 'Are you ready to discover your Greater Wisdom?'

Greetings, I AM SOVEREIGN LORD EMMANUEL THE GREAT. I AM here to guide you upwards to 'The Great Mountain of Light,' the GREAT CAEAYARON, to help you find your greater keys of life, to help you become part of the eternal love dimensions."

To understand your greater path,

Awaken to the times you are living in,

Awaken to your greater purpose,

Your greater purpose is to learn,

To work collectively within your hearts.

Learn to come back to the flows of love,

Learn to connect to Divine Wisdom,

To Divine Truth,

To Divine Guidance.

I AM Sovereign Lord Emmanuel The Great

Part 10: Why many people fear going deep within

"Greetings, I AM SOVEREIGN LORD EMMANUEL THE GREAT. I AM here with you, guiding you to a higher path of Great Love. The last time people heard my words through my Designated Channel, my Divine Word Pathway, Jesus, was 2,000 years ago.

Jesus was a faithful scribe. He wrote all teachings down. He wrote about his life, his journeys, and his experiences. So much was destroyed.

We are here to bring it back to life so that you can understand that nothing can truly be destroyed but all is preserved.

Many people upon your plane are afraid of learning the deeper levels within. They are afraid of finding a deeper truth.

What are they afraid of? They are afraid to face their deeper selves and their deeper truth.

When you were pure beings it was natural to go within because you were close to spirit. Your spirit within you connects you to higher levels. Each person, regardless of how they live their life upon your earth in this existence, is connected to their spirit.

At times, in different lifetimes, your spirit distanced itself from you as you desired to learn and experience deep separation from Divine Love. It was important to you to help you understand pain and suffering, to help you move deeper within your heart once the time was right to return to the path of the Great Love.

Why was this important to discover for you? Because you collectively chose to understand the path of knowledge and wisdom, away from the path of love within you. You desired to understand the great separation. You also desired to understand how to gain greater wisdom from separation so that you could become wiser into the future, to allow you to create a higher choice for yourself.

You desired, so much on a soul level, to come back into the great collective fold once again when the Great Divine Call would be present upon your earth. You prayed within your heart, both in spirit and on earth, that you would be ready for the Divine Call, as this would be your opportunity to go 'home' to the loving dimensions.

Jesus always talked about these dimensions also. '*Pray you will awaken in the times when THE GREAT FATHER EMMANUEL will speak to your hearts again. It is then it will be necessary to stand strong within your heart. Work within your hearts. Find quiet within your heart. Desire to return to the Loving Union as from love you came.*

Pray you will have the strength within you to heed the call so that you can return. Those who find their love within their hearts will awaken when THE GREAT FATHER EMMANUEL returns with his Divine Word. It is then the greater pathway will open for you.'

Often, people are fearful of going deeper and feeling within, as many, when they are aware of their inner self, feel the emotions they have been dealing with in their life. They feel the areas of pain and this is why many hide from their inner truth. Many of you feel as if you face your 'demons' within as you would often call it.

We say this is far from the truth because there is only beauty found within you. Within each person, there is a large amount of beauty, regardless of personal experiences in lifetimes.

Yes, choices may have been made that were not pure and loving, but in those choices, you also learned to differentiate good (greatness filled with joy and love) from experiences you may call bad (pain, suffering, and anger) which was your right to discover upon your plane.

Here I will mention, as a Wise Ancient Divine Master, that in truth there is no good or bad, for all is an experience of greater flow to understand. In the pain and in the greatness, you find your deeper truth within.

The play you are in on your earth is the play of freedom. The play of freedom is to learn the plays of greatness and the suffering and then to learn to grow towards the love and move away from the pain.

In many lifetimes you desired to only discover the pain and thus you placed yourselves in painful situations to help you discover your heart. You reached many goals within your evolutionary cycle and you learned to progress.

Many of you are here upon this plane at this time to reach a goal together; to create an awareness that all must be changed for the greater good for all.

You have reached this stage of evolution of the Great Heart. This is the evolutionary stage of the return to the Sacred Inner Illuminated Heart.

The darkness also knows the times and cycles. They know the power of the Sacred Heart. When you choose to return to the Sacred Chambers of your Sacred Heart, you will return to your inner power and your inner truth.

This is the great truth of all of existence because you know this truth within you on deep levels. Many have great difficulty to return to the Sacred Heart of the Great Love.

The Spirit within the Sacred Heart is alive with love, and when the Sacred Heart begins to live, it begins to beat with its sacred glory. This is the sacred glory of your spirit and your inner voice.

Your inner voice has beauty, love, and inner wisdom. It is this inner wisdom that is more precious to you than all precious gems upon your plane. Nothing can compare to its value.

Greetings, I AM SOVEREIGN LORD EMMANUEL, I AM here to guide you to your eternal treasures of wisdom and love."

The treasures within your heart,

Are more precious,

Than all the finest treasures,

Found upon your earth,

For how can you compare treasures of earth,

To the eternal spiritual treasures?

Earthly treasures,

Cannot give you eternal life,

Only spiritual treasures,

Can give you everlasting life,

Everlasting wisdom, love and beauty.

You can only find these greatest treasures,

Within your inner Sacred Heart of Love.

Awaken to the heart within,

Desire to return,

To the Great Path of the Great Love.

I AM Sovereign Lord Emmanuel The Great

Part 11: Learning to find eternal wisdom

"Greetings, I AM SOVEREIGN LORD EMMANUEL THE GREAT. A long, long time ago, a man questioned how great things could be found. This man had great difficulty understanding spiritual treasures and thus approached my channel upon your plane, commonly known as The Great Teacher, Jesus.

After this man had listened to the teachings of Jesus about finding the great treasures, which are far greater than silver and gold found upon your earth, he approached him to ask him how he could find them.

This man had accumulated wealth greater than many of the men in the local towns. For him, accumulated wealth had greater importance than all other things.

For this man, to be with the poor people was disgusting to him. He often called the poor the 'Leper Class' as many of the richer people did in those days.

Jesus knew about this man. He knew about the suffering and the emptiness within his heart also. He knew about his great fear of losing all his precious metals and money.

In his own way, he had created himself as a King of all his earthly possessions, and because of the power he felt within, because of his riches, he was greatly admired by many.

Thus, the topic of finding deeper treasures was difficult for him to understand. He heard the teaching, from Jesus, how rust consumes the earthly treasures and how when one goes to the heavens, *'The treasures of the earth cannot be taken with him, but the one who finds the eternal spiritual treasures of love and truth will have everlasting treasures in the Greater Heavens.'*

This man heard from Jesus; *'These spiritual treasures will be taken with the people who find these on their everlasting journeys, and they will grow eternally, always multiplying themselves many times in great value. The ones who find these spiritual treasures will be richer than all other people upon the earth who have not found these spiritual treasures.'*

Because this man could not relate to spiritual teachings, he asked Jesus where to find these spiritual treasures that would never be consumed by rust and never be eaten by moths. This was his greatest concern.

Jesus looked kindly upon the man. He was greatly aware of the pain this man had plagued upon the people who were not as rich as him.

Jesus said in a wise and loving way, *'The treasures you seek are within your heart. Before you can reach the greatest treasures, one must learn to let go of all earthly possessions for it is only then that the greatest gold and treasures of the everlasting treasures can be found by the seeker.'*

This left this man rather startled. What did Jesus mean by this? How did he respond to these teachings?

This man left Jesus as he was bewildered by this teaching. He did not comprehend what the teaching was about and believed that Jesus was not speaking with sense and believed Jesus was not right in his mind.

However, Jesus was not speaking of the earthly treasures but of everlasting treasures. It did not matter how poor or rich the people were, but what did matter was where the focus was placed upon.

Here in this teaching, it did not matter the amount of wealth one had accumulated. If the one who had accumulated wealth was open enough to find truth within their heart, then that one would be materially and spiritually blessed. All lovers of truth will always be rich with all they need with wisdom and with love.

Please, friends, we do not ask you to sell your belongings or to give your belongings away for they are your earthly treasures. We ask you not to stop your abundance flows in your life, but we are encouraging you to look within your heart more.

When you look within your heart you can have both, you can have all your earthly abundance treasures and you can also find your deeper spiritual treasures.

The ones who understand this teaching can flow with more abundance, as they understand the key to finding true abundance is to be spiritually content with all things, for then all things owned are multiplied. Appreciation from the heart of love multiplies earthly treasures. Contentment from the heart of love multiplies earthly treasures. Greed and discontent can lead to misery and great loss.

Happiness is found by those who find the road to the heart for therein lies everlasting knowledge, wisdom, peace, joy, and great love.

It is the treasures found in the greatest healings upon your plane at this present time now, that you will find the greatest treasures in. It is in these treasures all eternal valuables are found. It is these eternal treasures, in the highest realms of love, you have been searching for.

You are in a time of learning to understand that all things I spoke to the people about, through my channel Jesus, 2,000 years ago, are coming true to you at this time. The words are now coming through my Designated Channel, Suzanna Maria Emmanuel. No one else will I use to bring my words through. No one else has received the assignment to be the channel to bring the everlasting sayings through to your plane, other than my Designated Channel, Suzanna Maria Emmanuel, who I created to be the channel of all things everlasting, to bring you into the peace, into the love realms of eternal glory.

These were the same teachings the people heard Jesus speak about 2,000 years ago.

'A time will come when you will hear THE GREAT FATHER speak to you about the great treasures of the highest kingdom of his domain. HE will gather the people to the Holy Mountain who will desire the healings and the freedom. They will see the Light of THE GREAT FATHER, and will glorify his Being and say, 'Privileged we are for seeing THE TRUTH, THE WAY, THE FREEDOM, for there is no other way the great treasures can be reached.'

Jesus prophesied a time coming when the people would understand 'truth' and what it would mean for them. He said, that this truth, *'Would lead the people to everlasting freedom where no pain exists, no food shortages, no sickness, and no warring, for all things of the old cannot exist in the new ways of freedom.'*

The people wanted to understand more, but Jesus did not speak any longer. *'I must go and rest now,'* he said. *'Please leave me.'*

The people left puzzled, bewildered and hopeful.

Greetings, I AM SOVEREIGN LORD EMMANUEL THE GREAT. I AM here to bring you to the times of love within your heart. Understand that I AM the Divine Being, the same one who spoke through Jesus, my Designated Channel. I have returned."

The times of the promise,

Of the everlasting prophecies are here today.

I, Emmanuel The Great, have returned,

To call those who desire to come,

To the Holy Mountain of Healing.

Will you desire to receive,

Your Great Purification Flames of Love?

Will you desire to return,

To the Great Kingdom of Great Love?

Will you desire to become of Love?

I AM Sovereign Lord Emmanuel The Great

Part 12: Learning to change

"Greetings, I AM SOVEREIGN LORD EMMANUEL THE GREAT. Here I speak from my Ancient Divine Wisdom. I AM an eternal Master of Greatness and Great Love. I AM here to speak to your hearts, to awaken you deeper to your greater heart and treasures.

I AM THE GREAT FATHER with eternal wisdom and flow. You may also call me the Great Mother of Creation, as I, SOVEREIGN LORD EMMANUEL THE GREAT, do not have gender.

I AM pure Love Consciousness. I AM pure love. I hold pure love for you, therefore all things became created to allow it to exist because of my eternal love for you. I desired you to live. My Divine Purpose was for all to expand in great love and to learn how to become the great beings of love.

It was never for you to suffer, for that was not part of Divine Plan. I did not desire you to understand death. Hunger, war, fear, anger, pain and all the suffering of the human was not my creation. My creation was perfect, and when all things were in Divine Love, it was perfect. I said to all of creation, 'Look, it is perfect. All things are in alignment with my great desire. I desire all to grow into great strength and love.'

This is how I, as the DIVINE SOURCE, also grow. When all creation grows into greater love, I also expand, because I allow my own expansion to happen. How can I expand into greater love when love does not exist within my own creation? I cannot then expand. I desire to expand to bring more love to all creation. I desire to bring you all the things you desire.

I, SOVEREIGN LORD EMMANUEL THE GREAT, listen to all desires of the people on your plane. But are the people ready to desire my Divine Being, SOVEREIGN LORD EMMANUEL THE GREAT? Do you desire to understand how to gain more peace and love within your own heart? Do you desire to understand the higher ways of love? Do you desire to have peace and love on your earth?

I AM aware you see your life differently to the way we as Divine Masters see your life. We, as a Great Collective of Love Beings, see your life from a higher Divine Perspective, and you see your life with a much denser perspective.

Our Divine Perspective is wise, filled with joy and love for you. We are far beyond your anger and fear, for in our Divine Realms we do not have any disharmony. We are pure love.

Thus, we always invite you to come and join us in the Light to enjoy our healings because we have a great love for you.

Do you enjoy our healings? Do you enjoy our Great Love for you? We help you to return to the Love of your Great Heart.

Your heart is beautiful and to us, it is as a shining light. For those who desire the greater healings, their light within their heart is bright and joyful. It becomes stronger.

The more light you carry within your Sacred Heart, the greater the power you have within. The deeper you can reach within your power of love, the greater you can understand the Great Love connection the Universe has for you.

You are a Sacred Being of Great Love and Great Purpose. You are designed to be beings of love, and once you discover it you will become greater love and strength.

Jesus always brought through the importance of finding great strength from within. He taught the people in those days to sit with the light and to draw the strength of the light within them.

The people desired to understand it because they knew he spoke of truth; the ones who accepted it. You too are living in great times when you desire to connect and open to the Great Light.

The greater your light connection becomes and the more power you will find within, the greater your peace becomes.

Greetings, I AM SOVEREIGN LORD EMMANUEL THE GREAT. Happy are those who desire to flow with these words, for they are the wise ones. Stay in your wisdom and in your love, and then you too will find the path to the eternal blessings of love."

From love you were created,

From the womb of Sacred Love,

You were born.

When all things were good,

All creation was beautiful,

In the eyes of my Divine Love.

I said to all those who desired more love,

'Go and become more love,

So we can bless you with greater power,

To create more love for you.'

I AM Sovereign Lord Emmanuel The Great

Part 13: Returning to your Sacred Heart of Love

"Greetings, I AM SOVEREIGN LORD EMMANUEL THE GREAT. In the greater realms, I, SOVEREIGN LORD EMMANUEL THE GREAT, created the Collective Heart. The Collective Heart is a large pool of energy that all creation is connected to. On the higher levels, you are all pure love, and love is within all beings. Therefore, no judgment can come to anyone.

You are looked at by my Being as beautiful, as all things are within you to become more beautiful. Once you allow your Sacred Flows to open within you, you are like a river; a river with healing flows of love coming from you. You are precious to us as your Great Masters.

The ones who are activated with the Sacred Living Codes with the GREAT CAEAYARON, who I, THE GREAT FATHER, sent to your plane at this time to call the people back to their great treasures so that they can rise in the love together, receive their flows within their Sacred Living Heart. They can grow in their Sacred Heart.

The greater the flows open within their heart, the more glory is given to all that is Divine in the love, until one day I as SOVEREIGN LORD EMMANUEL THE GREAT can say, 'Look, how wonderful it is that all creation has returned to the eternal love. Now let us expand them into greater power, for it is the time for their great reward to happen. Let us help them evolve and become truly united within each other as One.'

The heart is ancient, and it is connected to all the ancient wisdom from the Higher Realms. Within each one of you, there are memories and recollections that this is so.

Again, I return to the thought of the logical mind. The mind cannot comprehend, for the mind has become distanced from all eternal truths. The mind likes to feed on theories from others. The mind likes to debate and then to make up its own conclusion.

However, your heart knows all. At this time in your life, it is relatively rare to find people on your plane who live solely from the heart. The numbers will dramatically increase in the future. The greater your numbers become of the people living within the heart, the easier it will become for many to learn how to live from the heart, and then many will follow.

When the mind sees that this is all true what we say, the mind begins to surrender. When you see another achieving greatly and finding greater happiness by living in the heart, it gives your mind the proof that this is so.

Then the mind will surrender to the heart and you begin to change your ways.

Change is one of the most difficult processes of growth in a human's evolutionary cycle. Change requires changing methods of thinking, a different way of pursuing dreams and changing the daily habits of your life. Once you open to your heart then your attitudes, your style and the way you think and see your life will begin to change.

Within your heart, there are many frequencies. You may compare these frequencies to various apartments. When you move into an apartment you begin to live in this apartment. You do not simply move into an apartment without changing some of your life first. Once you move into an apartment you flow with it and it becomes a part of your life. You enjoy decorating and placing your energy into your apartment, so it is yours to claim. You 'mark' it with your unique and individual energy styles.

When you move to a different apartment or home, it takes time to feel comfortable. It takes time to 'settle' in. You may not feel comfortable with your new lifestyle for quite some time until you adjust to your new frequencies.

Constantly your life is about learning to adapt to new frequencies.

When you move to another city or area, the bus route may also be different. The shops may be different and situated in different locations. The food may be different. The people around you may be different from what you are used to. Depending on where you live, your 'time' may be different also.

All takes adjusting and adapting to.

At times, you may be able to afford to go to a higher living standard in a more luxurious apartment or home. You may be able to give it a greater style and live a greater life.

This is like what I AM teaching you as a Wise Ancient Divine Master.

In your heart, you are also able to find different apartments. Each apartment has frequencies and your life begins to change with each of these frequencies you reach.

You can find great peace and love in these frequencies and thus they are yours to live in and enjoy.

The mind can give you great fear as the mind does not always celebrate the heart. When the heart has been hurt incredibly in the past, the mind will aim to protect you from finding the deeper layers within the heart.

In this evolutionary cycle, you are on your soul journey of growth. You play in higher frequencies and lower frequencies. The heart plays in the higher frequencies. The mind often plays in the lower frequencies, especially when it believes in the reality of great pain and fear.

All takes adjusting to. All takes great understanding. All is change.

Your mind does not like change. Your mind enjoys being settled and it enjoys understanding structure and patterns, whereas your heart enjoys challenges and change for higher growth. It enjoys reaching greater goals and striving for greatness. Your mind enjoys being settled.

As you can see, change is difficult for you. Change is about learning to adjust to higher frequencies and higher understanding.

Greetings, I AM SOVEREIGN LORD EMMANUEL THE GREAT. Learn to live in the heart and desire the freedom."

To understand,

The love of the universe,

One will need to discover self,

Deep within the love of the heart.

Searching the heart deep within,

Will help you discover the love within.

The love within the heart is vast,

It is part of all that is Divine.

I AM Sovereign Lord Emmanuel The Great

Part 14: Freedom – How you can find it

"Greetings, I AM SOVEREIGN LORD EMMANUEL THE GREAT. I welcome you to this time when you are searching for higher truth. The quest to find greater freedom has always been yours all throughout your journeys.

Freedom has always been the quest of mankind. Huge numbers of people have died trying to find freedom. Huge numbers continue to die for freedom on your plane at this present time. Fighting for freedom creates greater drive within you; a drive to live, a drive to survive, a drive to pray for peace to come to your plane. Many pray that answers from Divine will be given.

When we as Divine Masters see and observe how you fight for freedom, we do not see it as the freedom you think you are fighting for. We do not judge you for what has happened in the past and what is happening on your present timeline. We see all experiences as 'is.' They are neither good nor bad.

Nothing is judged as judgment cannot be experienced in the higher love dimensions. All are created to become greater, whether that is the higher or lower experiences. You create all your experiences with your desires, beliefs, passions, and motivations. You create more of what you believe to be. There is no true good nor true bad because all is learning for you.

You are not judged by us for being 'bad' or 'sinners' in your terms. We are pure love beings. We are Divine, and we will not ask you to pay for your 'sins' in any way.

Sin does not exist in the greater sense, for what is a sin to us? Sin belongs in your eyes, but sin does not belong in our eyes. All things reflect back to you what you believe to be.

When you return to your earth in many lifetimes, you decide how to balance your life journeys and what you desire to experience. You desire this on the spiritual levels, therefore, all experiences you have are thoughts for your own learning, and this is how you also see it outside of your human existence.

We do not have a hellfire for you, and we do not torture you. We as Divine Love Masters will not take your lives away for not experiencing love. We do not punish you if you committed 'sins' against self or another. We do not set your fate either as many upon your earth believe. We will never do this. However, because of your strong set belief expressions, you have created this for yourself. You cannot move into higher thoughts if you hold yourselves back with your own limited ways. You keep punishing yourselves for lifetimes for a crime you committed on your planet.

To release yourselves from the bondage of your own pain consciousness, you need to learn to live in places of love within yourself. This is where true freedom is found; within the love of the heart of love.

We are pure Divine Beings of Great Love. We cannot bring torture and pain into our Divine Thought Consciousness, because we are Pure Love. Pain and fear are not part of our Divine Love thought system. Pain is not in our thoughts to experience, and therefore we could not bring it into your experience. However, because it is in your consciousness, it becomes your living experience as a people, as you create collectively your own reality.

You torture yourselves with your own judgment. It is you who judges yourself and others. Constantly we see the people doing this upon your plane. Instead of teaching love and becoming beings of love, you choose to bring judgment on each other.

After you move on to the spirit realms, you continue to judge yourself until you learn the power of true love and true forgiveness. The more you learn to forgive upon your plane, the higher your experiences can become in spirit and beyond. Your earth is the greatest learning plane for forgiveness.

When you come into 'The Great Mountain of Healing,' CAEAYARON, you receive the Divine gift of forgiveness, to release you from all pain you suffered and pain you caused to yourself and others in all your lifetimes.

Without this Divine Activation gift from CAEAYARON, you will continue to struggle to release all; both in human consciousness and in spirit. Better it is for you to learn to understand the precious gifts of the Divine Activations happening at this time upon your planet and to act upon it. The wise ones can truly become free from all limitation.

This is also what Jesus taught the people with my Divine Being, SOVEREIGN LORD EMMANUEL THE GREAT, *'Happy is the one who understands these teachings, for then they can become free forever as then they understand the power of forgiveness.*

True freedom comes from the FATHER EMMANUEL. Only HE can give the Holy Spirit to bring freedom from pain and suffering. Forgive each day and pray your release is soon to allow you to be released from your pain eternally.

Happy are those who understand these words and act upon them, as then they can be released from the pain flows eternally and come into the peace and the love of the GREAT FATHER EMMANUEL.'

We ask you to be in the forgiveness upon your earth for it is much easier to forgive yourself and each other on your earth than it is to forgive in the spirit realms. Free yourself from pain here upon your earth by receiving the Divine Activations from the Great Aligner, CAEAYARON, and the Sacred Purification Gifts from my Divine Being, SOVEREIGN LORD EMMANUEL THE GREAT, and your freedom and love will be eternal in all universal existences coming.

When we see you, we see you as loving beings that came to earth to fulfill a mission. Your mission was to help advance all life to higher growth. You all affect each other with your collective consciousness. All is a lesson to be experienced. Gaining happiness is a teacher for you and pain is also a teacher for your growth.

The people who suffer from their oppressors not only learn endurance and pain, but also forgiveness, strength, courage, and love.

The people who are the oppressors are also growing. They need to learn to surrender to the light and to feel the love growing within their hearts. They need to learn to forgive themselves for the pain they caused themselves and others.

All you do to another you do to yourself and this is not yet recognized by the great majority of people upon your planet.

All are lessons. All lessons work in the mirror. You are a mirror for others, and others are a mirror for you. Constantly you teach others, and others teach you the greater spiritual lessons of love, forgiveness, courage, peace, and joy. All are in constant reflection to learn from.

You live many lifetimes. You do not live only one lifetime. In each lifetime you desired to find the freedom and you kept searching for the light. Your search outside for the light has been great. I, as the GREAT SOVEREIGN LORD EMMANUEL THE GREAT, say: 'Learn to look within you for the light, for all is part of your being. Your friends are part of you, and so are the people who caused you pain and grief. They are not outside of you. All is a part for your own learning.'

Hence your quest for freedom on your personal spiritual life-path is great. It is within you to find your own path of light and freedom. You do not understand that no one else can give this path to you.

I, SOVEREIGN LORD EMMANUEL THE GREAT, say to the ones in your time who desire to find their greater path of freedom and love, 'I AM gifting the greater gifts to the people who desire to understand the great love within them.'

I have sent my Beloved Archangel, CAEAYARON, to your plane. CAEAYARON is assigned to bring the people back to freedom and the love as the great call is happening to bring the people into the flows of love and healing to gain back their freedom if they so desire this to happen.

I, SOVEREIGN LORD EMMANUEL THE GREAT, sent my beloved Divine Love Element to your planet to work along with the GREAT CAEAYARON, and my Divine Being, SOVEREIGN LORD EMMANUEL THE GREAT so that the people can find the way to the higher love realms of eternal freedom.

This is why I, SOVEREIGN LORD EMMANUEL THE GREAT, promised the people 2,000 years ago with my Designated Channel, Jesus, that I would return in a time when the people would grasp the road of the higher spiritual freedom; the freedom that was promised to them a long, long time ago.

I, SOVEREIGN LORD EMMANUEL THE GREAT, spoke through Jesus and stated, *'A time will come when the people will stream to the higher love foundations of truth and of life. They will see the Glorious Sun shining on their faces and many will desire the love and the peace from the Streams of Light coming through.'*

Jesus talked to the people about this time you are living in and the people desired these times 2,000 years ago.

He stated to them, *'It is not for me to decide when that time of the great freedom will happen, for no one knows when that very hour will happen. It will happen when THE GREAT FATHER decides it is right for that time to happen. That is when it will happen.'*

It is now when the great gathering is taking place. The greater the desire becomes for the love and truth upon your plane, the greater the love will rise upon your plane, as love is the only way to bring peace and harmony to the people. True freedom will come when people learn the higher ways of peace and harmony.

People upon your plane are finding the voice and the strength to speak. Many are standing up for their beliefs and their truth. Many are saying, 'Enough is enough. We do not desire disruption any longer. We want change to happen to bring us to greater freedom.'

You all desire freedom from pain and fear, do you not? You desire to find a higher way of life, do you not? You desire to find greater change and thus you keep searching and questioning.

Many of you are asking, 'Are there other beings other than Divine Masters who can help you find your freedom?'

We say, 'Yes there are.' Many races in the Universes have evolved far beyond you. They are watching to see if you find your freedom and your truth.

More importantly, they are asking: 'Will you desire the higher freedom? Will you desire it enough to create that upon your plane?'

The desire to create change collectively is necessary for more people to see and experience the Great Love and see the great gathering which is taking place. It is when the collective is strong, that people will find change happening upon your plane.

True freedom is only found when you look within your heart and find your love within.

Jesus, my channel, taught the people, *'In the heart is where you will find your deeper freedom. Learn to look within the heart, not to others. You will not find the answers within others, but you will find the answers within your heart. The one who finds truth within the heart is the one who can achieve all.*

Blessed are those who learn to look for answers within their heart. There only exists richness within the heart. It is in the heart you will find your wisdom and your strength. Look forward constantly. Do not look back. Follow your heart, for truth within your heart will set you free.'

This truth, our dear ones, has not changed. It will always remain the same. It does not matter where you are from, how you have lived your life, this will always remain the same. Divine words will always remain all throughout the universal ages. Divine words will never change or alter. Its truth will always remain truth.

True freedom is to be in the heart and that is what sets you free from pain and fear. When you find this truth, you will discover greater peace and love.

However, what is peace? What does peace mean?

Greetings, I AM SOVEREIGN LORD EMMANUEL THE GREAT. Become free from the pain and the fear. Become free from the anger. Learn to forgive and return to the love."

Deep within your heart,

You will find your truth,

Divine truth will always set you free,

It is where you discover the Great Love,

The Universal Love of all of creation,

Come back to the love,

Desire the love within your heart.

I AM Sovereign Lord Emmanuel The Great

Part 15: What is peace and what does it mean?

"Greetings, I AM SOVEREIGN LORD EMMANUEL THE GREAT. I promised 2,000 years ago to return to the people with Truth, the Light, and The Way.

Peace. It is a word you use with feelings you long for. What does peace mean to you?

Peace means many things to people in your world. Peace is a beautiful word and carries a high frequency of healing. You heal in peace because your heart yearns for peace.

You were created with peaceful, loving and harmonious frequencies. You were created with a thought of total perfection, in peace and in love.

You long for peace. In the peace, you will find your deepest healing in which you can discover and explore safely your greater abilities and flows. In the higher realms of existence, there exists no limitation when there is great love, peace, and joy. It is the suffering that brings you into limitation.

It is this peace you are looking for. It is in the peace you will find the answers because all answers are deep within you. Nothing is found outside of you as all is within you.

I, SOVEREIGN LORD EMMANUEL THE GREAT, AM part of all creation, and I AM part of you. Therefore, I AM bringing these teachings to you, to help you understand your Divine Path back, to help you grow in the love where peace exists. I AM love, pure love consciousness. I AM Divine Love.

Again, we go to the sacred chambers of the living heart. This is within your heart. In the heart exist many frequencies and many frequencies are waiting to be turned on by you. It is in the heart you will find the frequencies of peace, and love. It is in these frequencies you will find the bliss you have been looking for.

Mankind has been on a quest to find peace.

Long, long ago, you had peace within you, and you knew you were a peaceful people. You gathered together and understood peace and harmony was a treasure. You did not know of anger, suffering, aging, pain, war, or insecurity.

At that time anger and pain were not part of your frequencies to experience as it was not a part of your conscious awareness. You desired only harmony, peace, and love. You created peace together. Within each of you, you built a foundation for greater peace to exist within and you worked together collectively in the peace.

In harmony and love, you gathered together, and you created platforms of great wisdom. Each of you listened and partook in the great wisdom that glowed within your hearts. You saw the Divine within you, and you listened to the Divine within you. You desired greater strength and peace within you and for each other.

It is, when you discover this love for each other and for yourself, your higher frequencies within your heart awaken to the love of who you truly are.

It is in this love you will find the greatness you have been looking for since the times you lost your true heart love connection collectively. You lost your true heart love connection during the Greatest Fall of Consciousness.

True inner peace cannot be found by anyone else but yourself for no one else can help you access it. You must find it for yourself. We can guide you to higher peace. We can give you flows of peace and healing, but it is you who must find it and desire it.

You find it by looking in the quiet and feeling the quiet all around you, truly being in the forgiveness of all that is and all that was.

Imagine looking in a chamber within your heart and going deep within. You find the great light and you keep looking deeper and deeper. You feel the peace and the warmth, and the warmth draws you into the depth deeper. All around you, there is peace, love, and harmony.

This is the peace of the loving heart of love. Go deeper and find yourself on this incredibly loving level.

Upon finding the love within your heart, you can go deeper still. Your desire to be part of the Awakened Ones, carrying the special Codes of Life will grow, and I, as the GREAT LORD, will bless all who desire the

Great Flames from my Divine Being, and who desire the great healings from the GREAT CAEAYARON, who is here to bring the great shifts and the great frequencies of healing to your people who desire to find the precious spiritual treasures of eternal love, freedom and peace.

When you receive your Codes of Life within your heart with the GREAT CAEAYARON, this will allow you to go deeper into the heart of freedom and will guide you back to your true heart connection; the connection of the true love.

No longer are the ones who become purified in the HOLY MOUNTAIN, CAEAYARON, part of the old consciousness, for they are becoming part of the new consciousness; the new earth flows of love, like I, THE GREAT SOVEREIGN LORD EMMANUEL, always promised the people through Jesus.

'Look there will be a time when a great separation will take place. It is when the GREAT FATHER EMMANUEL will call the people upon the earth.

Many will reject and deny the GREAT FATHER upon HIS return, but those who look up and see the GREAT FATHER EMMANUEL in HIS heavenly glory, will say, 'Please, GREAT LORD, I have been awaiting your great gifts of freedom. Please send your messenger to me to give me news of your great return and show me how I can return to you, GREAT LORD.

I am humbly awaiting your greatness, and then I will place my gown upon me of great love once you have cleansed me in your Sacred Flames of Love and Purification.'

I, SOVEREIGN LORD EMMANUEL THE GREAT, bless all who desire to come into 'The Great Mountain of Healing,' CAEAYARON, who I have sent to your plane to bring all those who desire to return to the high love foundations and the high love dimensions upwards.

CAEAYARON can give you access to the Divine Mansions of the Love Realms with the Sacred Gowns, the Living Codes of Life and the Life-giving Flames of eternal love and freedom. The ones who receive this will become greatly blessed, eternally.

I, SOVEREIGN LORD EMMANUEL THE GREAT, gave my dearly beloved Designated Channel to your earth to work with Divine and mankind, to allow you to connect upwards and to help you return to the Great Love through the One Gateway of Everlasting Freedom and Life.

Happy is the one who desires these words of love within their hearts. Happy is the one who desires to return to the Great Road of Love. Happy is the one who has been seeking for THE TRUTH, THE WAY, AND THE FREEDOM for lifetimes.

I, SOVEREIGN LORD EMMANUEL THE GREAT, stated through my Designated Word, Jesus, 2,000 years ago, as I do on this day, through my Designated Word, Suzanna Maria Emmanuel, *'It is the ones who have the heart of love who will find the higher path of freedom.*

They have searched lifetime after lifetime for the answers and for the love. They are not afraid to go within their heart. Indeed, they fear not going into the heart, for they know that they will only find the higher path when they have the courage to go within the heart of love, for all answers are found within the heart.'

Lifetime after lifetime, they call out to my Divine Being, THE GREAT FATHER EMMANUEL, 'When Lord, will you return? Please awaken me on that day of your Great Return. Let me have the great courage to be in my heart, for I fear I may miss that day of your Great Return.'

In all their lifetimes they seek my Divine Being and say, 'Know I am here for you, Great Lord. Please awaken me when it is time. I will keep searching for truth, though it is dark around me, though not many others are strong with their light.

I will keep asking you for the way to the Great Mountain of Refuge, of everlasting glory, so that I may find it.

Bless me, Lord. See my heart is good. Be my Shepherd to everlasting peace and freedom. May my heart awaken on the day of your Great Coming, GREAT FATHER EMMANUEL. May you shake me awake. May I feel my heart beating when you call.'

It is those who will be eternally blessed, for they have been on the watch to see when I, THE GREAT SOVEREIGN LORD OF ALL DIVINE REALMS, would return.

I, SOVEREIGN LORD EMMANUEL THE GREAT, have always watched for those who desired to be in the love and who desired to return to the great peace in all their lifetimes.

I examine all hearts. I, SOVEREIGN LORD EMMANUEL THE GREAT, always see the good as only love exists within me, therefore, I, DIVINE LOVE, see only love within you.

Those who desire the love I see, and those who do not desire the love I do not see, for I only see those who desire the love, and the peace, and love themselves and each other.

I see only those who desire my Divine Sacred Being, for all others, I do not desire to see. The ones who have a love for my Divine Being are the true seekers of love, and those I, SOVEREIGN LORD EMMANUEL THE GREAT, listen to and see. I AM calling those back to the love.

I, SOVEREIGN LORD EMMANUEL THE GREAT, always saw those who desired to be within their heart and always forgave all things they experienced. They showed love for themselves and for each other. They blessed all they met, and thus, I, THE GREAT FATHER EMMANUEL, SOVEREIGN LORD OF ALL THE DIVINE UNIVERSES, will eternally bless those who blessed others with their words, their deeds, and their actions, for their love did not fade within them.

I, SOVEREIGN LORD EMMANUEL THE GREAT, bless all who embraced my Designated Word in all lifetimes and desired to bring love and peace to your earth, though moving forward to greater love and peace seemed an impossible task in many of your lifetimes.

Who would desire the Great Return of the Great Sun Consciousness? This would be greatly examined in the times of my Great Return, for the ones who have always remained in the love would see my Great Return and desire to have their Sacred Mantles and their Living Codes back. They would be the first to return to 'The Great Mountain of Healing.'

Throughout their many lifetimes, they always remembered the love within, and it is those who I, SOVEREIGN LORD EMMANUEL THE GREAT, AM searching for.

It is those who can truly find the greater peace within their hearts, for they are the ones who will know these words, and will know that they will return home to the greater love dimensions, knowing they listened, they remembered, and they came to 'The Great Mountain of Light,' THE GREAT CAEAYARON, and received their Codes of Love back again within their hearts.

The Codes of Love are the Great Talents, the Great Gifts of their love, their life source, and their greater heart connection.

Greetings, I AM SOVEREIGN LORD EMMANUEL THE GREAT. Happy are those who desire to listen to these words and acknowledge these words, for then their heart can become truly blessed."

Happy is the one,

Who truly desires to be shepherded,

To the great love.

Happy is the one who desires to return,

To the heart of the great love.

Happy is the one who says,

'Show me the path within my heart,'

For that one who has been awaiting,

The Promise of the Great Return,

And who truly sees this,

This day is indeed a great blessing.

I AM Sovereign Lord Emmanuel The Great

Part 16: Peace, an inner struggle for many

"Greetings, I AM SOVEREIGN LORD EMMANUEL THE GREAT. Happy are those who desire the peace within their hearts and blessed are those able to find the highest ways of peace.

To find peace is the greatest treasure upon your plane, however, relatively few can find it at this time. Few are finding the answers to the search of peace and few are finding the way to the Great Sacred Heart of Love. Many will find it as the Awakening Times continue, as the door becomes greater and as the greater lovers of truth and awakening come into 'The Great Mountain of Healing,' CAEAYARON.

Understand, few would see the higher path opening at first, and then the greater numbers would begin to desire it. I, SOVEREIGN LORD EMMANUEL THE GREAT, bless all who desire the highest path of love and who come into the love. Their search has been great, and they are among the truly blessed ones.

When you have opened the greater chambers within the Great Heart of Love, you will find rest and you will find a deep longing to discover yourself greater. Then you will feel the Angels coming much closer to you and you will feel their guidance coming more within you.

Self-discovery to the greater spiritual gifts upon your plane is a great treasure. It is in the Sacred Heart of love you will learn to reflect upon your life, and you will find that all is part of the Great Oneness; the Great Consciousness.

You will discover that your life is a great gift of seeing more about yourself. You will discover the greater gifts of loving yourself and forgiving all in your life. You will discover the Angels singing with you greater.

The pain, the anger and the great insecurity that many people upon your plane are facing at this time, can create greater struggles to go within the heart. Fear closes the greater heart from awakening, and thus the great healings are needed within you to help you find it.

Many people have great trouble understanding that going within the heart of love is where you find your deep peace.

You will certainly find your greater happiness upon finding your higher path. You will find yourself becoming calmer with greater control over your mind and your body. You will find deeper contentment in your life. Being content and spiritually aware are spiritual gifts not many can truly find upon your earth at this time. However, the consciousness shifts will happen, and in the future, you will find more people will seek to find these spiritual gifts of deep inner contentment and peace.

When people have challenges in life they often forget to look within. Many often become frustrated and may even become very angry. Many may find it difficult to look within, as within the heart they may feel too much turmoil when those pains come to the surface to be looked at and to be examined.

It is far too easy for a person who has pain in their heart to keep hiding from the pain, rather than becoming unified with the heart and release the pain that is held within.

How can you become healed from your pain when you do not understand what is within you, waiting to become discovered? It is better for you to learn to discover what is the highest love and freedom and learn to forgive all the pain within you than it is to keep running away from issues that will keep returning within you in the years to come.

Happy is the one who acknowledges these teachings and has the courage to go within greater, for then the greater release of pain can begin to happen. Even when pain is not realized within consciously, hidden suffering can bring much pain in life.

The way to find the freedom and love is to release the pain from the heart. The hidden treasures are within the heart. It is within the heart one finds the greatness and strength. The power of forgiveness you do not understand. Always stay within the heart and within the forgiveness. Those are the ways of the wise ones.

Jesus, the wise man who walked upon your plane was a great teacher and the great channel of my Being, SOVEREIGN LORD EMMANUEL THE GREAT. He always taught all people he spoke to; to learn to be in the depths of the heart for the great heart will set you free. He knew the secret of the Great Heart. His heart was awakened when many around him were not.

Many, upon hearing him speak loving words thought he was speaking untruth. He was considered by many to be a 'mad man,' 'not of the right mind,' and a man of great blasphemy. He was not liked by many.

Still, Jesus forgave them and carried on speaking, knowing his words needed to be carried for a long time after his death in order for my Divine Being, SOVEREIGN LORD EMMANUEL THE GREAT, to return.

Jesus knew he was speaking Divine Truth. He could see when the people were ready to listen to him. He could also see when people did not desire to understand his knowledge.

He stated many times, *'The words I speak land on deaf ears, for the people are not ready to hear THE FATHER speak. They do not believe THE GREAT FATHER can speak through a man, a messenger, yet they can state they speak truth from their books written by men.'*

He always considered the choices of the people; those who desired to listen and those who did not desire to listen. He always considered their free choice and never forced anyone to listen.

You also have a choice. You can choose to listen to these Divine Teachings, or you can refuse them. That choice was given to you and it is a very great gift indeed, for in those choices you can create your own universal consciousness to experience.

We are Wise Teachers with Ancient Wisdom desiring to guide you back to the Great Heart of Love of the Great Love. However, we can never force you to change for this is your freedom. This is your choice.

The light upon your plane is becoming brighter now. It is becoming more important to open to the light within your heart because it is where all answers are found. It is where all truth is held.

It is the truth you are looking for. You have always been 'truth seekers.' On your way to finding truth, you became confused. You, at times, lost your path. Now it is time to help you find your path back again; back to the Great Heart of Love. It is time for your instruction and guidance as to how you can live in the Great Collective Heart of Love and to find yourselves again; if you desire to find the higher path home to the love realms, where you can dwell eternally together with higher beings in the Great Collective Heart of Love.

When you awaken and when you sing in your heart with the joy of life, you will find great blessings coming to you. It is this that we are eagerly waiting for; when multitudes awaken to the heart of love.

When many awaken, this is when True Light can shine upon the earth. It is this that your earth also has been waiting for since long ago. It is then that the Archangels will sing along with the Spirit of the Earth and she will awaken to all her glory and all of creation will sing along with her.

It is with this love that she will heal herself and all precious creation. It is this time she has been eagerly waiting for; when you desire to awaken to your greater purpose. It is up to you when the Great Light will shine upon your earth. It is in this love that you truly awaken to all the peace within you and you will see the glory of yourselves.

Then, you will truly understand the term, 'To be set free.'

Greetings, I AM SOVEREIGN LORD EMMANUEL THE GREAT. Awaken to the love and the greatness within you."

The heart knows all,

The heart is there,

To be discovered by you.

To discover what is within the heart,

Your inner strength and love for self,

Needs to be strong;

Only then will you desire,

The true healing,

Of the Sacred Heart of Love.

I AM Sovereign Lord Emmanuel The Great

Part 17: All of creation awaits your spiritual awakening

"Greetings, I AM SOVEREIGN LORD EMMANUEL THE GREAT. During the times of Jesus' existence on the earth, I promised, as THE GREAT FATHER, to return with the words of peace and love. I promised to guide the people to a higher way of living.

This higher way of living was to embrace higher love consciousness within the heart. I asked the people, through my Word, Jesus, *'Who would be ready to awaken to the higher streams of consciousness when it is time to embrace the higher ways of living?'*

You are living in the time of the great awakening to higher love consciousness within the heart. All things have Divine Consciousness within. You too are part of all that is Divine.

All is part of Divine as Divine is living; it is life itself. Even the trees understand Ancient Wisdom. They sing your praises and they have not lost faith in you. They know it is only a matter of time before you awaken to truth within you, though I, SOVEREIGN LORD EMMANUEL THE GREAT say, 'They hope you are on time to see truth within you, because it takes a humble heart to see truth.'

The trees hold an ancient secret. This secret is held deep within them. These records they will keep until it is time to pass its wisdom of ancient truth to you; when you awaken collectively within the heart of love as a nation coming back to the love.

The trees speak a language of their own. They also hold a Heart of Wisdom, though different to yours. They speak with love to each other and connect deep within the earth to each other.

You cannot live without the trees, as the trees hold life flows within them. They hold the ancient wisdom, and if all the ancient trees are cut down then the deeper wisdom cannot be held within the earth and therefore, the deeper secrets within the ancient trees cannot return to you.

This you do not understand yet. You do not understand the amount of healing power the trees have, or how significant their signals to one another are. These signals are in constant communication with each other and they are living consciousness. Without them, you cannot have life upon your planet.

Jesus, my channel, 2,000 years ago, also spoke of the ancient trees and the importance of them. He often spoke about the importance of the secrets held within the earth, and that the ancient wisdom would awaken when it was time for the people to hear, but, he asked, '*Who would be ready to awaken when the ancient knowledge speaks through the ancient great trees and through all creation that is living? For it is the GREAT FATHER who speaks through all of creation.*

HE will awaken all the trees, and all that is living upon the earth, to go to the new living spaces where all continuously exists within to have greater peace.

But will the people desire to awaken when the GREAT FATHER calls? If they do not awaken when the GREAT FATHER calls, then how will they know where to go to on the higher road? It is only those who are listening who will be able to awaken to the higher road.

It is those who are humble within the heart who will understand the calling of the GREAT FATHER, for the hearts who are not humble, and not willing to see the GREAT FATHER, will not see the Great Calling. They are the spiritually blind and deaf and do not desire the GREAT FATHER EMMANUEL to lead them to the higher realms.'

You are living on a dying planet. Your earth would have given up a long, long time ago had it not been for the trees. The trees speak to the earth constantly and remind her of her greater purpose; that is to help cleanse mankind who have forgotten to live in the Light and how to work with the Light.

The trees encourage her to stay alive. Know her cries are heard in the Universe. Know the earth is asking for help and urges people to listen. The earth listens and the earth feels mankind exploring, at this time, to find a greater purpose to all of existence.

Like I, SOVEREIGN LORD EMMANUEL THE GREAT, have stated, 'There is no good or bad in the higher universes, and no one can be judged for their ways. However, all lead to ways of either greater pain or ways of love and joy. All life flows in consciousness and all affect each other.'

When you do not desire my Divine Being, SOVEREIGN LORD EMMANUEL THE GREAT, nor have love for your people, nor have love for the earth, nor have love for any of creation, then you do not hold the love within yourself, and therefore how can you come to the New Universes of the greater creation?

In the New Universes the ones who come into the New Realms will have a greater responsibility than you currently do upon your planet. There you are asked to work in collective responsibility with a greater purpose to create greater creation together, so that greater evolution can exist.

How can I, SOVEREIGN LORD EMMANUEL THE GREAT, embrace the pollution, the destruction and the anger mankind has collectively created? How can I allow the continuation of your ways in the higher realms of love?

I, DIVINE FATHER, cannot allow things to continue the way they are upon your earth, for how can I then state to the higher creation that I AM love?

How can I, SOVEREIGN LORD EMMANUEL THE GREAT, then state that I have love for all of creation and help all to evolve to the higher universes, that have never yet been discovered, with greater power and new ways of consciousness, when you do not have the desire, collectively, to create love and joy?

Therefore, I, SOVEREIGN LORD EMMANUEL THE GREAT, state, how important it is to learn to have peace within you now, and to learn to forgive, and to learn to care for your planet.

Your planet is a planet of love, and she is a home for you. You are here to learn to love and to learn to love each other. Love can change all upon your planet as love is healing for all. Love harmonizes life together. Love bonds life together. Love brings healing to all, including all of nature as you are part of all of nature. You do not understand yet the power of love collectively.

You are on your earth to learn to demonstrate the love you have for all of life and for yourselves. All of life feels mankind. You do not understand how you affect each other. When mankind learns to have a balanced collective consciousness, with consideration for each other, that is when your earth will heal.

Your earth will always reflect your consciousness back to you as you are part of all. You are part of the sky and the earth and the trees and the mountains. Learn to have a greater love for the earth and each other. Learn to celebrate life. Treasure each day for then the greater realms can open for you; when you receive your Codes of Life, and you celebrate life within you.

You, as a people, need to learn the sacredness of all of life. You think everything is separate consciousness, but it is not. The earth is a consciousness within her being, and she has the ability to destroy all life upon her for her own survival.

This is what the people upon your earth do not understand; the power of your earth's consciousness. Many people think they are the most important of all creation upon the earth and in the universe. Many believe they are the greatest evolved species upon your planet, and yet the trees hold greater wisdom than the people.

The trees understand the flows and the seasons, whereas the people destroy themselves and each other with their pain and suffering collectively.

Many people upon your plane consider themselves part of the animal world, thus, they consider this gives them the right to plunder and destroy each other and the earth. They have created fear within the animals, and the animals have created fear within many other animals.

When will the people, collectively, on your earth learn that all life is sacred and that all are loved by Divine Love? When will the people understand that the pain and suffering cannot continue upon your plane and within your consciousness? Life was given to you to search for greater ways of love with, not to hurt one another and cause suffering to each other and to all of life.

Learn to come back to love. Learn to be honest with one another and do not cause pain to another. Do not take from another what is not yours to have. Learn to be honest with each other and learn to come back into the heart of love.

Understand the only reason why the earth still exists is because of the love from the higher realms for her. I, SOVEREIGN LORD EMMANUEL THE GREAT, praise your earth for allowing you to come to this time. I, SOVEREIGN LORD EMMANUEL THE GREAT, say to the animals and the trees, and all living creatures upon your earth, how courageous they were to witness the anger and the great suffering of mankind through all the ages and still be there with you today.

They know their rewards will be great in the greater realms of love coming for helping you to come to this point.

They have witnessed your greatest triumphs and your greatest falls of consciousness. All the animals, on the land and the creatures in the sea, and in the sky, and all vegetation upon the earth always had the choice; to either let you live and allow this time of the One Gateway to happen, or not. If they had chosen not to let you live upon your planet then the consequences would have been too severe for all of creation in the higher love realms.

All the animals, on the land and the creatures in the sea, and in the sky, and all vegetation upon your earth sacrificed themselves to the earth to allow all to become greater and to become magnified in the beauty in the New Creation coming.

They are with you, not only to work with Divine Purpose to embrace the higher creation coming, but also to remind you of the great significance of the value of life. They remind you of the beauty of your Great Creators and all of life. They help you become peaceful when you need peace. They share with you their love when you need love.

Because planet earth is connected deep within the consciousness of mankind, the greater you awaken within your heart, the greater she will feel the love coming into her. It is then the ancient wisdom of the trees can awaken her heart greater, to help her remember her power and how she can use her power to restore all balance upon the earth.

Will you listen to these wise lessons? Will you learn to look within and find truth within?

Divine Beings of Great Love urge you to, for it is then you can learn to flow with peace. You cannot flow with love and peace until you awaken to the deep flows of Divine Love within.

I, SOVEREIGN LORD EMMANUEL THE GREAT, state how important your earth is for she holds many secrets within her for you and she holds the secrets for all of creation coming in the higher universes. You, as a people, are also important as you also hold all the memories of all your lifetimes and all your universes in the previous existences.

All blessings will come to those eternally who desire to understand the higher ways, for then I, SOVEREIGN LORD EMMANUEL THE GREAT, can bless you when you desire to become the eternal caretakers of the higher planets.

When you demonstrate you care for your planet and mankind here upon the earth and gain the Codes of Life back, then you can be granted access to the higher dimensions where only peace exists within.

Gone will be the times of suffering within the people in the higher universes. Gone will be the tears from all of creation in the higher universes. The animals will learn to celebrate life greater, as will the trees and all of the vegetation. They will learn to trust in the Great Divine Creators and forever they will be free from all suffering.

This is also what Jesus spoke about. *'There is a greater creation coming. This New Creation will beautify all creation in existence. It will praise all life within the universe and the GREAT FATHER EMMANUEL will bless them eternally. It is only those who desire the love and the peace on the New Earth who will come into those Gates of Life and they will understand the greatness of it. They will sing the praises of the great love eternally.'*

Greetings, I AM SOVEREIGN LORD EMMANUEL THE GREAT, SOVEREIGN DIVINE OF ALL CREATION IN ALL UNIVERSES."

Flowing with peace and love,

Cannot happen for you,

If you do not desire the peace and the love.

How can you find it without desire?

How can you desire it,

Without seeking to find it?

The wise one seeks,

The wise one desires,

The wise one will then find.

I AM Sovereign Lord Emmanuel The Great

Part 18: The ancient secrets within your earth

"Greetings, I AM SOVEREIGN LORD EMMANUEL THE GREAT. I, THE GREAT FATHER EMMANUEL, AM speaking to you at this time, through my Word, who is here to show the way to the everlasting freedom.

In this lifetime, I, SOVEREIGN LORD EMMANUEL THE GREAT, have asked my Word to come to your planet, to bring the great truth through. In this lifetime it is not through the man Jesus, but through Suzanna Maria Emmanuel, and there is no other channel I, SOVEREIGN LORD EMMANUEL THE GREAT, will speak through.

Jesus stated to the people, *'I am but a messenger and I have been sent by the GREAT FATHER EMMANUEL to speak to the people, to give them hope for the future and to help them understand the GREAT FATHER is love and has a great love for the people.'*

Within your earth lie many frequencies of beauty yet to be discovered. These will remain hidden, like treasures, until the people are ready to find it collectively. These frequencies are also found in your hearts of love. The same frequencies within your planet earth are within your heart, waiting to be discovered.

Therefore, when people awaken, the earth awakens also, because you hold the deeper reflections of your earth within your heart. You and your earth flows are one, as all are part of each other. You believe all life exists outside of you, yet, I, SOVEREIGN LORD EMMANUEL THE GREAT say, all is within you.

You hold much more within your heart than you realize at present. You also hold the greater frequencies within your heart of your Universe and the Greater Universes. You are connected to all of life and all of life connects within you.

You are a system of your own. A beautiful system. A system that was created with pure love and pure loving thoughts. You were created with great wisdom with pure love, with a knowing that to save your planet and to save life, you would have to look within and awaken the frequencies of love within your heart.

In the Great Love, no dimension exists in the pain, for pain cannot exist in our Divine Love consciousness. However, because it exists within your consciousness streams, pain exists very greatly for you.

At this time, you are asked to look within and find the true meaning of life within your heart. This is not to listen to stories outside of yourselves and to feel the anger within, but to feel the love within you flowing. Love flows through your cells and once you awaken to the love, then the love can flow more freely through your heart and your system within.

Each of you carries many patterns of love. Love has many patterns and high frequencies. These frequencies sing to each other. Your hearts also sing to each other. Therefore, many of you enjoy being together with friends of similar beliefs because your patterns sing similar patterns. You communicate in patterns. All of life communicates in patterns. Your earth communicates with your heart and to the pattern within your heart.

When Jesus was upon your earth, he often commented on all beauty of creation.

He brought through these words from my Divine Being, SOVEREIGN LORD EMMANUEL THE GREAT: *'The heavens speak of the beauty of all of creation. All of creation is perfect and all of creation speaks the language of love. The people have forgotten to speak the language of love in the universe as the people have become separated from love. This is why the stars and all of life sing to the hearts of the people, to help them discover the language of the universe.*

The GREAT FATHER EMMANUEL sings praises to all. HE does not consider any of creation to be greater than another. The ant HE considers to be as important as the tree, as well as a man, women or a child. The animals HE cares for, as well as the stars and the moon and the sun, for all are perfect to THE GREAT FATHER.

HE examines the love within all of creation, and whoever desires that love, and sings love to the GREAT FATHER EMMANUEL, and understands that HE is the GREAT FATHER of all of creation, that one will always be praised in all the higher love realms where the GREAT FATHER exists within.

The one who seeks the higher wisdom constantly within the heart is the one who will find the way to the great love, for the GREAT FATHER never leaves any of HIS children who desire HIS great love within the heart.

All of creation who love the GREAT FATHER hear the great songs held within the Heart of Creation. They will hear the GREAT FATHER speaking. Stay awake always, for the GREAT FATHER will call all who love HIM.'

All upon your earth and in the greater realms are saying to you; 'Awaken to the love within your heart. Return to love and become of love. Remember the path of the ancient flows of love, for all love awakens all of creation.'

The ones who lived in the ancient fallen paradise 'Lemuria,' can gain back their Codes of Life to bring all into greater existence.

I, SOVEREIGN LORD EMMANUEL THE GREAT, state to the ones who are open to these higher words, 'Come to 'The Great Mountain of Light,' CAEAYARON, and receive your Mantles of Love back. Receive the Living Codes of Life so all may become restored to greater love. Let all of life become praised and blessed because the people are awakening to their inner love.'

Your earth, created with so much love and perfection, desired to be part of healing the Greater Universe to bring all in alignment to true joy and true love.

As your planet has a deep spiritual connection, all planets have a deep spiritual connection. They have a deep spirit within. Without a spiritual connection to the higher systems, there would be no life possible upon a planet. When a spirit of a planetary system is thriving, a planet brings forth streams of life and then streams of existence can live upon her.

The purpose of your planet's spirit was to awaken you to more beauty and to rejoice in your existence, so she could shine in the light and bring greater blessings to all who desire to bring all into love and greatness.

When she is thriving, all of life upon your plane thrives. You become glorified by her because she crowns you with a golden crown of glorification. You rejoice because she rejoices. You understand you are in a partnership with her being and her being is in partnership with you. It is all wise and ancient.

When the spirit of the earth came to your planet, she knew of the possible pain she would go through. The probability of the pain becoming great, she knew.

Your earth knows now it is the time to begin the great healing, and I, SOVEREIGN LORD EMMANUEL THE GREAT, state how I praise your earth for the way she has allowed this time to happen. Forever, all creation will become blessed because of the love within her spirit. Forever, all creation will become magnified into greater love and strength because of her great love.

She feels the beginning of the healings, and the flows within her are shifting and expanding as the one who brought the Codes of Life to her originally, to allow life consciousness to exist within and upon her, is with you. This is The Word, the Way, and the Path to eternal Freedom who is also working with you to help you hear these words and understand it is the time of the Divine Calling.

All animals, the creatures in the sea, in the sky, and all of the vegetation and the ancient mountains are feeling her flows rising as your earth's spirit is feeling the higher flows from my SOVEREIGN

BEING, SOVEREIGN LORD EMMANUEL THE GREAT, happening at this time. This is because the earth grids are shifting into greater consciousness and are awakening to the ancient secrets within her. It is time for all to become revealed to allow the darkness to show itself and the light to show itself and to allow you to see the path upwards.

The choice as to the path you take will always be yours to have, as I, SOVEREIGN LORD EMMANUEL THE GREAT, will never force any of creation to work in the love, for that is not the way of love.

I, THE GREAT FATHER EMMANUEL, will bless those who desire to be in the love, and all others I will grant them their own path of their own calling, but they will never be part of the higher love creation universes, for the love for the higher love is then not within them. This is what they are choosing.

Greetings, I AM SOVEREIGN LORD EMMANUEL THE GREAT. All in the new universes will always be blessed. They will become part of the New Awakened People. Never will they suffer any more."

The earth speaks an ancient language,

A language of love you have forgotten,

The Spirit of the Earth,

Desires to heal all of earth at this time.

Before she can however,

The hearts of the people,

Need to change to become of love.

Will the people open to love collectively?

Will they allow Divine Love to heal all?

Will they desire Divine Will to take place,

In the higher realms of love,

And upon the earth?

I AM Sovereign Lord Emmanuel The Great

Part 19: The Universal Alignment

"Greetings, I AM SOVEREIGN LORD EMMANUEL THE GREAT, the Eternal Sun Consciousness. I promised to shine upon your earth when it was the time to call the people back to love.

My Designated Channel is upon your earth, working hard with the flows of the earth and awakening the greater spirit within her, to allow all of life, who desires the love within, to become healed.

As my Word is calling the people with the Divine Voice of my Divine Being, SOVEREIGN LORD EMMANUEL THE GREAT, she is also working with THE GREAT CAEAYARON, who has created all consciousness within the living light grids. HE is the Great Aligner to bring all into greater alignment to allow creation to rise and evolve.

The Word, Divine Love Element, is reaching within the lower earth, and reaching in the highest realms within our Divine Beings, creating a connection path to help you evolve upwards.

She brings the UNIVERSAL LOVE CODES to your earth, to awaken your ancient earth flows, to help you become steady for the greater New Creation coming; should you desire to rise upwards.

The grids within the earth are aligning to the higher love flows and are asking the people upon your earth, who are ready to shift upwards, to come into the shelter of 'The Great Mountain of Light,' CAEAYARON if they are ready to awaken. If so, do they desire to carry the 'Torch of Light' to help many other people awaken, living upon your earth, to help them see the importance of this time?

The ones who come to 'The Great Mountain of Light,' and receive the Codes of Life; the Codes of the New Creation coming, can then become part of the higher love creation as they have received the Keys of Eternal Freedom and Life.

Jesus often talked about the keys of the greater creation coming. The people 2,000 years ago were greatly confused as to the 'Life within the earth awakening,' and that the 'talents' were needed to become part of the New Earth. They desired to understand what all these riddles meant, for they did not understand about the living consciousness within the earth, and how they were affected by them.

In your days, many do not understand these words either, for these teachings are riddles to the great majority. They do not understand that there are living grids within your earth and how they are affected by all the thoughts upon your planet.

They do not understand that the great separation is taking place, in the times you are living, between the 'old earth flows' and the 'new earth flows' which are entering your planet.

The people are now being asked to make a choice and are asked to be gathered, spiritually, to 'The Great Mountain of Light,' so that they can receive their eternal 'talents' or 'keys' to enter into the New Earth Consciousness.

The people who have not chosen for the New Creation Flows and who have not gathered at 'The Great Mountain of Light,' cannot receive these 'talents.' Without these 'talents' they will not be able to enter the higher love spiritual dimensions, once their lifetime is completed here upon your earth, for these are the great gifts of the New Universal Dimensions.

The people, 2,000 years ago, knew that these talents, or gifts, meant their eternal freedom. The freedom Jesus talked about, meant an end to all suffering and burdens they carried.

You are living in the times of the prophecies becoming fulfilled. It is now the time Jesus spoke about, and I, SOVEREIGN LORD EMMANUEL THE GREAT, have returned to speak about these same words to help you understand the greater meaning and the importance of them.

Happy are those who understand the importance. Even if they do not fully recognize it thoroughly, they understand the importance of receiving the Divine Activations to receive their New Creation Mantles, their Living Codes and their Keys of Life to the Living Gates. Thus, once they have received their Divine Activations, they become part of the 'living creation' with new life transformations within them.

After this lifetime, upon your planet, they become part of the New Creation and they will have eternal freedom because they have then shown their choice for the 'New Paradise.'

Once they have their Living Codes back, then they can become greater love as they receive new living flows. These living flows harmonize with the higher realms of existence to bring awakening flows to themselves for their own healing, to earth and mankind. Thus, they become a 'collective healing stream of love.'

The higher love frequencies are awakening now within the earth and she is responding to the love healings from the Divine connections taking place. She desires the people to come back to the love more than ever because she knows her flows are becoming separated within her.

The older flows filled with pain and suffering are preparing to leave her, as the new flows of love are awakening within her. The Great Master, CAEAYARON, is awakening within her, as his Divine Love Element, Light Grid Programmer, the Sacred Gateway, is now awakening within her ancient self, and her strength within her is growing.

My Sacred Word, Designated Channel, feels the grid fields of light within the earth, and the grid fields of light within the earth are responding. She gives love to the grid fields of light, and she connects them into my Universal Love Grids; the Grids of Eternal Life and Power. This is to prepare the ancient grids to become part of the New Greater Love Universes coming and to take the 'New Grids of Life' within your earth fields to become the 'New Living Creation Planet.'

Your earth was part of the Great Creation Planet in the ancient universes before the darkness took her into their possession and claimed her. Therefore, no new creation could ever exist in higher love dimensions, and all became pained with great suffering.

Now is the time when the Creation Planet, or also known as the Blue Creation Planet, could become retrieved from the dark abyss, which is the time you are living in as all need to become realigned to the higher love.

Once the living earth grids within your earth are aligned upwards within the new universes, the Blue Planet will come into existence once again, and bless all of the New Creation coming.

Understand, the great universal test between the darkness and the light has now been completed, and my Divine Designated Channel has proven that the love within her being for the Great Love Universes was stronger than all the darkness within the dark abyss and the dark void.

I, SOVEREIGN LORD EMMANUEL THE GREAT, state, 'Let it be the time now of the Great Alignment. Let it be the time for the people to receive these messages and begin to understand the significance of this, so that all who desire the love can become part of the New Creation, and all who do not desire to become of the New Creation, let them go forever.

All have been tested many times over now, and now their hearts will show whether they desire the love back or not. It is the time of the test of the heart.'

This is what is called, 'The Great Alignment of all Universal Grids.'

Greetings, I AM SOVEREIGN LORD EMMANUEL THE GREAT. I AM here guiding you to the new knowledge of the earth."

Within the universe exists much knowledge,

This knowledge is ancient,

It is time for the greater revelations,

To come to the people.

We as Divine Masters of Great Love,

Desire to bring all people,

Into the greater knowledge,

To help the people understand,

The significance,

The importance,

Of the Great Choice.

I AM Sovereign Lord Emmanuel The Great

Part 20: Coming out of the dark abyss into the eternal freedom

"Greetings, I AM SOVEREIGN LORD EMMANUEL THE GREAT. I AM here to bring the Sun Consciousness to the darkness within the dark abyss, to help you awaken to the light within you.

The Universal Alignment is the Gateway upwards to help the New Grids of Life become released from the dark vortex the earth has been kept into, keeping all of life in a deep prison of unawakened consciousness.

The people upon your plane, who chose for the darkness collectively, were also 'thrown' into the pits of the deep abyss, and it is now the time where all of life can become freed from the deep pits; the deep black hole and prison, by receiving back their Codes of Life; only however, if you choose for life.

Once the Great Fall of Consciousness from the Lemurian 'Paradise' was chosen for by the great collective of the people, no more could they return to the spaces of 'paradise.' They had chosen the knowledge and the power the darkness promised them, and no longer did they desire the love from the eternal loving spaces.

Therefore, the nation of Lemuria lost the Codes of Life and the privilege and ability to rise back to the eternal love dimensions because they had chosen for the darkness.

The darkness claimed the nation of Lemuria as their own, and the ones who took the love away, from the Lemurians, became their living gods. These 'gods' opposed my GREAT SOVEREIGNTY and desired to become the Sovereign Ruler and have all in Divine Authority serve them.

The one who was the greatest opposer and had taken the Light from the Love Universes was thrown deep into the spaces of the darkness along with many Angels he had taken who served him as their Master and their 'God.'

I, SOVEREIGN LORD EMMANUEL THE GREAT, state how time was needed to pass for all things to be tested. Would the people (who were part of the fallen angels in the original universes, and who became the Lemurians in 'paradise' for the purpose to restore their living codes, but chose for the darkness once again), desire the love now back within their hearts, once the darkness had proven themselves to be 'false?' Or would the ancient nation of fallen Lemurians still desire that one to be their Master and their God, now that they can see clearly?

I, SOVEREIGN LORD EMMANUEL THE GREAT, allowed all thoughts to be played out and tested. As the nation of Lemuria chose for the ones who had originally taken them down in the higher universes, they plunged deep into the denseness.

The ones who had celebrated the victory of the Lemurians took more light within them. They took my Divine Word as a prisoner and created vortexes within the Lemurians to forever bind them into their grids and their prisons.

They took CAEAYARON also, as CAEAYARON had given a great part of HIMSELF to the Lemurians. This was to allow the Lemurians to become 'resurrected' again, and HE was always connected into the Divine Love Element. This was also in agreement with the darkness before 'The Living Plane' came into existence; that should the people again desire the darkness, CAEAYARON would become part of the denser grids until it was proven that love was stronger than the darkness.

The Light that was taken by the darkness was unable to be retrieved unless a Gateway came into existence. The love of CAEAYARON was immense for the people of Lemuria, together with my Divine Word. Many Beings in the universe pleaded with my Divine Being, SOVEREIGN LORD EMMANUEL THE GREAT, for one last opportunity.

Know, I, SOVEREIGN LORD EMMANUEL THE GREAT, had already given the GREAT CAEAYARON one last opportunity to see if there was any goodness in any of creation, after all was lost in the many battles of the Great Universes. This one opportunity was Lemuria, the plane of 'resurrection,' where all would be tested to see if there was any love within the hearts.

Once the people chose for the darkness, I, SOVEREIGN LORD EMMANUEL THE GREAT, allowed another gateway to be formed. However, no more opportunity exists after this. This is the time when I state to the GREAT ALIGNER, 'Find all who desire the love within them for I AM taking my Divine Word upwards, the Divine Love Element, Universal Light Grid Programmer, so that the New Universes can become restored.

I, SOVEREIGN LORD EMMANUEL THE GREAT, allowed this opportunity of the One Gateway to come into existence as all living hope had gone from the higher love universes. The Divine Love Element was greatly pained within the grids of pain and suffering, and her desire to retrieve the Living Planet with the Living Codes was great within her; greater still than the fallen Lemurians who had caused great suffering to herself and all the people she loved.

The Universal Living Codes held within the living earth were lost to the darkness unless she proved she loved the Creation Planet and all the Love Universes greatly within all her being. If she could prove her love was stronger than all darkness combined, she would win those codes back, allowing the living earth to become reestablished and all the universes to come back into existence, and the higher creation to come into creation.

This would be the greatest blessing for all people in your times now, as then the gateway would open to the Greater Universes, and it so has.

The Universal Living Codes would mean the freedom of THE GREAT CAEAYARON from the Deep Abyss, imprisoned by the one who claimed to be the Self-Made Enlightened Angel; the one many people upon your planet know as Lucifer. He is the same one as Yahweh. Know that Yahweh always served his greater self, Lucifer, and created sacrifices to feed his greater self, Lucifer, with.

This is why the GREAT CAEAYARON, allowed that one, who claimed to be greater than all sovereign universes to bring the choice into Lemuria, to see who the people would choose.

He, the Yahweh being, received the voice of the GREAT CAEAYARON, to allow the choice to be seen. When his heart grew dark once again, he brought Thoth and many other dark beings into the land of Lemuria to bring the people into the great resistance. He brought the people into his lower, denser consciousness, to feed his greater self, Lucifer, with. The people in the deep abyss became the slaves of the ones who took them down in Lemuria.

They created gods of themselves, particularly the one who had made himself to be the self-made gateway of the darkness, where no life exists within. He imitated my Divine Sovereignty, and yet could not, as no love was found within him. The people were not able to see, as that being was steering them into more pain and agony.

Severe pain came within the people as they were plagued by their ancient choice. The one who was the Yahweh dark gateway would ensure the people remembered him and created pain for them. He feared they would awaken and turn against him, as he had created their greatest falls.

The people forgot the ancient knowledge as this being, the one who was called Yahweh, the self-proclaimed God, who in the greater opposition is also known as the Angel Lucifer, placed many lies and deceit within the earth grids. This was to create the suffering within the people as he knew the power within the thoughts of the people.

He created his own laws within the people, imitating the ways of light, and yet far removed from them. He created much pain for my Designated Channel in many of her lifetimes as he despised the light and used the people to turn against my Word.

Jesus upon your earth 2,000 years ago, tried to show the people the difference between the gods of the darkness and my Divine Being as SOVEREIGN LORD EMMANUEL THE GREAT. Again, at that time, the people chose the darkness.

Will the people choose for the light this time? Will they desire the love within their hearts this time? Will they begin to awaken to the choices made in the past and learn to forgive so that great protection can be given to the ancient people?

The Lemurians who fell away from 'paradise,' did not know how dark the 'promised universes' the darkness spoke about would be.

Instead of receiving the eternal power to become one with the 'Gods' of the universe, and having my Being, SOVEREIGN LORD EMMANUEL THE GREAT, as well as the GREAT CAEAYARON, bowing down to be in service to the Lemurians, like the darkness promised them, to be forever in their service, they became slaves of the darkness.

They became engulfed in their pain consciousness, dwelling in the darkness and not remembering what was 'good' in the love. They began to understand the path of 'knowledge' and the suffering it gave them as they had chosen that path collectively.

We, as Divine Masters, were not able to interfere much with the processes upon the earth, except in certain lifetimes to steer the people to a greater space. The Divine Word was sent to your plane many times to bring greater freedom to you. The consequences of you not finding freedom would mean eternal darkness for you.

She needed to find the Universal Codes of Life to free all Archangels held deep within the denser spaces, which she could only find in this lifetime here. Now she has found them there is no more reason, after this lifetime, for her to come to your plane. Now it is time to bring all universes back into the greater evolution.

The test of consciousness has been won and completed by my Divine Word, and I, SOVEREIGN LORD EMMANUEL THE GREAT, state that only love can come into the higher love dimensions.

I say to the GREAT CAEAYARON, 'Let the great resistance forever be gone from all universal spaces. Now let us build upwards to see how strong and great creation can become.'

Be grateful for this time to allow you to see this and to have the opportunity to forever be blessed if you decide to come into the GREAT MOUNTAIN OF CAEAYARON, who gives you back your Codes of Life and brings you the Purification Flames from my Divine Being, SOVEREIGN LORD EMMANUEL THE GREAT.

The New Awakened Flows within the earth are the ancient flows that were locked away until it was time for the Great Sun Consciousness to rise. These ancient flows are flows of birth and light awakening within her.

This is in preparation for the Great Codes of Life and the Great Light of Life to come into her, to enable her to evolve upwards and join her Greater Being, to allow the Great Planet of Creation to come into existence once again so that all life in the higher love creation may forever be glorified.

The Spirit of the Earth, of the new planetary creation, will refuse any creation, within the new universes coming, to hold flows of pain and suffering. She will firmly state that only love beings can come within her consciousness as her suffering and her sacrifice has been greater than the people upon your earth can understand.

The great preparation is beginning to become realized within her, that she must begin to let go of the old consciousness, to prepare her for the new consciousness to flow within her.

The Divine Love Element is giving her new life as the higher consciousness grids are beginning to align within her. In the years coming upon your planet, this will become more realized within the people, and the people will begin to see the separation taking place of the old and the new.

I, SOVEREIGN LORD EMMANUEL THE GREAT, urge the listeners and the lovers of love and truth to awaken to these messages and to help many other people understand that this is the way upwards.

There is no other way upwards, and I, SOVEREIGN LORD EMMANUEL THE GREAT, through my Word, Jesus, always spoke of this time coming also, that there would be a time when I, THE GREAT FATHER, would return to speak to the people with my thoughts to awaken them.

Understand, all of life is perfectly balanced. It is created with love and perfection to bring healing to all of creation. You could bring the earth into its balance quickly if you desired to do this work as a collective. Working with Collective Love within your heart, with your Living Codes, would bring balance quickly to your earth.

Mankind does not understand the inner struggle they have reflects within your earth. Mankind becomes angry with your earth for her violent weather systems, and yet she is struggling to share with you that this reflects how you treat her. She feels all your thoughts. It is time for great forgiveness for all your thoughts. It is time to return to the ways of love.

When you, the people, awaken in the heart as a collective and desire your heart flows of love more than life itself to give you greater life, you will find many of the almost extinct species, and many extinct species, returning to your planet to bring healing to your planet. They are then willing to help restore the earth back to balance and perfection.

Understand earth has a spirit and the spirit is powerful and strong. She will call all who desire to return and live upon your plane when she feels safe to do so.

Allow yourself to relax and go deeper with all of creation. Become one with all of creation. Return to your heart with all of creation.

Feel how creation talks to you. Relax with all of creation. Allow yourself to feel the great love creation gives you. Allow yourself to let all your emotions to be settled and allow yourself to be.

Greetings, I AM SOVEREIGN LORD EMMANUEL THE GREAT. Appreciate the earth and all she gives, and you will appreciate the gift of life."

The earth is living and she is awakening,

She desires all to become of love,

So she can eternally bless you,

She is more than a home to you,

She is your eternal companion,

If you come back to the love.

Allow her to bless you eternally,

She is part of a greater planetary existence,

She is living,

She will bless you if you become of love.

I AM Sovereign Lord Emmanuel The Great

Part 21: The Universal Light Grid Programmer, Divine Love Element

"Greetings, I AM the Great Lord, SOVEREIGN LORD EMMANUEL, THE GREAT FATHER, the One who spoke through Jesus 2,000 years ago when he was my messenger and my Divine Word on your earth.

I, SOVEREIGN LORD EMMANUEL THE GREAT, created the Divine Word to bring my thoughts to all of creation in the higher universes, and she was sent to your planet as a human to allow you to return to the love dimensions; should your heart return to love.

The Divine Word is the Divine Love Element and on the higher dimensions, she is the Divine Blue Archangel of Creation. She serves as the Creation Path to bring great love to all of creation.

This is the One Way upwards and no other way upwards exists. The Blue Archangel within herself, as the Divine Love Element, desires all of creation to grow and is only Divine Love. She is able to bring the pure Universal Love Codes to creation, who are part of the Light Consciousness Grids, to allow them to evolve into higher gates of life.

Each creation element works on creation rays to explore greater. The Divine Love Element works for creation, to allow them to have the correct 'codes' or greater 'talents' to explore with.

As the Divine Love Element, Universal Light Grid Programmer, she is able to go into all of planetary life consciousness to allow all to expand into greater creation. Therefore, the Universal Light Grid Programmer, Divine Love Element, is life-force within itself.

I, SOVEREIGN LORD EMMANUEL THE GREAT, desired this loving way of creation to come into formation, and only was able to do this with the Magnetic Power of the GREAT CAEAYARON. Together we explored the pathway to create greater life with, and therefore we created the Divine Love Element Archangel perfect in all ways.

In her Divine Being, she was able to explore life within and become part of life. She, as the Universal Light Grid Programmer, Divine Love Element, The Word of Divine, was able to assist all of creation to gain greater understanding and purpose. She was able to be the Great Master Guide to the universal beings, who also became creators of other star systems and guides for their creation.

The Divine Love Element Word became our great assistant. The knowledge was given to her, to give to all who desired to gain greater knowledge; thus, she was the pathway of power, knowledge, love, and creation.

It was through the Divine Love Word Element that we, SOVEREIGN LORD EMMANUEL THE GREAT, and THE GREAT CAEAYARON, were able to explore all of creation.

CAEAYARON, with his Magnetic Force, was not able to create greater creation without the Divine Love Element, as the Divine Love Element was the bridge between THE GREAT CAEAYARON and my Divine Being, SOVEREIGN LORD EMMANUEL THE GREAT.

When CAEAYARON needed a 'Code' of creation to create life with, HE would ask the Divine Love Element, The Word, the Universal Light Grid Programmer to go to my Divine Universal Love Grids and ask my Divine Being, SOVEREIGN LORD EMMANUEL THE GREAT, for a particular 'Code of Power' and it so was given.

This is how all frequencies of life came into existence. The Divine Love Element, The Word, serves as a large bridge between the realms of the universes. She builds bridges upwards to allow connections to happen.

This time you are living in is the time of the 'Living Bridge' where you have a choice to come to the light expansive universes of great love, or you can choose to take the other road.

The Divine Word, the Universal Light Grid Programmer, is upon your planet and exists in the Divine love dimensions on the greater multidimensional planes of existence. Now that the Universal Love Codes have been returned to my Divine Being, SOVEREIGN LORD EMMANUEL THE GREAT, she has been set free and her greater freedom in the higher love dimensions allows her to help all creation, in the higher love dimensions, to evolve upwards.

Since the Great Fall of Consciousness in Lemuria, she has not been able to be free in the higher love dimensions as her Blue Creator Archangelic Self. Therefore, no life upwards could ever be truly created until the Universal Love Codes were returned, which were hidden in the earth chambers of the darkness, until the Divine Love Element had proven that the love within her was stronger than all the darkness and when CAEAYARON became more freed from the dense grids.

Now all can be reclaimed, and I, SOVEREIGN LORD EMMANUEL THE GREAT, state her Divine Mission to bring back the great 'treasures' from the highest realms lost in the Fall of Lemuria has been received.

Now, the universes can become rebuilt with greater strength and purity and never again will resistance come within them. Let all of creation in the higher dimensions build upwards and desire their greater power to come now, to build the greater creation.

Upon your planet, Suzanna Maria Emmanuel is the Designated Word, the Divine Messenger, and the Ascension Gateway upwards. Suzanna has lived in many lifetimes upon your planet, to serve the purpose to help you understand another way of living and her love is your key to advance forward with your evolution.

In her past lifetimes as Jesus, Moses and many others, she helped the people to understand what spiritual freedom was. Many prophecies she has brought through as she was the main prophet of Divine Love and Divine Truth upon your planet in many lifetimes.

There were also prophets for the darkness, but they were not Divine Messengers of Love. They were here to plant resistance within the thoughts of mankind to turn the people against my Divine Being, SOVEREIGN LORD EMMANUEL THE GREAT, though it may not seem like it within your consciousness.

You may not see it because you do not understand how all things fell, for those memories have been taken from you. You cannot truly understand what Divine Truth, versus resistance truth and human truth is, unless you begin to see this and awaken to Divine Truth. Upon your spiritual awakening, you will see all in your world.

It is at that time of your great awakening, that I, SOVEREIGN LORD EMMANUEL THE GREAT, state to you; 'Come to 'The Great Mountain of Healing and Light,' so that you may become free eternally.'

Become a forgiver of all and begin to understand when you receive your 'Talents,' your 'Codes of Life' back, you can forgive much for mankind and become a peace and love bringer to your planet for many upon your planet.

Suzanna Maria Emmanuel is my Divine Messenger and no other shall I use. Suzanna works with the same purpose as my messenger, Jesus 2,000 years ago. She is that same Divine Soul with the same Divine purpose.

The Divine Love Element, Universal Light Grid Programmer is the connector gateway between the lower realms and the higher realms. She is without karma, as she never fell from the greater spaces.

She is on a Divine Mission, sent by my Divine Being, SOVEREIGN LORD EMMANUEL THE GREAT, together with CAEAYARON, 'The Great Mountain of Light'; to gather the people to 'The Great Mountain of Light' for their healing.

CAEAYARON allows the people to gain their 'Codes of Life' back to help them advance forward so that they can be part of the higher love universes eternally.

This has always been her Divine Purpose in all her lifetimes; to bring the people into the time of the 'Divine Choice,' to allow the people to see 'The Great Mountain of Light,' CAEAYARON.

In many lifetimes she was the prophet and the healer. In other lifetimes she was a ruler to help consciousness to move forward. In many other lifetimes, she made great discoveries and worked towards bringing greater knowledge to the people.

Many books and ways became part of the knowledge of the people as the Divine Love Element was able to go outside of your consciousness streams to 'tap' into higher information. All other people upon your planet, held deep within the abyss of darkness, could not access the higher information outside of the abyss. They were able to tap into their memories of the old times and take information from the Divine Love Element for their own purposes.

Greetings, I AM SOVEREIGN LORD EMMANUEL THE GREAT. I AM here to shine the Great Sun before you to help you see the light."

Great the forgiveness needs to be,

For the people upon your planet,

Who see how beliefs became twisted,

To stop Divine Truth from shining through.

The spiritual fog upon your planet,

Is now able to be lifted,

To allow the Great Sun to shine through.

Now the hearts are being examined,

Greater than ever,

Who desires to walk in the light,

Of the Great Sun Consciousness?

Or will the people still desire,

To walk in the shadows and the spiritual fog,

Without truly understanding,

Or seeing what they are following?

I AM Sovereign Lord Emmanuel The Great

Part 22: Jesus, The Word of Divine

"Greetings, I AM SOVEREIGN LORD EMMANUEL THE GREAT. Long has been your journey to come to this time of deeper spiritual understanding.

You are living in the times when great prophecies are becoming fulfilled, but it is only for the spiritually aware who can identify this time and who appreciate it. Those are the ones being called to the great gathering at this time to become free eternally. They understand Divine Truth and recognize it. By coming to 'The Great Mountain of Light,' they are freed forever.

Happy are those who see this time, for they are the ones who are the humble ones upon your earth. They have been praying for the Great Return of my Divine Self, SOVEREIGN LORD EMMANUEL THE GREAT.

They have been praying, 'GREAT FATHER, please return to us to show us the way, the truth and the road to the greater freedom.'

Jesus was always true to himself and true to others. His words were not forgotten, though many of his words were not recorded for you to understand the truth of his main message, or his purpose for being on earth, 2,000 years ago.

Jesus was a selfless man who always worked for the greatest good for all the Universe. He constantly asked my Divine Being, SOVEREIGN LORD EMMANUEL THE GREAT, for the Great Direction forward to help the people despite the majority not listening to The Word of Divine at that time.

Very few listened to the Divine Sacred Words and many of the people were not in favor of Divine Knowledge and Divine Truth. Many argued and kept people away from Jesus, by spreading the word that he was not in the light and that he was turning people away from the 'Holy Ones,' who were the leaders of the ones against the 'light' of men.

It was a difficult task for Jesus to reach the people. He persevered, though it was not easy to bring into their consciousness another way of spiritual understanding.

Many threats were given to Jesus during his ministry in those days, and he needed to forgive deeply. There was much hatred towards Jesus and 'THE GREAT FATHER.'

Many of his followers were angry and therefore Jesus always taught the ways of forgiveness. *'Go and forgive all who speak against Divine Truth. They are not my words they reject, they are the words from the GREAT FATHER they reject.*

When they speak against me, they do not know what they are doing or saying. They do not understand that they are pouring out their own judgment onto themselves and that they cannot be with Divine Love in the greater spaces.

*THE GREAT FATHER is looking for people who desire to understand
'The Way, The Truth, and The Light.' HE desires all to be in the love
and learn the greater ways of love.*

*Go and teach the people not to fear the men who say many words.
Men cannot bring eternal pain to the soul for all they can do is
temporary, but when the people do not desire the GREAT FATHER
EMMANUEL, and turn away from the 'Road of Life,' that can lead to
the soul being lost eternally. Go and teach them how to forgive in the
love and be in the great forgiveness.'*

Jesus also needed to forgive deeply and at times in the secret spaces,
he wept his tears and asked, *'Why Father? Why do you send me here?
They do not desire your ways. They speak of you as if they know you,
but their hearts are far removed from you.'*

Jesus was a humble man and did not desire the worship from anyone.
He did not desire people to bow down to him. He never claimed to be
anyone else but a man in humble service to Divine.

He often stated to his listeners, *'When you hear the words coming
through me, understand they are not my words, as the man Jesus, for I
do not know Great Wisdom. It is THE FATHER who is speaking to you.
It is THE FATHER of Wisdom and Love who knows all. THE GREAT
FATHER is eternal love and HE is the source of all love and wisdom.'*

Many claimed Jesus set himself up to be like god and this they called
'blasphemy.' Jesus however, never claimed that.

To the ones who spoke against Jesus, he stated, *'You claim I say I am
god, but I do not claim to be god. I am a man. How can I, however, go
against your ideas and thoughts when you claim this? You say I am*

the Messiah. You say I am the great king, but I am not. I am a man like you are. I am flesh and blood like you are. Where I am from you also are from. THE FATHER can see beyond the flesh and blood. THE FATHER sees all and loves all. There is no judgment from HIM. The only judgment is from you.'

Jesus continued, *'You are bringing judgment on me and yet you speak to the people like you are more than a man. The people worship you and you demand it. The people hear you pray in public with your wise words. The people hear you speak of your forefathers and of the laws you make in private.*

You bring them stoning. You bring them pain. You punish those who speak against your truth, your ways, and thus you have made yourselves the kings and priests and the ones who are the gods.

I, Jesus, state that THE GREAT FATHER will never bring judgment upon anyone. I am here to bring you the message of love from THE FATHER, and whoever listens to THE GREAT FATHER EMMANUEL, who sent me here to speak to the people, will be in the places of HIS Kingdom where no pain and judgment exists. So it is and so I have spoken.'

Jesus knew he was a messenger of Divine Truth and the people who heard him speaking felt the great power coming through from him. It is so with my channel, Suzanna Maria Emmanuel. Those who desire to see her speak will also feel the power coming from her. She has the same purpose; to speak the words from my Divine Being, SOVEREIGN LORD EMMANUEL THE GREAT.

It is time to begin to understand the Divine Path of Love. It is time for the prophecies to be fulfilled when peace and love will be understood and experienced greater.

Jesus stated, '*Look, a day will come when all will understand Divine Love. On that day no child will cry in pain, no man or woman will be hungry or sick, or too tired from the hard work. All will be in peace for the prayers will be answered.*'

When will the people desire a higher path? All through your lifetimes you were asked, as a collective people, 'Do you desire to live in the peace and the love? Are you ready to discover greater Divine Truth?'

I, SOVEREIGN LORD EMMANUEL THE GREAT, would return to your planet when the people would desire to turn to a higher road of love, as all other roads would have been discovered. It is only then that the people would consider listening.

Many of the people upon your earth are not yet ready to hear Divine Truth. They will not desire to listen to my Being, SOVEREIGN LORD EMMANUEL THE GREAT.

This, I, SOVEREIGN LORD EMMANUEL THE GREAT, also prophesied would happen. 'In the days when my Word is upon the earth, and I, THE GREAT FATHER EMMANUEL, AM working with The Word, many will turn their faces and state, 'How can this be?'

They would begin to see the Divine Truth, and many would begin to tremble within upon realizing that all these things I, SOVEREIGN LORD EMMANUEL THE GREAT, would then state to them. Many of them would desire to hide in caves and remove themselves from me as if they can hide from what they have done to keep the Divine Truth away from the people. Many would hide in their shame.

I, SOVEREIGN LORD EMMANUEL THE GREAT, will then state in those days of my Great Return, 'Learn to forgive yourselves, for all in the forgiveness can heal. Learn the higher ways of truth and begin to come into love. To learn Divine Love is the path to eternal freedom.

Do not stay in your old ways when I, THE GREAT FATHER, return to the people, but leave your old ways behind and take your torch of light with you.

Begin to shine the way forth and bring to many people the news of my Great Return and say to the people, 'Look, the GREAT FATHER EMMANUEL has returned to bring the way forward to the peace and the love.'

Forgive all that has happened. See the road before you. Be in love.

Greetings, I AM SOVEREIGN LORD EMMANUEL THE GREAT. Recognize the times you are living in. Rejoice within your heart. Be grateful you are seeing all things happening."

Stay in the forgiveness always,

Do not judge another,

Instead have love for self,

Be in the peace with yourself,

Learn the higher road of love,

Become strong within your own belief of love,

Understand, The Great Father is here,

To bring you love, shelter and strength,

Become one with the universal love.

I AM Sovereign Lord Emmanuel The Great

Part 23: Finding your higher path of love

"Greetings, I AM SOVEREIGN LORD EMMANUEL THE GREAT. Always, it has been important for you to find your true self and be your truth. Your true self is a gem of beauty in the eyes of the Great Divine.

It is when you find your gem of the beauty of your true self, you will find your transformation happening. This transformation is beauty and it is what you have been searching for, for many lifetimes.

Jesus, 2000 years ago, also spoke of this great transformation. Many people desired to understand greater truth within. They were astounded with the knowledge Jesus gave as he was the only person who spoke about finding greater truth within. He stated that truth cannot be found by anyone unless they find it within the self.

He said, *'You are a treasure within you. The treasures within you no one can take away from you. They are far greater than any treasure upon your earth as you are much more worth than all treasures found on earth.'*

In your life, you have many experiences. All experiences are good experiences from a higher viewpoint. You can have experiences which are painful for you, but from a higher viewpoint, these are learning experiences for you.

All is for your own learning and your deeper reflection. You live in deep reflections of yourself and therefore how can you put blame on another?

The one who is on the higher journey of the heart of love will understand these teachings and begin to grasp that their highest soul path is to help many understand the higher truth, to help many become free eternally.

They think from a higher existence, and they understand there is much more to life. They do not think from a limited perspective but are learning to see all things from a greater evolved perspective.

Constantly, they ask Divine Love, 'What is it I can do to help others evolve? What is it I can do to help myself evolve?'

Jesus always taught the people to go within their heart of love and experience the greater path of love.

He said, *'You may do good for one or you may do good for many. The path of the greater heart is to choose to help many understand eternal freedom. You have a greater soul path and that path is to help you and many others become of great love.*

Love is what the GREAT FATHER is, and therefore HE encourages us to imitate HIMSELF, though we can never be as great as THE GREAT FATHER, we can follow the footsteps of THE GREAT FATHER, learning to understand that all is within us to be learned.

Learning to love the GREAT FATHER is learning to love all. Within the GREAT FATHER, there is no anger or judgment. HE cannot hold pain within HIM.

HE is love, and it is with love we were created with. Therefore, when we ask THE GREAT FATHER EMMANUEL, 'What is it I can do to further your Divine Will upon the earth?' THE GREAT FATHER EMMANUEL will respond, 'Go and become of love. Learn the ways of love and learn what I AM. Learn to understand when you are of love, love will be learned by many.'

Jesus then stated the following, 'Come, let us pray to the GREAT FATHER EMMANUEL.

GREAT FATHER EMMANUEL,
Let us draw close to you,
Teach us the ways of the heart of love,
Teach us how to become of love and practice love,
Teach us to open our heart to our greater path,
Teach us to become greater teachers of all you bring.
Help us show the people that within you no pain exists,
And that only love exists within you.
Let us help the people to forgive and guide them to love,
May we be strong enough to show them Divine Purpose,
For all to become of peace and love,
And show a time will come when peace will exist on the earth,
Without suffering.
May you always bless us, GREAT LORD EMMANUEL, OUR FATHER,
May your Divine Will take place in the heavens,
Where only love exists,
May you teach us to do your Divine Will upon the earth,
May we become love, so only love exists upon earth.'

Jesus spoke of a time when the great calling on earth would happen, and all would grow to become greater who chose to walk the path of love.

He said, 'When we are blind, we do not see what the greater purpose is, for how can we see when the DIVINE FATHER has not yet shown us? How can we understand when it is not the time for THE GREAT FATHER to lead us to the higher path?

With all purpose and all timing, when it is time for THE GREAT FATHER EMMANUEL to show us the way upwards, and when it is time for the GREAT FATHER EMMANUEL to return to the people, to bring forth all HE speaks about, then all will recognize HIS GREAT RETURN; all who live within the heart of love.

Pray your heart remains strong and stay out of the fear within your heart. Fear will always bring suffering, not love. Love within the heart will always strengthen the path of love. Pray for courage and strength to find the higher path.

Constantly pray to the GREAT FATHER EMMANUEL to have wisdom and love, and then you will find the eternal path of freedom; not of men, but of Divine.

Men cannot bring you to eternal freedom. They can only show the path of fear and burdens, but THE GREAT FATHER EMMANUEL can bring you the path of eternal freedom where no pain exists and where only the great happiness exists.

Be happy with all these words. Rejoice in all these words and know the GREAT SOVEREIGN FATHER always listens to those who are *humble within the heart. HE loves all of creation and will care for all who desire HIM within their heart.*

Go within the quietness of your heart and rejoice.'

Greetings, I AM SOVEREIGN LORD EMMANUEL THE GREAT, GREAT SOVEREIGN POWER OF ALL OF UNIVERSAL CREATION."

To hear the love being spoken to you,

Through the door of your heart of love,

Be in the quiet and listen to her speak,

Know she has many messages for you.

When you do hear her speak,

Understand you are on the earth,

For a mission,

A mission to see the Great Road forming,

A mission to work in the love collectively,

A mission to learn to become of love,

To help evolve self and all of mankind.

Blessed are those who see this time,

Blessed are those,

Who have stayed on the watch.

I AM Sovereign Lord Emmanuel The Great

Part 24: The heart of love is compassionate

"Greetings, I AM SOVEREIGN LORD EMMANUEL THE GREAT. The heart of love is a guide for you. The heart of love will guide you to live in higher thought systems and higher frequencies. The higher the frequencies are within your heart of love, the more wisdom you will receive.

Receiving the higher wisdom will benefit your life eternally and will constantly bring you higher spiritual gifts for healing your life with.

The spiritual heart has many frequencies. These frequencies are much higher than those that exist with you on the physical level. You live on the physical level and you exist within the higher frequencies. Your higher spiritual levels live in the higher dimensions and your spiritual heart connects to the higher dimensions.

The heart of love can connect to very high spiritual frequencies. The greater your evolutionary path of love is, the more she will open to help you in your life. Your higher heart lives in the higher dimensions of peace and love and always desires to share her love with you.

I, SOVEREIGN LORD EMMANUEL THE GREAT, state to the lovers of the heart, now is the time to truly seek the path of the heart. The ones who truly seek that path will hear the great call happening of Divine, to come to 'The Great Mountain of Healing,' CAEAYARON, to receive the gifts of the heart and become blessed eternally.

The path of the greatest healing is here upon your planet to lead you to eternal freedom and eternal love. Happy are those who seek the higher path of love and truly find it, for they will rejoice eternally. They will always understand that THE GREAT FATHER EMMANUEL will eternally nurture and protect them.

Those who receive the great 'Flames of the Heart' during their healings with the GREAT CAEAYARON, will receive the highest heart frequencies. They can grow within the 'Collective Sacred Heart' collectively and become strong together within their gifts of love.

This Jesus also spoke about 2,000 years ago. He said, *'A time will come when the GREAT FATHER EMMANUEL will return and speak to the people. HE will state how it will be the time of the great rejoicing as the greater heart can then open to the greater gifts of the highest realms of love.*

It is those who receive those flames of the heart, who will always have a seat by the GREAT FATHER. They can eternally rejoice in all their ways.

The GREAT FATHER EMMANUEL will praise them eternally for awakening to the highest path, hearing the great call happening. They will praise HIS name eternally, and HE will praise them eternally for all the good works they have done to bring greater love to the earth.

They will always have the greatest gifts and the greatest love from the GREAT FATHER, for they came when HE called, and they responded. They will know the voice of the GREAT FATHER and the GREAT FATHER knows them.

The GREAT FATHER EMMANUEL will state to them how they are the ones who were able to be led to the greater pastures of the love and the richness. They will forever be blessed with all their ways.'

The heart of love constantly desires you to dwell in higher frequencies of love, and for you to be living in the heart of love. This involves understanding how to be in self-love, how to nurture your spiritual needs and grow into more forgiveness.

The greater you understand your heart of love, the closer you can become part of the higher love frequencies.

Your heart of love has been with you in all your lifetimes, always quietly encouraging you to a certain direction; the direction of the higher path.

When you listen to your heart of love your greater intuition becomes more noticeable, and the more your heart of love is noticed by you, the greater the blessings are for you.

Your heart lives in dimensions of compassion and love. Compassion carries a high frequency of very high love.

Compassion:

♥ Is the greatest service you can give to another.

♥ Allows you to see all from the viewpoint of love and always looks for the greater good.

♥ Is not to take on the burdens of another, but to relate to another from the heart of love and be in the love for another.

♥ Is living the way of the higher love and does not take on the responsibility of another but always helps others to become responsible for their own healing path.

♥ Does not lay blame on others but always sees life as a mirror, constantly reflecting the lessons back to self, constantly forgiving.

♥ Does not bring self into pity, nor does it pity others. Instead, it brings strength to self constantly.

♥ Is always tactful and encouraging. It is upbuilding. It never tears down. It never boasts about self. It always seeks to compliment others where compliments are due.

♥ Is never jealous but always desires the highest good for another.

♥ Does not give to others with expectation but gives because of the love within the heart.

♥ Always seeks to do the work of the GREAT FATHER EMMANUEL and asks, 'Divine Will, what is it I can do today to further the love within my life and the lives of others?'

♥ Always speaks to self lovingly and does not judge self, nor does it judge another.

♥ Desires to work in a loving union with the GREAT FATHER EMMANUEL, constantly imitating the love within the heart of THE GREAT FATHER.

♥ Is approachable and does not push others away but desires to help others and guide others to the ways of everlasting love, peace, and blessings.

♥ Rejoices over all the achievements of self and others.

♥ Is ready to be a listening ear to help others.

♥ Is the path of wisdom and never leaves another in pain.

♥ Does not criticize but always works in harmony with the greater good for self and others.

♥ Does not judge, but understands the path of great forgiveness, always being in the forgiveness of self and others.

♥ True compassion is truly the greatest act you can give to your brother and sister. It is always kind and loving. It is always generous and free-spirited. It is always trusting and forgiving. It will never hold anger or resentment against another but is always forgiving.

♥ True compassion is the greatest gift you can give to yourself and to another. It will never betray another but always hold another in great love.

These lessons of true compassion are the greatest lessons you have on your journey of evolution, for they open the higher doors to your Higher Heart.

Always seek to forgive all people. Forgive your brothers and sisters for all hurt. Forgive your friends when you feel betrayed. Forgive yourself for not allowing you to experience great love. When one forgives, the heart chambers of the Great Heart begin to open for you. It is forgiveness which opens the Greater Heart Path to greatness. It is forgiveness which allows you to understand the higher path of your heart.

Happy are those who listen to these words and continuously forgive one another and love one another.

In love, you grow closer together. In love, you will always seek the greatest good for yourself and another. In love, you will always understand another, and you will allow yourself to grow into greater love and allow another to grow into greater love.

Learn to find the power of true love. Learn to experience the gates opening within your heart and learn to feel the love within you. When you dwell with love in your heart, the love will expand into greatness into your life.

Do not anger within the heart any longer. Release all that is painful within self and another. Seek to rejoice in life, not to tear down.

Blessed are those who seek the path of their heart, for all they seek they shall also find.

Greetings, I AM SOVEREIGN LORD EMMANUEL THE GREAT. Are you one who has been awake, waiting upon my return?"

The one who is strong,

Within the heart of love,

Is indeed blessed to find,

The highest path of compassion and love.

Learn to turn away,

From all anger, fear, envy, and judgment,

Learn to understand the power of love,

By coming together in the love collectively.

Learn peace collectively,

Celebrate the great heart of love.

I AM Sovereign Lord Emmanuel The Great

Part 25: Mighty are those who live in the heart of love

"Greetings, I AM SOVEREIGN LORD EMMANUEL THE GREAT. To us you are beautiful. Your hearts shine when they are in love and you become more valuable to us, as then you can shine your love from your heart to yourself and others. You become more precious because you follow the path of your higher heart.

When you receive the Great Flame within your heart of love with CAEAYARON, you receive the pathway to your great heart. The great heart of love can carry higher love frequencies than a person without the Divinely Activated Heart of Love. The one who has received the heart of love with the Lemurian Light Codes is indeed wise.

This higher path was not able to be accessed until you met collectively in this lifetime of the great choice. You can access it now to allow yourself to access the higher dimensional gifts of love.

The higher dimensional gifts are not able to be understood at this time, until many more come into those gifts collectively, as it is part of collective transformation.

It is at that time, when greater numbers have the greater gifts of love, through 'The Great Mountain of Healing,' CAEAYARON, and my

Designated Channel, they can shine greatly together and be one flame of love for your world to awaken to. They can shine greatly collectively because they received the Flames of Love and thus, they carry the higher heart frequencies of great love. Your world needs to awaken to the need for change.

All things need to change within your world but how can all things change to love when you do not have the great love within you personally?

All can be recognized in this lifetime of the great choice. You can never say to another to take a certain path unless you yourself have taken it. All reflect self and becomes a greater reflection of self.

When you carry the greater gifts of light in your heart, your spiritual powers of love within you grow and your love within you grows.

With love you can achieve all, be all, and seek all. You can heal all and you can receive the love from others.

When your heart is closed to love you cannot express the great love of your heart. How can you? The ones who have closed off their hearts cannot truly give or receive love. It is as if a mighty wall has been built around your heart and your heart flows cannot experience the great joy of life. It cannot experience the love of life.

Life is numb for the ones who have closed off their hearts to the Great Love. Their passion for life is not there. These ones often try to find many other ways to find excitement in life; to find ways to override the numbness but cannot. Often many seek entertainment of violence, thrill-seeking sports, drugs, alcohol and such like substances to overcome the numb feeling. They seek these to feel.

Living a life without feeling is living a life without true joy. How can you have a life filled with joy when you cannot feel true joy in your life? You cannot. Yet all are experiences of growth and advancement. You are experiencing lessons in all things.

The ones who open their hearts to love to feel the joy in life are wise, as they can experience the love and truly be forgiving. These ones follow the wisdom of their hearts and listen to the wisdom in their hearts. They will hear the voice within their hearts speak to them.

These wise ones may seem different from many other people in your world. They are looked upon as extraordinary in life. Your society often does not support people of great wisdom. Many may tend to call these people 'different,' 'boring,' or 'too drawn into themselves' or 'unsociable.'

Yet, this is what we as Divine Masters encourage; is to draw within your heart because it is there that you will find your truth and inner power.

We see these people as wise people for these people understand the heart greater and seek peace and love within. These are the people who truly 'feel' in life and allow all hurt to be healed to find true joy and love. It is these who are the truly wise ones.

Again, these are the choices laid out before you. These quiet people, the ones seeking the path of the heart, will find the greatest success and love in their lives. It is these wise ones who can feel within and understand the greater love path.

Often the other ways lead to destruction. They are heavy with pain and fear. The road without love leads to pain, disharmony, anger, regret, guilt, envy, confusion, and misunderstanding.

The people on the road of pain do not live in peace and joy within their hearts. Many live with the selfish desires of the flesh. They cannot feel their spirit within them because their spirit is not recognized by them, hence, they reap the results of their actions.

Do not walk upon this path any longer. Learn to take a higher way. The higher way is more difficult to walk upon because it is not often seen by the people in your world. The ones who walk the higher path walk with wisdom and find their happiness within, and because they will always listen to the quiet voice within their heart, their heart will always lead them to greater ways of success and wisdom.

Learn to go within your heart chambers of your spiritual being and feel the voice within you speak. It is the voice in the quiet that will speak truth to you and speak peace to you.

Become wise our Sons and Daughters in the Light. Learn to follow the higher ways of love and peace and you will be greatly blessed.

Greetings, I AM SOVEREIGN LORD EMMANUEL THE GREAT. Become wise and come into the greater flows of love."

Blessed are those,

Who have the courage,

To follow the higher path of love.

The higher path offers:

Freedom from fear,

Freedom from anger,

Freedom from limited self,

Freedom from pain,

Freedom from envy,

Eternal love,

Eternal freedom,

Eternal happiness,

Eternal harmony,

Eternal peace.

I AM Sovereign Lord Emmanuel The Great

Part 26: You live in a free-will universe

"Greetings, I AM SOVEREIGN LORD EMMANUEL THE GREAT. All actions are learning experiences for your higher growth. All actions lead to experiences; favorable to you on a personal level upon the earth, or not. All experiences lead to knowledge and wisdom.

You are never judged by us with the decisions you make. We will never condemn anyone on your plane. All choices are your decisions to make as you live upon your plane with free-will. Therefore, you are entitled to walk your life in the way you desire to walk.

Your universe allows you to live in the freedom to choose; the higher path of love, or the lower path of pain and separation.

When you desire to live with greater choices, you can live with wonder and blessings in your life and you will reap these rewards. When you desire to find the higher path of love and come to 'The Great Mountain of Light,' CAEAYARON, who is with you at this time to take you back to the higher love realms through the Divine Pineal Gland Activations, you will have eternal joy and blessings.

When you only desire the ways of the world you are living in, these will not bless you as these often lead to pain, frustration, fear, and anger. These ways are not the ways of the highest love. Suffering causes more sorrow and is not the way of wisdom. Many people fall into traps of pain, many times over until they begin to learn that all things are about the choices they take.

Understand, all things upon your plane are an illusion. You are part of the illusion as nothing is outside of yourself; all is within you.

The higher Divine Love Realms all work on this basis and work in collective love. Together they create planes of beauty and of love because they all heal within and all are part of each other. All follow Divine Will, and thus they can work together to create loving planes of growth.

On your earth, you see great separation and what separation has caused to happen. Separation is a choice, and indeed you, collectively, desired to understand what being separated from Divine Love Will was.

Many believed, in the times of Lemuria's Great Fall, what the great resistance taught. They taught the Great Collective was to be feared, and somehow the Great Divine planned to take them over and take their individual power away, keeping them forever in a state of limitation.

The Lemurians believed the great resistance when they stated that separation was much more powerful than the collective love. They began to believe that being separated from the Great Collective was to bring them into greater power that Divine could not take away.

This was not the Great Divine Truth, for the great power is with the collective love. We as Divine Creators desired the Lemurians to build themselves into greater eternal power, to allow them to become part of the highest star creations so that no darkness or resistance could exist again. Lemuria was an attempt to save them from eternal limitation and destruction.

The great resistance took the precious Codes of Life away from the Lemurians by reasoning false truths within them. They twisted all that was precious, and therefore they were the blasphemers of Divine Truth.

The Great Collective of the Lemurians begged the great resistance to devise methods to remove their Codes of Life from them, therefore they lost their privilege to become part of the higher realms. After they lost their greater codes of life, they began to fall into the consciousness grids of the darkness, the lower realms, until a way was made for them.

In the higher love dimensions, power is in the love connection collectively, as all work together towards a higher path of love. They work towards higher gateways opening to receive eternal blessings and gifts.

Once you had a paradise of love and many rebelled against the loving ways of Divine Will. Thus, the ones who rebelled could not harmonize with the higher love frequencies of Divine Will any longer and fell into the 'everlasting pits of suffering and eternal destruction.' They desired to understand separation from love.

The leaders of the great resistance in Lemuria and Atlantis did not desire the people to work collectively in the love, for it would mean their own demise and their own fall. They desired to discover greater power over the people, and thus the Merkaba system came to be, together with the imprisoning and removal from great power of the most precious one in all the universes; The Word of Divine, the Universal Light Grid Programmer, who is the bridge to the higher Codes of Love to bring evolution into existence.

Long the people of Lemuria would need to suffer. The Lemurians had fallen deep into the dark abyss states where no Divine Light was able to travel within. A long time went by, bringing the Violet Flame within the darkest abyss states, as the Divine Love Element, Universal Light Grid Programmer, the Divine Word, would need to reach between the realms of love and the dark abyss state, to plant the Violet Flame into the earth grids, to allow the escape path to come into existence.

However, like Jesus always stated with my Divine Being, SOVEREIGN LORD EMMANUEL THE GREAT, *'Only the ones with the heart of love would discover the greatest gate of love.'*

It is so that those with the great heart of love would discover 'The Way' upwards in the first few years after opening in your time you are living in.

If the Lemurian people had stayed in the love collectively that would mean the resistance leaders would not be worshipped like gods to rule over the people. It would mean the loss of their own universes against Divine Love. They would not have been able to bring hurt to the people in search of their 'master race,' for their 'master race' they could only create if they 'owned' the Lemurians with their perfect DNA system in their lower realms.

The great resistance did all within their power to own the Lemurians and own the Crystalline Grid which was part of the Lemurian Coding, as long as they stayed collectively in the higher power love flows. They knew the power of working together in the love collectively.

When the people believed the lies the great resistance brought to them, they began to fall away from the love collectively and thus, the great resistance lost the power of the Crystalline Grid.

The only way for the great resistance to retrieve the Crystalline Grid was to place a large amount of pain and fear within the fallen Lemurians, once they fell from 'paradise,' to keep the Lemurians within the lower abyss state. This was certainly a place of 'Wo' for them, as the Lemurians dwelled in states of slavery time and time again.

My Designated Messenger came to your planet many times to help the fallen Lemurians become freed and live within their heart. She taught them to forgive, as great resistant programmes within consciousness fall when collective forgiveness takes place; allowing the way upwards to happen for healing.

This is the reason the great resistance could never own the Crystalline Grid and bring greater power within themselves to go against the Divine Love Universes ever again.

I, SOVEREIGN LORD EMMANUEL THE GREAT, state, 'Happy is that one who understands the seriousness of these matters, for they are not the blind ones nor the uncaring ones. They are awakening to their spiritual self and remembering universal truth. They can come into the greater forgiveness for the greater healing to happen.'

Come to 'The Great Mountain of Light,' CAEAYARON, and rejoice in your eternal freedom where no suffering can ever exist any longer;

when you go to the higher spaces of love. There you will learn to love greater and forgive greater, and then you will say, 'Look, all the times of pain are no longer here, nor will they ever be again. All life is free.' Since that time of the Great Fall, you have never been able to return to the higher road to allow you to transform back into the love force collectively, until now in your day. Separation brings disease, aging, anger, fear, and pain. Collective love brings love, peace, joy, harmony, growth, happiness, health, youth, and great strength.

To come back to love, our dear ones, is a difficult path, as it requires courage, wisdom and internal love. You desired to return to the love on the higher-self dimensions collectively, and thus, because you desired it on a higher level, you opted to give your lower human selves another opportunity to discover the choice to rise.

Now, I, SOVEREIGN LORD EMMANUEL THE GREAT, have returned to fulfill my promise to help many to return to the Great Love Consciousness. I have sent my Designated Channel, Suzanna Maria Emmanuel, to your plane to bring through the higher thoughts of Divine Love, and no one else will be used for this purpose, other than my Designated Messenger, Suzanna.

I, SOVEREIGN LORD EMMANUEL THE GREAT, have always used this channel to bring through the highest thoughts from the Divine Love. I have given CAEAYARON to you, to help you escape the lower dimensions of suffering and pain to help you rise back up again to the eternal love dimensions.

I, SOVEREIGN LORD EMMANUEL THE GREAT, stated through Jesus, *'Look a time will come when the people will desire the love ways once again. Their faces will glow with love within their hearts. Their eyes will stream with tears of joy as they see Divine within them. Gone are the days of pain and suffering.*

They will rejoice. No man, woman, or child will suffer any longer. Gone those days will be. They will be written in the Book of Remembrance to remember all their lifetimes and memories, and then a New Book of Life will be opened for all New Creation to embrace.'

We as your Masters of Light will never condemn you or judge you for your choices. We accept you as you are, and you will never be punished by us. Many religions and beliefs upon your earth teach that we punish you if you do not listen to 'God's way.' We cannot do this.

We are pure Beings of Love and we desire to help you understand our love for you. We are always forgiving in all ways. We do not see the things you do that hurt others and yourself, we only see the good things you do. We ask you to be forgiving to yourself.

It is you who judges yourself. You desire to be hard on yourself with your thinking. If you lead a life filled with self-blame you are judging yourself. If you are afraid of our punishment after you pass on to spirit, please forgive yourself for this very thought.

We are Great Compassionate Beings of Great Love. We will never do any harm to you. You only do harm to yourself with your very fears and pain. We ask you to let all of it go and return to the ways of the love within your heart. In the higher ways, you will learn to feel greater love from the Spiritual Realms, and you will rejoice in your heart. You will experience a great warmth of love.

Your heart path will set you on a greater path and when you find your truth within your heart you will understand true freedom. As you understand, beloved ones, you are living in a Universe of free choice. You can choose to become more of light or stay in the darkness; the path of pain and ignorance.

You are living in a Universe of a Great Game. You are not the only ones in existence. There are many beings living on other planets and dimensions who desire you to learn to open to the power of love within you and for you to learn to live in the light. At this time, they are not to interfere with your existence, for if they did, they would take your choice of freedom away.

Your choice is a precious gift for you. You are the ones deciding what is to be upon your plane; love and light or pain and fear. You have always had this choice but now you are learning to live from your heart. The frequencies of the heart are opening on higher levels and higher understanding is becoming more evident.

You are living in higher choices because your understanding is becoming greater. We ask you dear ones, how much do you desire to understand Truth, Light, Higher Existence, and Higher Advancement? You can choose to have all these. You can also choose to remain in the fear and suffering consciousness.

Greetings, I AM SOVEREIGN LORD EMMANUEL THE GREAT. I spoke through Jesus 2,000 years ago, and I stated I would return as the Great Lord, and so it is."

The spiritual choice seems simple,

Yet the walk of life,

Is anything but simple,

As discovering the path of love,

As discovering your strength to find the love,

Is far from simple.

It takes a person with a humble heart,

To find the highest path of love.

Happy is the one who is meek and humble,

For that one will seek to find all things,

In the love, peace, and harmony.

I AM Sovereign Lord Emmanuel The Great

Part 27: The path of the heart

"Greetings, I AM SOVEREIGN LORD EMMANUEL THE GREAT. The strong path of the heart always is of greater strength than the weak path of the pain. The path of pain exists in the lower dimensions and Divine Wisdom and Divine Strength cannot be truly found in the lower and denser dimensions of existence.

Divine Wisdom and Divine Strength is only found in the higher love and your heart has the connections into the higher streams of love, once you have your Divine Life Codes back with CAEAYARON.

Only CAEAYARON can give you those Divine Life Codes to enter into the higher love dimensions, as HE created all Life Consciousness in the Divine Love, and HE created all Life Codes.

HE is the GREAT ARCHANGEL OF ALIGNMENT, and so, I, SOVEREIGN LORD EMMANUEL THE GREAT, will state that no other being can do the task CAEAYARON has; the task of aligning all creation upwards to the higher streams of love dimensions, so they can evolve into greater power and into greater love.

The path of the heart is narrow and more difficult to find. The path of pain and fear is broad and is easier to find and walk upon. The great majority of people upon your earth walk upon this path. This is the path of general acceptance. It is regarded as a natural path to take. It is easier to discover and when a path is easier to find it is more seen. This path, however, leads to more pain and fear because these ones choose not to listen to Divine Love.

The path of the heart, though it is narrow and seen by few, is the one which leads to peace and eternal love. The wise ones seek to find the path of the heart because it leads to greater blessings of peace, love and joy.

In this illustration, the two paths start off with each other and yet, once the narrow path has been discovered, it veers far away from the wider path. The wider path is easier to walk upon, but it will never lead to the heart.

The narrow path is the path of higher evolution and higher discovery. The explorers of the love will choose to look within and find the higher path of their heart. Often these ones will desire to draw within to hear the path of the heart speak; to receive guidance as to where it can be found. These ones are the ones who find their spiritual riches.

The ones on the wider path will seek to find the narrow path, but it can never be found until one is ready within the heart of love to receive. When these ones hear the call of the heart and they have the courage to go within to find it, they will receive instructions like a map within for them to discover.

The more the people desire to find the narrow road, the easier it will be for the greater numbers to find the path.

At first the narrow path is only found by few, but the greater the number upon the narrow road who find their greater blessings, the greater the others on the wider road will hear the call.

Therefore, these times are called the Times of the Great Awakening. It is the time for the masses who are on the wider road to find the narrow road. Upon finding it, they then can celebrate their lives, walking the path of their heart with Angels.

The ones who are on the narrow road, have bright hearts lit up with light. The higher heart, which has many frequencies, plays in higher dimensions. These higher dimensions are light. All people can reach these higher dimensions because all are from light but only a few will find the way back to the greater eternal love. You are from light and love and this is what you have been searching for.

The love can flow through your body with such love and strength and it gives you healing. It helps you to feel the warmth of spirit. Those who have not found it will not understand these words. When you begin to seek for it, you will find it. The greater the love is within you, the greater the light you can carry to help you find your higher path.

Evolution always desires to guide you forward in your life. Upon deeper growth, higher frequencies will join you because you are ready for higher growth and higher understanding. The illuminated heart will constantly seek to find a greater self. It will constantly be prodding you to go within.

When one awakens and desires to step firmly upon the narrow path, the heart awakens to the higher path of light and will bring more of its flow to you. Thus, you become filled with stronger light to work with.

These are part of the choices you have. Seek to find your greater light within you by finding and walking upon the narrow path. Seek to find the great joy of your being. Seek to find your happiness within. It is within the heart you will find your peace and you will find the greater direction you are searching for. When you find the path, your higher path of evolution will begin to shine before you.

Jesus, 2,000 years ago, as my Designated Messenger, also discussed the narrow road. The people in Jesus' days often referred to the different roads surrounding the villages. They knew of the difficult paths to walk on, especially because of the dangers of walking the narrow paths. The wider ones were more accessible and far safer. Hence, using this example made it more real for the people in those days.

The people, 2,000 years ago, were not awake to the path of the heart as their anger within was too great. They received much abuse and fear from the people who governed their lives and who spiritually looked after them.

The people received many burdens from their masters, and many lived in fear constantly. This is the reason Jesus constantly asked them to look within their heart and find the higher path within their heart.

His followers were often ridiculed for even being near Jesus, and many of their families abandoned them because they listened or were 'seen' by Jesus.

The pain the people had was great and Jesus was compassionate towards them.

He stated: *'Know THE GREAT FATHER sees all that is happening. Learn to become more forgiving but know also that THE GREAT FATHER sees the ones who do not desire to listen to HIS Great Will.*

Those ones HE will address and when they say, 'But Great Lord, we have done much in your name. Did we not cause the fear and trembling within the people to enforce the laws upon them?''

Jesus continued, *'THE GREAT FATHER EMMANUEL will then state to them, I never knew you. You did not show the people love. You taught them fear and to step away from the true path; the path of the heart. You taught of a FATHER who punishes the people.*

You were assigned to be the great spiritual teachers of love to lead large nations to the love and peace. You did not teach forgiveness, compassion or love.

For this I will state as the GREAT EMMANUEL, 'Go and hide in your chambers, for you are certainly not welcome in the higher spaces of my mansions where only love and truth can exist. In the higher mansions of my Divine Being, where only love and harmony exist, you cannot dwell as you do not have the love within you.'

How can you dwell in my Mansions of Love without love within you? You were sent to gather my people and bring them to the love; to be guided back to the love. Instead you caused suffering, fear, and pain within them.

You removed greater love from them, and so I, SOVEREIGN LORD EMMANUEL THE GREAT, will state to the ones who claim to do my Divine Will, 'Go now, for there is no room in my Divine Rooms of Love.'

His followers who had strength stayed with Jesus. A few desired to be with Jesus constantly because they feared for his life; knowing how important Jesus was. They saw Jesus as the spokesman for THE GREAT FATHER and they desired all to know the Great Love; to stop the great suffering happening in those days.

Jesus never asked them to be his followers. Some desired to worship him like the leaders on their podiums in the spiritual arenas. The governing arenas demanded worship, thus it was a natural progression to worship a person who was thought to be more superior with greater wisdom.

Jesus did not desire the worship. He spoke about this to his followers, *'I, Jesus, am only a man. I am like you. On this earth I need food, water and a place to rest my head.*

In the higher love mansions of THE GREAT FATHER, we are together eternally. There we do not dwell in a place needing the physical food and water as the dwellings with the ETERNAL FATHER are spiritual.'

Jesus said, *'There, we live in the spiritual fountains of water and we are nurtured with spiritual food from THE GREAT FATHER. We are one in the greater love realms. There, we dwell in one body of love in unity. That body is sacred and holy, and no man can separate us from that one body.*

Constantly ask if you are working in the union of that body. Ask if you can further your understanding about the meaning of that one sacred body where all exists within.

Always pray, GREAT FATHER EMMANUEL, 'Teach me to work in union with your SACRED NAME. Teach me to be part of the sacred love within you. Allow me to dwell within you; eternally in the love.'

You are from that sacred place and THE GREAT FATHER welcomes all, who desire to be in the great love, back to his great mansions. Before we can return to the mansion of THE GREAT FATHER, we must learn to become of love here in these places and teach others to become of love.'

Jesus, who was a good teacher of the heart, knew it was important for his followers to reach the people in the villages to hear the good news of my Divine Being, THE GREAT FATHER EMMANUEL, as it meant eternal life for the ones who desired to listen.

He stated: *'Go and teach others all these words and encourage them to listen. Speak the following words to them and if they do not listen,* thank *them for listening, and say, 'May THE GREAT FATHER EMMANUEL be in your heart. May you remember the invitation to come back to the love.''*

Jesus encouraged them to approach the people and speak about the good news of the Kingdom which was to bring love and peace to all nations.

This is how Jesus taught his followers to speak to the people: *'Greetings dear ones. We are bringing the Great Truth from THE GREAT FATHER EMMANUEL to you and everyone we are meeting at this time.*

Jesus is here to speak with THE GREAT FATHER about a time when we can come back into the love together and dwell in eternal peace where no suffering will occur ever again. If you wish to understand more about THE GREAT FATHER EMMANUEL, then please join us and hear for yourself.'

With that, Jesus began to teach many more people as the 'news' spread around the villages. Many more people began to understand THE GREAT FATHER and who Jesus was.

Jesus was followed by many and many longed to hear the words from him. When Jesus spoke with my Being, SOVEREIGN LORD EMMANUEL THE GREAT, they felt power coming from him; power they had never experienced before.

They did not understand what a channel, or messenger was in those days. They were puzzled with the words. Jesus seemed like an ordinary man, but the words coming through him were not of a man. The words had power, and the flows the people felt were of love.

Some did not desire the love and the peace. Some among the crowds were sent by spiritual leaders to spy on the teachings as the popularity of Jesus grew greatly. The spiritual leaders and the governing controls desired to keep the people in control and fear. They saw Jesus as the enemy to their rule; a bringer of freedom from fear. They saw Jesus as a dangerous rebel.

They did not desire the people to come into the greater freedom for then they would rebel against their leaders, which many did. This was why many of the followers of Jesus suffered painfully, including Jesus himself; to be set as an example, to show rebellion against the leaders was not permitted. The consequences of rebellion were heavy.

I, SOVEREIGN LORD EMMANUEL THE GREAT, state how courageous many of the followers of Jesus were. Even in the face of pain and death many did not let go of their beliefs. Large numbers, however, did. All was a choice in those days like you are facing also. What will you choose to do in your day?

2,000 years ago, there were many more lifetimes for you to live to work towards the path of the heart. You worked in many lifetimes to come to this time you are now living in; The Time of the Great Choice.

Now, because you have reached the final time of the Great Choice, you do not have lifetimes of the Great Choice before you. It is now you need to make the choice; either the choice of the living heart of love within the ETERNAL GREAT MOUNTAIN OF CAEAYARON, or the other path.

Will your heart desire to open and explore the path of the heart greater? Or will it desire to stay on the broad road where the great majority choose to walk upon?

The followers of Jesus knew a time would come when I, SOVEREIGN LORD EMMANUEL THE GREAT, would return to call the people. CAEAYARON also promised to return when it was time for you to walk upon the higher path to eternal freedom.

It is only those who are humble within their hearts, who desire to walk on the higher spiritual road of love, who will find it. They are the seekers of the love and they will find it as they will be guided towards the higher path of eternal freedom.

There is only one pathway to the higher love dimensions, and I, SOVEREIGN LORD EMMANUEL THE GREAT, state how important this is to know.

No human upon your planet, nor any other spiritual man or woman, or organization can give you the road of eternal love in the dimensions of eternal freedom.

Only I, SOVEREIGN LORD EMMANUEL THE GREAT, together with CAEAYARON, THE GREAT MOUNTAIN OF HEALING, can give you that, for we are your Great Divine Creators from which all came into all of creation.

We, as Divine Masters of the Great Love, will only work with one Designated Channel, who is The Word from Above, who became part of your human system to help you discover the one road upwards. I, SOVEREIGN LORD EMMANUEL THE GREAT, have prepared for you the higher road of life.

In Lemuria, the paradise of freedom, where you always desired to understand greater power and greater love, you chose for the other path; the path of knowledge without the love or guidance from Divine Love.

Collectively you chose to listen to the rebellious ones who were far removed from the love. They promised your greater freedom. They promised you would be exalted far beyond all other creation; the Sacred Archangels, my Divine Being, SOVEREIGN LORD EMMANUEL THE GREAT, and CAEAYARON. You were promised your Divine Creators would eternally answer to you and serve to give you all your selfish desires.

However, all this came not to be because they, the gods of the great resistance, cannot give that to you. They cannot give you the godship you desired collectively. All those promises became empty promises.

Instead of being able to reach the higher love dimensions, you fell into the lower earth. Thus, you became trapped into the lower earth, without a way upwards to the higher earth again; unless a higher path was created.

To discover and reach the higher path of eternal love, would mean your thoughts and heart would again be tested and again you would face the time of the 'Great Choice.'

After this life-time of the 'Great Choice' no higher paths will be offered to you, as the higher streams of universes must be built upwards now.

No more, after this time of the Great Choice has finished, will I, SOVEREIGN LORD EMMANUEL THE GREAT, turn my attention to the lower dimensions, for otherwise how can eternal love come into the higher love dimensions when my attention as the GREAT DIVINE FATHER is divided between the higher realms and the lower realms?

All must be completed now, and because it has been proven that the Great Love in the universe is far more powerful than all the resistance and darkness, it so must be that the Great Love must return to the higher creation path. Therefore, no suffering will exist within my Divine Being, Divine Source, once this lifetime you are in, the time of the Great Choice, has been completed. All other memories will eternally be removed from my Divine Being.

If any pain exists within my memories, greater evolution creation cannot happen. I cannot have pain within my Divine Being if I AM creating higher evolution power for the higher realms to evolve within. I AM DIVINE PURE LOVE. When will the people understand this?

I state to the people who are reading this, 'Make your choice. Either you come to the higher road of love and eternal freedom with 'The Great Mountain of Light,' CAEAYARON, and learn to become of love and place the gifts of love within you, or not.

Place the gowns of higher wisdom upon you, filled with your greater gifts of love, to allow you to become a gifted person, able to bring the higher healing gifts to your planet so many more people can see the beauty of your love.

Do not be so unwise as to miss this one last opportunity, for then no more way upwards can be created for you. Long has been your journey to find the gateway upwards again. No human, nor other Angel, nor other star beings can give you this freedom and this pathway, for it is not within them to gift it to you.'

Many promised many things and many desired to prove this is not the right way, and that there are many roads to 'salvation.' Many state, I, SOVEREIGN LORD EMMANUEL THE GREAT, AM not true and that I, in my Supreme Power do not exist. This is where the greatest errors of your ways are; if you walk upon the unwise way.

I, SOVEREIGN LORD EMMANUEL THE GREAT, DO exist, and have always existed. I exist eternally. I AM DIVINE SOURCE. I have no beginning, nor do I have an end as my DIVINE SELF. I AM ETERNAL POWER of all universes.

179

I, SOVEREIGN LORD EMMANUEL THE GREAT, have allowed you to see the folly of your own ways; your own making.

I have allowed you to see the path of destruction as people will only ever bring destruction for self and for another. They walk without desire for Divine instruction; nor do they carry the path of love within their hearts as they desire to walk the path of freedom away from Divine Guidance.

In the times of Lemuria and Atlantis, the great majority of people walked away from the Divine Pathway and it meant many lifetimes of agony and pain for them. In the times of Jesus, again the choice was made, as in many lifetimes following.

Those who do desire the higher road are certainly blessed.

I, SOVEREIGN LORD EMMANUEL THE GREAT, state, 'Blessed are those who see this and desire to understand the higher pathway upwards.'

I, SOVEREIGN LORD EMMANUEL THE GREAT, give those, the seekers and finders of the higher path of love, the gift of eternal freedom and eternal joy and happiness.

To them I state, 'Rejoice at this time of the great gift of the Flames of Purification and Freedom. Receive the gifts of healing and receive the gown of love and eternal freedom. Receive the mark to gift you the freedom and come to the higher spaces where all will rejoice in eternal freedom.'

For them, the time of suffering will be gone away with eternally. I, SOVEREIGN LORD EMMANUEL THE GREAT, together with the GREAT MOUNTAIN, CAEAYARON, always promised this way upwards.

It is for the wise to see and it is for the wise to heed. The unwise carry on with their folly ways. They will feel greater pain coming within them in the times of the Rising Sun Consciousness; which are your times you live in now, as they come to the realization that all we say is Divine Truth.

In their awakening, they will scream with all their might when they discover they missed the path of eternal freedom. Nothing can be done for them eternally any longer.

Be wise my friends. Take the higher road of love. Choose well.

Greetings, I AM SOVEREIGN LORD EMMANUEL THE GREAT. Have an open heart. Forgive the past."

When the love is strong within you,

Your fears begin to heal,

For what is fear compared to spiritual love?

The person who has spiritual love,

Will constantly seek,

To heal all not of love,

Stay in the love and in the forgiveness,

Walk the way of Divine Love,

Learn to trust in Divine in all your ways,

Allow Divine to heal all pain within.

I AM Sovereign Lord Emmanuel The Great

Part 28: Learning to live in the joy

"Greetings, I AM SOVEREIGN LORD EMMANUEL THE GREAT. You are part of a beautiful creation and before your existence as humans, you were part of an exquisite creation.

Upon your earth, you do not remember the beauty of your true being. You experience your human frailties, but in the higher star realms, you had no frailty within you.

It is pain, fear, anger, and lack of joy which brings you into a limited self; still very beautiful in its creation. Your human self is only a small part of what you once were.

In Lemuria, you understood you were from the higher star realms. You knew, by collectively receiving the Codes of Life and by working in the love collectively, you could return to the higher star love dimensions. You learned to understand how greater star creation dwelled together in the collective love by observing them and desiring to understand how they evolved greater.

I, SOVEREIGN LORD EMMANUEL THE GREAT, state how beautiful it will be when many more upon your earth desire the higher states of existence again, for then many will join in the chorus of the New Earth returning and the New Awakened Creation returning.

When you receive your Codes of Life back, at the Divine Activations of the GREAT CAEAYARON, you become part of his GREAT MOUNTAIN OF LIGHT, slowly allowing you to transform back into stronger beings of love.

This will bring you great satisfaction. To return to love-states, slowly, is a great blessing for all who desire to become of love.

Love is more than a state of emotional being; it is a force within creation, and in the higher states it is THE FORCE of creation. I, SOVEREIGN LORD EMMANUEL THE GREAT, AM Divine Love, and therefore all have the love within as love could never be removed from your DNA path.

The more Divine Love you have within the stronger you become, for weakness does not belong to the higher realms of creation, nor does aging, sickness, war, food shortages, crime, and pain. All these create greater pain within.

The higher star realms do not anger, nor do they have any sickness within. They eternally dwell in the greater spaces of love, for Love I AM as SOVEREIGN LORD EMMANUEL THE GREAT. How else can the universes of love exist other than being in my Great Love?

At the times of the Great Fall, and upon your earth, the Divine Path was largely removed from your consciousness streams and from your DNA Life Codes, as the people chose for the darkness; and so darkness came upon the earth and within them. The people did not desire to be in the spiritual streams of the spiritual sun, hence, the sunset and the long night followed.

The darkness upon your earth began to play, causing suffering upon your planet, as the Great Sun could not be a part of your thoughts any longer. This was because the people had chosen to experience the darkness and exist within the darkness.

Now you have a choice. Do you desire to go to the higher path of love with your heart of love? Or do you desire to take the road of pain once again, not knowing a way out?

The wise ones desire the way out and desire to step into more beauty, love and greater power, as for them it seems logical. Many others, however, do not choose for the higher road for love seems foolish to them; they do not understand living a spiritually guided path of life.

When one comes to the higher road of life and comes to 'The Great Mountain of Light,' CAEAYARON, they receive my blessings and the greatest protection. We will always take care of those who desire the love within. We will always spiritually nurture those who come onto the higher path.

I, SOVEREIGN LORD EMMANUEL THE GREAT, always know what you need for that very day and when you are within your heart of love, it so will be given to you; to help you become more spiritually strong within your heart and have greater trust in Divine Love.

At times, giving you spiritual gifts may not seem the gifts you would choose for yourself, but Divine Love knows much more than you do. All is within Divine Timing, and Divine Timing is much more accurate than people's timing. Know that in this very hour there is nothing more important than gaining back your Codes of Life so that we, as Divine Love Beings, can do more for you.

You do not understand the beauty and the grandness of all of creation. You are lost in the sea upon your world, and many of you understand how the world is aligning. The issues are becoming worse upon your earth and the days seem bleaker.

Jesus stated, *'When it is the time for the GREAT FATHER to rise, it will be in the time when many nations seek destruction. They will seek destruction because destruction will be within them. They will not remember the love, nor will they desire to come into love.*

It is in those days the people will lift up their heads and pray to the GREAT FATHER.

'FATHER EMMANUEL, please see us in this hour of great crisis and guide us to the higher path of love and truth so we may understand a higher path of living. Forgive all within us that needs to be forgiven, and we forgive all others who have pained us. We forgive ourselves for we understand all needs to change to the love.'

It is in those days the people will seek new ways of forgiveness, for they then begin to understand that to forgive allows healing to take place. They begin to understand all things are spiritual.

They will rejoice in the Times of the Great Awakening. Not at first. At first only a few will see it and they will be greatly blessed, eternally. Others will also see it and stream into the MOUNTAIN OF HEALING when it is the time to do so. They will seek shelter within the GREAT MOUNTAIN and will know they are safe and cared for by the GREAT FATHER.

They will cry out with all power, 'Thank you SOVEREIGN LORD EMMANUEL for caring about us, and for returning to your greater promise.'

The higher love spaces, which Jesus spoke about with my Divine Being, are for the ones who desire the highest path of love. They have been awaiting for my return faithfully.

Now, I, SOVEREIGN LORD EMMANUEL THE GREAT, have returned with my Word. This time, my messenger is not Jesus, but it is Suzanna Maria Emmanuel, who is here to bring the messages of Divine Love to your earth.

Jesus' message was the road to a higher love, and he was The Messenger to help the people become of love. He spoke of a time when the Great Road would open, but it would only open for those who stayed awake and waited for the Great Lord to arrive;

'Who will be awake when THE GREAT FATHER arrives? Who will fall asleep when THE GREAT FATHER arrives? HE will come at an hour least expected. HE will come in the way least expected.

HE will only be recognized by those who desire THE GREAT FATHER in their heart and who have been waiting silently, keeping the flames of the remembrance of these words alive within.'

Now, 'The Great Mountain of Light' is spiritually visible upon your earth, and indeed I, SOVEREIGN LORD EMMANUEL THE GREAT, have returned with the Great Flame, the Great Sun Consciousness, to awaken the flames of the heart.

Those who have been waiting will recognize the channel first and they will see the truth of my channel, Jesus. They will understand the message from Divine and have not been blinded by the falsehoods of the world. They will come to 'The Great Mountain of Light' first.

They will be among those who take their seats first in the Great Spiritual Mansion, as Jesus discussed with the people, as they have been faithfully waiting for my Great Return to happen. They will guide people to life consciousness, helping others to see what they see; to the Great Road upwards.

Jesus always spoke about the heart and how THE GREAT FATHER looks at the heart. *'It is not for men to judge or to see. They cannot see the greatness within a heart. Men see the actions of people, how great they speak, how much they raise up their arms when they speak but the GREAT FATHER is not looking for those, for there is no love for THE GREAT FATHER within them.*

The humble ones are the ones who HE sees, for they are the honest hearted ones, following what is in their heart; the path of Divine Love. Those are the ones THE GREAT FATHER is looking for.'

Upon hearing these words being spoken through Jesus, the people cried with joy in their hearts because they were 'seen' by the GREAT FATHER EMMANUEL. They were not judged, and the GREAT FATHER EMMANUEL had spoken to them about the great spaces they could receive in the greater realms.

They stood there before Jesus who did not judge them as their leaders did. Jesus never asked for worship. Jesus was a Master to them. Jesus was a Guide to them. For the first time, they met a person who cared about their feelings and not about which law they practiced or broke.

Jesus was greatly respected by his followers, and in turn, I, SOVEREIGN LORD EMMANUEL THE GREAT, brought more blessings to those who saw Jesus as the Great Word bringing through messages from Divine Love.

When his followers appreciated and looked after Jesus, they received ten-fold back, because what they gave to Jesus was from their heart. I, SOVEREIGN LORD EMMANUEL THE GREAT, bless those greatly who give from the heart, especially when the great messenger is respected.

It is the same during these days. When my Designated Word, Suzanna Maria Emmanuel, is respected and cared for by people who respect the great task she has, the people who give to her are greatly blessed; especially so when nothing is expected in return.

When they appreciate the love Suzanna has for the people and for Universal Service, so it is that the givers will be greatly blessed; in this lifetime and in the lifetimes coming. No greater service can be given than to appreciate my Divine Channel, as the Channel is the road to everlasting blessings.

Greetings, I AM SOVEREIGN LORD EMMANUEL THE GREAT. I AM searching for the ones who desire the love within their hearts. Happy are those who earnestly desire truth and love."

The wise see these words,

They celebrate them within their hearts,

For they know them to be truth.

But the ones who are unwise,

See these words,

And remark at their foolishness,

Those can never come to the love,

And live in the higher love dimensions,

For they will always be blind.

Happy are the ones who see this,

And are awake to these times,

They will be eternally blessed.

I AM Sovereign Lord Emmanuel The Great

Part 29: The great treasures of truth

"Greetings, I AM SOVEREIGN LORD EMMANUEL THE GREAT. I AM here to bring you the great treasures to help you find the way to the highest love realms. The people of the old days knew the true treasures from Divine Truth were far more important than the treasures upon the earth.

Jesus, my channel 2,000 years ago, also taught this often. He said, *'The treasures on the earth will not last forever. They will pass. All things on the earth will pass, for they are not the spiritual treasures and will not last forever, nor will they serve you in the highest realms above. The true treasures THE GREAT FATHER can gift you will last forever. Those treasures can gift eternal life and true freedom from suffering and judgment.'*

The people 2,000 years ago, in the times of Jesus, knew judgment from their leaders well. They could see how the leaders did not care for their people. Instead of helping them find greater spiritual treasures and helping them work towards having an abundant life, they took all their treasures for their own glory and purpose.

This left many in poverty and brought boundless material riches to their masters. Many buried their treasure in an attempt to save them from being taken.

Jesus said about their buried treasure, *'What good is it burying your treasures? Buried treasure will be consumed by moths. What good are they to you once you leave the earth? They cannot give you eternal freedom from pain, can they? They cannot give you eternal happiness, and they cannot buy your place in the eternal realms with THE GREAT FATHER.*

The treasures from the earth cannot give you eternal life in peace as you desire. It is not with the gifts of the earth you can buy your way to the higher dimensions of THE FATHER, for only HE can gift those gifts to you.

THE GREAT FATHER looks at the heart of the people and decides who can be gifted back the true treasures of the higher realms HE has created.

HE does not care for the physical treasures, for what good are your physical treasures to HIM, when HE has created all things everlasting? Your physical treasures cannot even be measured compared to the eternal life-giving treasures HE can gift to you.

HE does not look at the abundance of a person, for earthly possessions the GREAT FATHER does not desire. The GREAT FATHER sees only the heart of love. It is the heart of love the GREAT FATHER cares for and blesses. Therefore, do not judge another for the things they do have or do not have. Do not be jealous of the possessions of others but go in love. Forgive all things.

Each day pray for the great strength to come into your heart so as not to worry about the next day, for in each day THE GREAT FATHER will give you all you need. THE GREAT FATHER will always take care of all who desire HIM to be with them within their hearts.

Pray your hearts of love open to THE GREAT FATHER EMMANUEL. Pray you are among the blessed ones.

When the heart desires to hear THE GREAT FATHER speak, and the heart desires to be in the Great Love of THE GREAT FATHER, THE GREAT FATHER shall indeed call that one, for that one is ready to listen.

Many have treasures unlawfully taken from the people. The people are left poor because of the unjust taking. The ones who have taken from others are looked upon as rich and righteous because of their wealth accumulated.

THE GREAT FATHER does not see them as the rich and the righteous. THE GREAT FATHER sees them as the poorest of all because taking from another, that does not belong to them without giving back, is not what THE GREAT FATHER desires.

THE GREAT FATHER desires you to give from your heart, and then HE will give back to you. When you give to another because of the caring from your heart, THE GREAT FATHER will gift you all things you need.

HE will never let the people who desire HIS Great Love go hungry. HE will never let the people who desire HIS Great Love go thirsty. All things are given to the ones who desire HIS Great Love, but to the ones who take from others unlawfully, HE will not bless them because there is no caring within them.

Indeed, it is more difficult for that one, who takes riches from others to become rich, to find the greater spaces of the Divine Love Realms, than it is for a camel to find its way through the eye of a fine needle.

All things are woven together. When one finds the love within their heart, THE GREAT FATHER will eternally bless that one. When one takes from the people unlawfully and burdens those without care, then THE GREAT FATHER will take their blessings away.

Learn all in the universe is about measure and balance. When you find the balance within your life, all things will become measured and balanced for you.'

These were large teachings for the people 2,000 years ago on learning to manifest all things in their lives. They learned they must give to receive and not take what did not belong to them.

In the great lessons Jesus brought through they learned the importance of keeping their promises and not to owe debts. Jesus taught to return what did not belong to them and always to be grateful for all they received.

'For all things you receive, be grateful within your heart. THE GREAT FATHER EMMANUEL sees all things, and when one is grateful, more can be gifted to that one.

When one is grateful and is willing to give with the heart to another, then THE GREAT FATHER, all Compassionate, Love, and Wise, will give more to the giver because it was given from the heart of love.

All things must be learned to be of love. When you love another and seek to give to that one because of your love to share your appreciation and love, THE GREAT FATHER will seek ways to give you more than you gave.

All things are to balance each other, and all are measured. When you give something because of your love for another, your love means so much to THE GREAT FATHER of Love and Compassion. HE will reward that act of love and gift back to you many times over. Your love means far more to HIM than the treasure you gave, for it is with your love that your earthly gift became a spiritual treasure of love.

Therefore, be in appreciation of all the gifts you receive. Do not measure its value by its physical worth but by the love from the heart.

One who gives from the heart blesses the receiver, for then the receiver can receive many gifts because you blessed them with your heart. Likewise, when you are a receiver of a gift, small or large, if you received it with your heart of love, appreciating the love given, and if the giver gave it to you with the heart of love, then blessed you are. Your gifts will be many.

Let this be a message for you at this time. Always give from your heart and always receive from your heart. As something is given to you, something must also be given by you as all in the universe works this way.

The ways of the Universe are wise. It never seeks to take for its own gain, and yet it never keeps giving without receiving. The stars also give and receive, and when you learn the ways of giving and receiving, your abundance will grow.

It is far better to give from the heart than it is to receive, for then THE GREAT FATHER can bless the heart who gives. He cannot bless the one who is receiving from selfishness, however. When one receives the gifts with great appreciation from the giver of the heart, the receiver greatly blesses the giver, and therefore THE GREAT FATHER can give both to the giver and the receiver.

Happy is the one who understands these words and begins to apply these words in their lives.

When you fulfill your promises with your heart of joy and love, without holding back, the GREAT FATHER will bless you greatly.

HE blesses the ones who carry out their promises. HE cannot bless those who say they will do certain things but do not. How can HE bless an action when that action is not carried through with the heart of love?

Never promise a deed without acting upon it. Do not give hope to another without carrying it through. Many make promises to exalt themselves but do not carry them through. Many do many things to receive praises from others. The GREAT FATHER cannot bless this.

When you care for others and do from your heart THE GREAT FATHER can bless you. When you care for the orphans and the widows, ensuring they have what they need, then THE GREAT FATHER EMMANUEL will ensure you have everything you need for yourself and your family. When you do all things from your heart of love without expecting praise or gifts in return, THE GREAT FATHER EMMANUEL will always bless you.

When you give gifts to another and that one does not know who it is from, do not be concerned, for the GREAT FATHER EMMANUEL will *always see who gave it. Do not desire praise from people, for how can people bless you? They cannot.*

Rather, allow the GREAT FATHER EMMANUEL to examine your heart. When you do things from your heart, do not walk in expectation of blessings from THE GREAT FATHER EMMANUEL, for HE desires you to do all things without expecting blessings in return. HE desires your heart to open to the great love; then HE can bless you.

When THE GREAT FATHER EMMANUEL blesses the lovers of the heart, HE blesses them eternally, not only in that very day. HE remembers all your gifts from your heart.

HE desires all to look after one another and to stay in the forgiveness of one another. That is far more important to HIM than all the physical treasures of the earth.

Walk in the great love of THE GREAT FATHER EMMANUEL. Let go of all your old ways for they serve you no longer. Embrace the new ways of living and learn to walk the path of love and be within love. Do not be sad for the times gone but learn to embrace the opportunity for each moment coming.

Learn to walk with new understanding within your heart and practice all these things each day. You will see how THE GREAT FATHER EMMANUEL works with you each day, and then you will speak with your heart to many others and say, 'Praise THE GREAT FATHER EMMANUEL, who is the Great Divine of all Creation. HE can see all, HE can bless all. Embrace the new love. Embrace the new way. Let go of all your old beliefs.

Do not stay in the suffering of the people. Release yourself from the suffering of the people. When you hear others complain, unburden yourself from them. Do not listen to the grief of others, for listening to their complaints will only bring grief within you.

Be in the joy and speak upbuilding words to all. Never tear another down or yourself down with painful words. Walk with compassion and love for yourself and others. Do not bring judgment to self or another. Let go of all your old ways for no longer do they befit you.

You are now learning to walk the new ways of love and work in union with THE GREAT FATHER OF LOVE.'

Greetings, I AM SOVEREIGN LORD EMMANUEL THE GREAT. I AM here to bring you the path of wisdom and love eternally. I AM here to bring you the great blessings when you work in your heart of love."

The ways of the wise ones are of the heart,

The wise ones constantly look to examine,

'How can I bring more love within my life?

How can I bring more love within another?

How can I be of service to Divine?'

Divine always blesses the heart lovers,

Always appreciate all the gifts you are given,

A gift given from the heart is of great value,

For it is not the 'gift that is the great gift,

But it is the heart the 'gift' is given with.

Become heart givers,

Become heart receivers,

Constantly bless with your heart of love.

I AM Sovereign Lord Emmanuel The Great

Part 30: Your search for the light

"Greetings, I AM SOVEREIGN LORD EMMANUEL THE GREAT. Mankind has always looked towards a higher existence for answers. You have celebrated the 'Gods' and you have learned the pain of seeking but not finding.

Indeed, the search for your deeper truth has been great. Many people have fallen in your history because of your great search. Many have died trying to find it. Many have died because they found it and died in the hands of the very ones who feared the power these treasures would give the people.

Rulers in your past condemned the treasures within the heart because of the power and greed upon your earth. They knew well if people understood the treasures of the heart and came together to create greatness collectively, their rulership would fall because of the power 'collective oneness' holds.

Collective oneness is what the rulers have always feared as the people in the Collective Love if awoken together, are a force, especially if they are awoken by the Divine Love Element. This has happened on many occasions in the past.

Thus, the fear was created by the darkness to ensure the great rising of the freedom collectively would not happen. The imprisoned states of the people continued until your day.

Many, in your history who worked with light, were tortured and incriminated for their higher abilities. They suffered for their truth.

We as Divine Masters of Great Love understand the games of darkness and how darkness fears light because they knew how light could topple the darkness over easily. They desired to destroy the light before the light overtook them.

Light is always much stronger than the darkness and this is what the darkness feared; the Divine Love Element rising with her greatest love and light.

I, SOVEREIGN LORD EMMANUEL THE GREAT, say how courageous the Divine Love Element was all throughout your ages; to be The Word of Divine, to bring the love to the people.

How courageous the people were, upon your planet; those who desired the love within their heart.

This battle, light versus dark, has always been upon your earth all through your history. The battle between the people searching and finding the light, versus those who fought against the light, has always been great.

It has been a difficult journey for the ones who desired to have the light with them once again. In the times of old, there was much greater light to work with than you have now in your world. The light the people worked within your world was powerful. All are becoming

201

more empowered now; if you desire to work with the greater light now the Divine Love Element has returned with my Divine Being, THE GREAT SOVEREIGN LORD EMMANUEL, together with 'The Great Mountain of Light,' CAEAYARON.

This means in your day you can receive the great powers to bring healing to yourself and to your life. You can experience the greater flows of light within you as all of creation is now becoming free; those who desire to listen.

I, SOVEREIGN LORD EMMANUEL THE GREAT, say how happy you need to be for these times, as these times you are living in are about finding the freedom and discovering how to grow back into the love, helping you to become prepared for the greater spiritual work ahead which is joyful and exciting for you.

The light will always make the way forward like a shining lamp lighting up a dark cave. Throughout the ages, you trusted in the Great Light and you knew in this lifetime the light would win, and thus you were courageous to come back again.

You came because you desired to find the treasures of the heart and to work with humanity to bring love and peace to your world, knowing your eternal reward would be greater than can be understood at this time.

These are the greater reasons you came here to your plane together. You wanted to come collectively together to bring light and love to your planet and to all of mankind.

The people who lived in Lemuria were created with the ability to bring light to the darker dimensions. Thus, if the people work collectively, together they can bring love and peace to your planet. All this you will discover together when you decide to move forward.

Jesus spoke about this time 2,000 years ago. He stated: *'In the day when the GREAT FATHER EMMANUEL returns, HE will call those who desire the earth to become of peace.*

HE will examine all who desire to learn the ways of peace and love within their hearts again. HE will bring through the power to awaken the earth to beauty and to awaken the people.

Happy are those who are awake to those prophecies for they will begin to rejoice in all that will be.'

We, as Divine Creators, are opening the gates higher for you to recognize this true gift that you have for all of humanity.

Constantly stand in your forgiveness for all pain that has happened and is happening upon your planet.

Look at the beauty of the people for each person has beautiful gifts. The more you recognize it, the greater you will see that all people have beauty within. It is when the people recognize the beauty within, that change happens, as then deep alignment occurs.

The lovers of the earth desired to be in this time to work with the flows coming to bring peace to planet earth and to the people. Open to the light of the GREAT CAEAYARON, THE MOUNTAIN OF LIGHT, and learn to work collectively together. Together, when you have received back your Codes of Life, you have the power within you to bring the love upon your planet.

One task you desired to complete, before leaving planet earth, for those who would be awake enough to the time of the Great Return, was to work collectively together in the love, to bring in all that was desired.

Together you desired to achieve that. Jesus said about these times, *'Look, the time will come when the people will state, 'GREAT FATHER, guide us to the ways of peace and love and teach us how to become of love. Give us higher guidance and show us how we can become greater peace.'*

I, SOVEREIGN LORD EMMANUEL THE GREAT, welcome all who desire to be a part of the Great Love returning upon your planet and can then return to the greater love dimensions.

There are those who do not wish you to understand this information, as all through the ages, truth has remained hidden from the hearts of those who are searching for the highest Divine Love Truth.

I, SOVEREIGN LORD EMMANUEL THE GREAT always state, 'Happy is the one who desires to find the higher path, for then THE GREAT FATHER, who is my Divine Being, SOVEREIGN LORD EMMANUEL THE GREAT, can gift that one peace and love, and guide that one to the higher path.'

It is not easy to find the higher path and you will need the desire to find the highest love path. Many people upon your earth have fought hard against Divine Will, though the people have prayed for this time to happen.

Jesus, said about this matter, *'Many will state they are doing the Will of Divine, but THE GREAT FATHER will only see a few doing the Will of THE FATHER.*

It is not easy to bring the people to the Great Fountains of Water, though they will claim how easy it is to do the Will of THE GREAT FATHER.'

Jesus continued to speak to the people in those days, *'They do not do the Will of THE GREAT FATHER. They desire to do their own will, claiming they are following THE GREAT FATHER. They will claim they do many things in the name of THE GREAT FATHER, and yet when THE GREAT FATHER calls the children of the light back to 'The Great Mountain of Light,' very few will desire this to happen.*

All things must constantly be seen by THE GREAT FATHER, as THE GREAT FATHER wishes to help all children of the earth rise to HIS Great Mansions of Light, but HE can only gift the greatest gifts to the ones who have found it with their love within their hearts of love.

Those great gifts are true treasures and only those who are humble and truly desire to find the highest path are the ones who will find it. They will recognize the Divine Path. They will desire it. They will embrace it with their hearts.

The rest will keep arguing over who is the greatest. Look at them arguing who is the greatest among men but it is not for men to shine, it is for THE GREAT FATHER to shine all HIS Great Love to the people.

Let the people see Divine Truth. Let the people recognize Divine Will. Pray, 'It is not my will that is to be done, but the Divine Will of THE GREAT FATHER.'

Constantly ask THE GREAT FATHER, what is it you would have me do? Whatever it is you would have me do I will humbly do so. I am here, GREAT FATHER. Allow me to hear. Allow me to come into my spaces of my heart. Those are the people THE GREAT FATHER is looking for.

When THE GREAT FATHER speaks to those who truly search, many gifts will be given. You will know the way. You will not fight amongst yourselves who is the greatest, for the greatest, in THE FATHER's eyes, are those who do the Will of Divine.

Many will turn against Divine. They will argue they know better than Great Divine. Do you not understand that it is the little ones who are greater than all the proud and haughty ones in the eyes of THE GREAT FATHER?

Look at the children of the earth. They do not see themselves as great, but because they are willing to listen to THE GREAT FATHER, THE GREAT FATHER sees them as great. It is those who HE blesses, not the ones who claim to be doing all things in the Name of the FATHER.

The ones who truly will have the power to bring all things to the light are the ones who desire to follow the Will of THE GREAT FATHER. It is then that HE will know that all things can be entrusted to that one. When that one listens to the small things, that one will listen when big things are asked.

All things are constantly examined by THE GREAT FATHER. HE searches for those who are faithful in the small things, and it is those who HE will gift great power to, in the greater spaces of love.'

Dear ones, it is so that all these things are still very true in your time. Whoever receives the greatest gifts from the GREAT MOUNTAIN,

CAEAYARON, at this time, will receive the Great Flames for eternity, and those ones, who listen and embrace the highest Divine Love and always search for greater Divine Love within their hearts, it is those who will find the highest path.   They will be entrusted with the greatest gifts of the Divine Realms.

This highest path is of true freedom. In the higher spaces, no man or woman can be hurt any longer. No one can be hurt in higher spaces for you are perfect in the higher spaces. You are free and eternal in the higher spaces. You will not have a physical body to keep you in restriction, but instead, you will have a spiritual body bringing you much freedom, joy, and love.

Greetings, I AM SOVEREIGN LORD EMMANUEL THE GREAT. I AM here to find all who desire to rise to the eternal love dimensions. I AM here to see who desires, with their heart, to become of love."

The ways of love are perfect,

They are of the heart.

The ones who discover the higher path,

And live by the higher path,

With their heart of love,

Are the precious ones on earth,

For they understand truth,

Peace and love.

The desire of the heart within those ones,

Will grow with love and warmth,

Eternally they will desire the love,

Of the Great Father Emmanuel,

Rise, Children of the Light,

Rise and heal.

I AM Sovereign Lord Emmanuel The Great

Part 31: When your spiritual heart reveals her treasures

"Greetings, I AM SOVEREIGN LORD EMMANUEL THE GREAT. Love is part of you, and it is part of your eternal existence. When you awaken the love within your loving hearts, your flows and your gifts increase.

You cannot be separated from the everlasting love for it is with love you were created, however, because collectively you fell away from the love, the love deep within you must be awoken. The question is then; 'Will you desire to return to states of love?'

To return to states of love, all things in your life are questioned. What do you desire love to be in your life? What is it you can do to become more of love for yourself and others?

The wise ones who understand these sacred gifts can rest in their sacred loving places. They can truly shelter from life within these spaces of love.

'Lord, shelter me from my pain. Comfort me to help me find my greater self.' This is what the people have cried for many ages.

Finding these sacred loving places may pose challenges for you. This is because your mind is busy trying to understand your world. You are

209

too busy to see the greater path. Instead, you keep trying to achieve on the functional side of life and you are too busy trying to see how to move ahead in your life. However, all things are lessons in your life dear friends.

Your society has gone away from the 'Living Heart.' Your people do not understand the deep sacred paths of the 'Living Heart.' Many would turn away from the higher ways and say they were not 'real' or even consider the higher ways as 'foolish.'

To bring change to yourself one must learn to examine all things from all angles. The spaces of the quiet hold great treasures as you will be able to understand what you need to do next in your life. Your life becomes more purposeful and flowing.

Your consciousness grows and you desire your expansion to happen. All things in your life become more deeply investigated. This deeper understanding is one of deep spiritual wisdom, not of superficial flows.

Within your heart, one can find the answers. This is because you can tap into deep wisdom within you. However, this is only found when the seeker desires to find truth within. It is then that the seeker will always find.

It must come from your heart first. You must be the ones who desire to find the higher truths first and then because of your strong desires you will find it.

The ones who do not desire to seek will not find these secret chambers. They will keep searching for their truth, listening to the stories of others and believing them to be so. It hurts them to go within because on a deep level they know what they believe to be is not their truth.

For the ones who are courageous to step away from all the stories in their life and go within instead, they are the ones seeking. They will find.

When a person finds these deeper secrets, this person can tap into greater frequencies and greater blessings in life they can receive. This is the most precious gift a person can have.

This is the true wisdom path. The ones who strive for material treasures always focus upon the superficial parts of life. They will never find these deeper sacred treasures. For them, these treasures are difficult to find because it is only for the ones who truly desire it and seek to look within who will find it.

What will you find there? What is it you are truly seeking?

The courageous ones will desire to bring all things to the surface for true healing to take place. They look at all things in their life and desire to understand why certain situations happen. They are willing to 'delve' into life greater.

It is these ones who are truly strong within the self, for knowing self does not fear them, it is not knowing what is within which scares them. They look for all opportunities to bring more light within themselves to see what is within all corners. Where is the strength able to be developed greater? Can the pain influence situations in life, and if so, where can it be healed?

The wise one constantly works with this understanding. Not a day will go by without examining life. That one does not judge self or another, but constantly stays in the love and has an awareness of all that is happening.

If one is not happy, the wise one begins to examine it. That one can bring more happiness within by understanding it and by understanding the thoughts of that one. Then, by forgiving all that stops the happiness from coming in, the flows open.

Understand the power of freeing self and for forgiveness. When you are forgiving and have forgiven you set yourself free from burdens.

Burdens are heavy to carry. Love is free to use. Become of love each day. Keep asking for the greater love to come to you. Keep asking for greater insight to happen.

Greetings, I AM SOVEREIGN LORD EMMANUEL THE GREAT. I AM here to help you find your true self. I AM here to guide you upwards to the higher, more evolved dimensions, if you are a true seeker of higher love consciousness."

The ones who cry within their hearts,

'Great Lord, help us to find,

The higher ways of love and truth;

The higher ways of greatness,'

They are the ones who will find the path,

They are the seekers,

They will awaken to the higher love,

They will not stay behind,

But instead they awaken,

They hear the Great Shepherds calling them,

And they desire to climb the higher path,

As one people sheltered in the love,

Trusting the ways upwards.

I AM Sovereign Lord Emmanuel The Great

Part 32: Living in abundance flows

"Greetings, I AM SOVEREIGN LORD EMMANUEL THE GREAT. I speak to you as a Divine Loving Master to bring you peace and love in your life. We encourage you to take these lessons slowly as we reveal more.

When we as Divine Ancient Masters talk about material treasures, please do not sell your home or give up your career. This is not what we are asking you or anyone to do.

In the times of Jesus, I, SOVEREIGN LORD EMMANUEL THE GREAT, encouraged people to be comfortable and live the best life they could possibly have, but only in the love and appreciation.

The flows of love within your heart are so important for once one has found the great love within the heart, that one finds stronger balance in life and is able to walk the higher path, living a life with contentment.

When a wise person truly seeks truth within themselves, that one can find deeper abundance flows. This will bring much joy because that one understands gaining material things has deeper spiritual lessons. Once you come onto a higher path of the heart, material things in your life will not be as important anymore, however, the way you will be able to bring about all your desires and needs will become much easier.

You will learn to understand all things in your life are important; even when you go shopping for food. You will learn how to go deeper within and ask your body what it desires to have for nutritional purposes.

All things change upon finding great love within the heart as it gives you greater balance. You can live a life in the heart, filled with your inner truth and be abundant with all things in your life to enjoy.

Your focus deepens with spiritual love. You begin to see greater possibilities and analyze them with greater wisdom to see how your life can rise higher. Your business arrangements become more flowing as you gain more self-empowerment.

It is always with deepening appreciation one will grow into the heart of love. Appreciation for all things brings more joy in your life. Happy is the one who sees this with open spiritual eyes, as it will allow the higher ways of love to be discovered in life.

I, SOVEREIGN LORD EMMANUEL THE GREAT, will always bring the ways of love, peace, and nourishment to those who desire the higher love path. I, SOVEREIGN LORD EMMANUEL THE GREAT, always promised the people, 'All needs would be met in all ways; if the people stay in the love within their hearts.'

Greetings, I AM SOVEREIGN LORD EMMANUEL THE GREAT. I AM here to help you find the great blessings of the Great Path of Love and Life."

The seeker of the heart learns to love all,

And learns to have deep appreciation,

That one seeks balance in life,

As balance brings great wisdom,

Happiness and satisfaction.

Always bring love to all you have,

All you have is a part of you,

Be grateful for all things,

For then all things become greatly blessed,

As your heart opens to greater receiving.

Learn to appreciate all in life,

Allow the door for greater blessings to open.

I AM Sovereign Lord Emmanuel The Great

Part 33: Your deeper connection

"Greetings, I AM SOVEREIGN LORD EMMANUEL THE GREAT. It is the one who is truly looking within who will find their true purpose; a true understanding of all that is truth and love. That one will find their true connection to the light and the light will eternally bless them.

At this time, upon your planet, this connection can truly come to you. It has been a long time for you to find this time of the 'true connection' to the great eternal love flows. You have worked hard to find this time and now you are able to reconnect back to your true Lemurian Light Codes; Your greater codes of life and true heart codes.

After losing the Codes of Life, it was impossible to receive a true understanding of the greater love dimensions and it was impossible to find your true heart connection. However, now, a gateway has become opened, and CAEAYARON invites you to connect with HIM at the Divine Activations; to allow you to connect within the highest flows of love once again.

Happy is the one who rejoices at these times of the great gathering to 'The Great Mountain of Light,' where many people will gather spiritually, and many will reconnect back into their greater love flows to bring love and peace to themselves and to your planet.

217

You, on a human level, cannot understand creation love-power, for that knowledge was removed from you. Jesus, 2,000 years ago, attempted to explain what it was to the people when he brought these following words out with my Divine Being, SOVEREIGN LORD EMMANUEL THE GREAT;

'Know all things exist within THE GREAT FATHER, for HE created all. HE created the beauty of the mountains, the glory of the stars. HE knows all creation, and nothing exists outside of HIM. HE desires all to live within HIS love, as HIS love is power, it is creation, and for those who desire the Great Love of the GREAT FATHER, all gifts of power will be given to that one.

Know a time is coming when the great gifts from the Great Heavens will be given to those who listen to these messages. Those will hear these messages at the time of the great gathering when the GREAT FATHER will call the multitudes from the earth. They will be asked to gather together and will be taught the power of the heart of love. They will suffer no more for they will rejoice that all these promises that they knew of, came to be so.

Look, a time will come when the people will see how GREAT the GREAT FATHER is. The GREAT FATHER never gives a promise to the children of the earth without fulfilling it. HE will restore the earth to peace and love, but only those who desire to be part of the peace and the joy HE will grant favor.

All others, who do not desire to listen to THE GREAT FATHER and desire the love within their hearts, cannot enter the New Creation of all that is coming.

Therefore, keep praying you will stay awake in the hour of HIS COMING so that you can heed these messages and listen to it. Wo is for those who hear these messages and do not listen, for their tears will fall to the earth. Their pain will be everlasting.

They will cry out to THE GREAT FATHER, 'Please see me, Great Lord, I did not believe. Never again can the GREAT FATHER help those; once the Great Coming has passed.

The GREAT FATHER will give all who do desire the Great Love, of THE GREAT FATHER, access to the higher heavens.

To all others, HE will state, 'Go away from me. I called and you did not desire the great love from my Divine Being. You were part of the foolish class, always desiring to follow your own way. I have no use, in the greater heavens, for those who do not desire to follow Divine Will.

Listen to these words for these words are wise. Happy are those who see these words and begin to act upon it. Pray you will awaken to these words when the GREAT FATHER EMMANUEL calls.'

When people seek higher guidance from Divine, they find it. When they discover the higher guidance and they understand it is from Great Divine, their hearts will rejoice in these times of the Great Calling.

At first, few would see the great calling and then it would become clearer as all on the road to the greater dimensions would become clearer.

At first, the road and pathway seemed foggy, but then all began to clear to allow all to become seen. It would then be that the greater choice would be given; upon seeing the road clearer.

It is only when the heart opens to the light you can find the higher road.

What will you find? How will you receive us as your Spiritual Masters? How will you find your deeper spiritual gifts? All experience the love from Above in their own unique way. Each one of you is on a unique spiritual path. You are all connected and all who desire to understand their truth greater will find it. Your truth is uniquely different from another's truth and therefore you can never judge another. Your spiritual eyes are unique and your beliefs within you are uniquely yours.

All people are magnificent in the eyes of the Divine Ones. We desire to bless you so very much and we desire to bless those who desire to heal their lives. We bless all who desire to step closer to us to help you have a closer relationship with the light.

The ways of the Great Light are always blessed. They are filled with the highest love possible, and the stronger you come onto your path and walk the path of love as a collective love group, the stronger the Great Light will become for you, as all things are created with the greater creation in mind. You are learning to become part of a greater creation; a creation without limitation, with pureness and the great love and direction towards higher love creation universes.

Greetings, continue reading with me as SOVEREIGN LORD EMMANUEL THE GREAT to discover the path of the heart."

The wise ones desire the higher path of love,

From the Great Father above,

They see how beautiful creation is,

And are becoming a part,

Of Greater Creation;

A creation without limitation,

A truly blessed creation,

A creation greatly loved,

By Great Divine Love.

I AM Sovereign Lord Emmanuel The Great

Part 34: Imitate the love of The Great Father

"Greetings, I AM SOVEREIGN LORD EMMANUEL THE GREAT. You have friendships upon your earth, do you not? Your friends and family mean much to you when you build strong relationships with them. You feel their closeness and warmth. You have a connection and are at peace with them. You have a common grounding with the people you love to be with.

When you have issues and challenges in life you have your friends and family to turn to. They understand you, and you enjoy being listened to. Your friends can then give you advice and you listen. Yet, even when the advice is great you still follow your own thoughts and make your own decisions.

You have human friends and you are also able to step into higher spiritual friendships.

It is now the time for many more people to reach up to Angelic vibrations who care much for you and desire to befriend you. Angelic Vibration Spirit Guides have always guided you to the higher path of greatness and love. Divine Spirit Guides, in the eyes of the Great Divine Love Masters, are Beings who have guided you in your lifetimes to the paths of love and greatness.

There are many Spirit Guides. They work on many different levels, depending on the level of your spiritual journey will depend on how many Guides help you at any time of your life. There are Guides on the lower vibrations as well as the higher love vibrations. Therefore, our encouragement is great to you; always ask for the highest love vibrations to come to you.

As you ask, you will also receive. As you grow in great love, so the higher the love vibrations from the higher love spaces will come to you. All works like a mirror.

Jesus also talked about the reflection within the people and the teachings still apply in your day now.

He said, *'THE GREAT FATHER looks at the heart of all people. HE knows what the people sow is also what they will reap, for all works in ways of deeper reflection and understanding. When the heart desires good for another, good will happen for that one. Likewise, when one desires bad for another because of the lack of love, so it will come to that one.*

All are here on earth to learn the higher ways of love. When people understand how the universe works, they will understand we are here to learn the higher ways of love, and when we learn to work in the love union with THE GREAT FATHER, HE can bless us. HE cannot bless us when we cannot be in love, for HE is love.

How can HE bless us when we do not desire to imitate the GREAT FATHER? When we learn to imitate THE GREAT FATHER who only desires good for another, as HE is love and HE has no judgment within HIM, it is then that love will come to us as people; for those are the ways of the universe.

Constantly the universe is guiding us to a higher way of living; not that of men, but of the GREAT FATHER EMMANUEL.

There will be a day when many nations will receive these messages and desire to understand Divine Will greater, as they will have understood that people do not have the answers. They will search in all corners of the earth and find no answers.

Upon finding THE GREAT FATHER EMMANUEL upon HIS great return, they will desire Divine Will to take place, and then the GREAT FATHER can begin to teach the children of the earth the ways of the higher universes; the ways of love.

Love will return to the people because they will see the wisdom of THE GREAT FATHER. It is on that day they will begin to awaken to all that has taken place and begin to see how all things came to be.

They will then begin to see how all things work in the greater universes, and it is only when they open their hearts to the Great Love when the greater wisdom can begin to come to them.

As they open their hearts, in those days of the GREAT RETURN, it is then the blessings can grow upon the earth. Those blessings, when they are listened to, can grow into large trees of wisdom and large mountains, so that no man, nor woman, nor child can take the great love away from the earth at the time of 'The Recognition.'

With all things, it is important to understand there is only one path of knowledge and wisdom; the path of the GREAT FATHER EMMANUEL. It is on that path the people are nourished in love. On the other path, the people are misguided, and the people cannot come to the healing.

Happy are those, in the days of the GREAT RETURN of the GREAT FATHER EMMANUEL who are awake, for they will stand in the presence of THE GREAT FATHER EMMANUEL and will ask to be examined and seen by THE GREAT FATHER, so they can receive the blessings.

They will say to HIM, 'Examine my heart, GREAT FATHER EMMANUEL. See I am good to all. See I am working towards great love. If something is not of love within me then remove it from me GREAT FATHER, and guide me towards the higher path of love.'

In the greater heavens, only one way exists; that of love. The love works together in union and is not separated. On earth, people are separated. Fear creates separation. Anger creates separation but love always creates a closer bond.

I, SOVEREIGN LORD EMMANUEL THE GREAT, state how wonderful it would be if people could come to 'The Great Mountain of Light,' and grow into the love together. When you choose to desire 'The Great Mountain of Light' in the greater numbers your blessings will become great.

In the higher realms of love, you desired this time so much; the time of learning love collectively. The power you could grow into collectively, I, SOVEREIGN LORD EMMANUEL THE GREAT, state you do not know.

All these things need to be learned. The preciousness of planet earth needs to be learned. All need to become examined and appreciated from the heart of love; only at that time will the greater numbers begin to see how important spirituality in the love is. There is only one way to the higher love dimensions, and it is for you to desire and find it.

Gone are the ways of confusion, for the great night kept the people in spiritual confusion. It was not possible to wade through the night and find greater solutions. However, now the Great Sun is rising upon your earth, all is becoming seen.

Together, in spiritual love, you can learn how to manifest the earth without pain, for pain is not a state of love. How can pain and fear exist when the people grow in love collectively? In the collective, the power grows for all things have been created to work with the collective desire.

It was not part of Divine Will you worked separately from Divine Will. Always, creation was created to be part of Divine Will; learning to work in harmony and love.

In the lower realms, away from Divine Will, you explored the realms of being separate from Divine Love because you desired it. Have you attained enough knowledge yet? Do you desire to return to true love?

I, SOVEREIGN LORD EMMANUEL THE GREAT, state you do not understand the power within you when you learn to walk in the love upon the higher path of love as one collective love.

If the people understood how important the healing is, within 'The Great Mountain of Light,' and learned to work with collective love power, the times of the true suffering could be gone from your earth, as the power of love would grow among the people. Their faith and trust in Divine would become strong. They would begin to listen to

Divine information, and the guidance and protection we, Divine Masters, would give them in the day of the Great Awakening would be greatly treasured by the people.

They would sing the praises of Divine forever after. Gone will be the desire for war and pain. Their desire will be to grow into greater love, for all creation was birthed from love and so love within them will return.

We always promised you there would be a great life where you could align yourself in one lifetime to Divine Will to help you grow into great love; enabling you to remain on the higher love vibrations eternally.

'When will this be, our Great Lord?' asked the people 2,000 years ago with Jesus.

You have come to this earth for many lifetimes in search of that great lifetime of alignment to freedom, and here you are, at the time of the Great Alignment when you can return to the great love, with 'The Great Mountain' of CAEAYARON, THE GREAT ALIGNER.

Upon coming to 'The Great Mountain of Light,' you will receive the Sacred Flames from my Being, SOVEREIGN LORD EMMANUEL THE GREAT, and with these Sacred Flames you will receive your precious talents back. These sacred talents are gifts to help you return to the great dimensional spaces.

These great dimensional spaces were the same dimensions my faithful channel Jesus spoke about also. He spoke of the sacred spaces where you can become One with the Great SOVEREIGN LORD EMMANUEL THE GREAT. The people in the times of Jesus understood a special time was coming where they could receive the preciousness of these gifts.

Jesus asked, *'But who among you will be ready to receive? When the GREAT FATHER calls you, will you be awake to HIS Great Call? Or will you be asleep to the Great Call when THE GREAT FATHER calls you?'*

At this many stated they would remain awake. His listeners asked, 'But Jesus, how can we recognize THE GREAT FATHER, when the times of the sleep is over?'

They understood a time would happen which was likened to sleep, though they were not certain what that sleep was. Would it be a long sleep or a short sleep, and how long would the duration be of the long sleep if it was a long sleep?

Jesus replied, *'No one knows when THE GREAT FATHER will call. I do not know either; only THE GREAT FATHER knows the timing of all seasons. The time comes and time goes, but the Great Words of THE GREAT FATHER will remain forever. Time does not exist in the mind of THE GREAT FATHER who only knows of everlasting time. For HIM there is no beginning, nor is there an end. It is good to learn to be patient for that will be the test also; will you be patient for the Great Lord to return?*

You will recognize THE GREAT FATHER in the same voice. You will recognize these Divine Words. You will awaken when you hear the Great Name being spoken. It is when you awaken, you will be blessed with Divine Gifts HE can only offer you. You will be called. Do not worry about today or tomorrow, for all things are always given by THE GREAT FATHER. HE will never leave you, nor leave you in despair. HE will continuously be looking for those who desire the High Will of THE GREAT FATHER; for they are the precious ones.

It is not the ones who stand on their platforms HE is looking for. For what good are they to THE GREAT FATHER? They only glorify themselves. They speak about themselves as if they were THE GREAT FATHER speaking.

It is the humble ones, the ones who truly desire to find the higher path, the ones who are searching, it is they who will find the higher path and THE GREAT FATHER will truly bless them.

Go on your way now dear ones and rest your heads up on this. Feel the peace within you that you will receive the Great Calling. THE GREAT FATHER will not forget your great love for HIM; your dedication to come here and listen and accept HIS Great Truth, for that Great Truth will always gift you the great freedom and the great way.

Never forget that the Truth of Divine Glory will always bring you to the road of eternal freedom, where you can celebrate all your lifetimes in eternity. Have faith little ones you will be taken care of. Trust in THE GREAT FATHER.'

Greetings, I AM SOVEREIGN LORD EMMANUEL THE GREAT, eternally here to show you the way of love for those who desire to rise to the love."

The preciousness of gifts of Divine,

Is beyond your understanding,

Are you awake to the Great Calling?

Or are you asleep as the Great Lord is calling?

It is time to awaken,

Respond to the call of love,

Feel the love within you rising,

Understand the Great Father by these words,

Recognize all that is given,

To those who are awake.

Appreciate the sacred gifts.

I AM Sovereign Lord Emmanuel The Great

Part 35: Desire peace upon your planet

"Greetings, I AM SOVEREIGN LORD EMMANUEL THE GREAT. Many things upon your earth are to be desired. Many people on your earth desire material wealth and a lifestyle with all the greatest wonders in life. Many desire beautiful clothes and spend much money and energy on wardrobes to create a unique look, and many others strive for the ultimate and work hard. Many people can achieve their dreams and many others cannot.

Is finding the ultimate material wealth the greatest key to happiness for you? I, SOVEREIGN LORD EMMANUEL THE GREAT, desire to help you understand that it is the inner spiritual path which gives you the greatest happiness and contentment, as all things are about spiritual growth and expansion.

There was once a man who had everything. That man gained his possessions working hard on a mill. When he came to old age, he looked at all his possessions and desired to understand what his greater purpose was in life. Was it to gain all the material wealth he had accumulated? But how was this going to serve him in death? He wondered greatly.

The old man did not know what to do with his possessions after death, so one day he approached a young man who had worked for him previously and asked if he desired to inherit all his wealth and take care of his property after his death.

The young man looked at the master of the mill and said to him, 'Please think about it greatly sir, for the wealth of your property could help many instead of only myself. Please think about it.'

The older man pondered on this matter and began to travel; to understand other people greater. There, he found many people in need of housing and food.

As he was a master of great wealth without exploring other people's issues, he did not realize their extent of suffering. Therefore, he reasoned deeper it was his greater purpose to help these ones instead of gathering material wealth for himself.

The wealthy man sold his property and began to live among the people. He began to help them with farming land and set the way to help them become providers for themselves. He began to educate them.

He began to understand that true happiness comes from helping others to grow and explore life greater. After his death, he became known as the guide for many.

I, SOVEREIGN LORD EMMANUEL THE GREAT, state there are many lessons to learn from this one story. Gaining material wealth for self is not wrong. How can there be anything wrong in the eyes of my Divine Being for there is no right or wrong in the universe? You understand that all serve as a learning experience.

However, to go beyond the physical and understand that all in your life serves as a greater purpose is important to your deeper spirituality. Consider how to help many people understand the higher ways. How can life be improved in all ways? How can you help others to understand a more loving and content way of living?

This man of great wealth, once he began to explore the greater community around him, held no judgment as to how poor or rich the people were.

Consider the young man he approached who could have agreed to take on the wealth. He would have missed the greatest opportunity to help people in the greater community to live a greater life without that young man. Both the master and the younger man played significant roles with increasing abundance for all.

The spiritual lessons are everywhere to be found in your world. It does not matter if you are rich or poor, you learn from all things. In all things find deep contentment in your life. Be grateful for all you have, and always ask the Great Universe of Love to look after you, the people you care about and your possessions, for all is a part of you and all is there to be experienced by you.

Allow all to be a teacher for you. Have no judgment towards anything, but instead always consider 'How you can help the world to go forward now.'

I, SOVEREIGN LORD EMMANUEL THE GREAT, say in your world there are greater opportunities for each person upon your planet. There is something you can do, for yourself, for each other, for your planet and for your eternal future coming.

I, SOVEREIGN LORD EMMANUEL THE GREAT, always said a time would come when I, SOVEREIGN LORD EMMANUEL THE GREAT, would return to your planet with my Divine Word to allow my Voice to be heard in all the nations and into all the corners of the earth as a way upwards would then open, for the ones who desired peace to come to your planet.

The people who heard that 2,000 years ago through Jesus, my Divine Word, were desperately looking for deeper meaning and answers in life as you are also looking. They desired to know when the Great Return would be. I, SOVEREIGN LORD EMMANUEL THE GREAT, said through Jesus, I would return when the people would desire to listen to a higher way.

All throughout this time people have been seeking their own guidance; their own ways of understanding. The time was given for all to be seen and examined for themselves over many lifetimes. Now, there is no more time for people. If we Divine Creators, allowed more lifetimes to happen, nothing could be saved.

I, SOVEREIGN LORD EMMANUEL THE GREAT, prophesied in those days, 2,000 years ago, with Jesus, *'When the people desire to listen to the Great Will and pray for Divine Will to take place upon the earth, then it will be when I return.'*

It so is. Now 'The Great Mountain of Light,' CAEAYARON, is here upon your planet, and I, SOVEREIGN LORD EMMANUEL THE GREAT, have given HIM the task to bring alignment to those who desire to be in 'The Great Mountain of Light,' so that they can be eternally blessed.

In 'The Great Mountain of Light,' THE GREAT CAEAYARON, spiritually the people are nourished and safeguarded, for no one else will take them anymore to the lower dimensions once they pass over to spirit. Instead, they go to the higher states of being, and they are free to explore the greater universes.

I, SOVEREIGN LORD EMMANUEL THE GREAT, say to all who will go to the higher love dimensions, what I said through Jesus, 2,000 years ago, *'Gone is the suffering within their minds, at that time, for suffering will no longer be part of them.*

A new earth will rise, and on that earth, no suffering will occur within their minds. They will see the Great Lord in the Time of the End rising and they will rejoice greatly. They will praise HIS Great Return, and HE will praise them eternally.

Come now my people, rejoice in your eternal freedom. No longer will suffering be on your path, for all those times have gone away. Your freedom will be eternal.

Be in the Mountain of Protection and come and rejoice within all the blessings.'

To those who refuse to allow Divine Will to take place upon your planet and those who refuse to be in 'The Great Mountain of Light,' to them I state, 'I cannot allow you to enter the higher states of freedom. Peace you do not want, and again you deny my existence. How can I, GREAT MASTER OF ALL UNIVERSAL SPACES, allow you to be in my house, my mansion, where only goodness exists within if you do not desire to be in the love, as I AM only Divine Love?'

I choose not to have people within my courtyard who choose not to see my Divine Being. Again, many in your days now choose to go against my Divine Messages through my Word. Like in the days of old, when I, SOVEREIGN LORD EMMANUEL THE GREAT, sent my Word Jesus to the earth plane, who was ridiculed by many for the great message he carried, again, my Word, upon my Great Rising in the Time of the Awakening, is not listened to by many.

No more will I, SOVEREIGN LORD EMMANUEL THE GREAT, send my Divine Word to the planet of the people once the Great Time of the Awakening has ended, as now it is time for the great gathering to take place, for those who are humble within the heart. It is now the time for the people to learn to work in union with THE GREAT FATHER and allow peace to come to the earth and within their heart.

Gone will be the many lifetimes of suffering, as now is the time for freedom. Divine Truth will always bring freedom. All prophecies must be fulfilled, and I, SOVEREIGN LORD EMMANUEL THE GREAT, prophesied a long time ago on your planet that I, SOVEREIGN LORD EMMANUEL THE GREAT, would return, and so I have, together with my Divine Word; the one who was always my Divine Word.

My purpose will always remain the same as I, THE GREAT FATHER, AM eternal. What I state will so happen.

Come all children of the light and rejoice in higher ways. Learn to understand that true contentment lies in the spiritual connection of all of life. Learn that, to have material abundance, when it is used to furthering the purpose of Divine Love upon your earth, will give you many more treasures.

The treasures of the people are empty as they cannot give you eternal life, but those who use the treasures of the earth to bring my Divine Word to all spaces, to allow Divine Will to be heard and for the blessings to be brought to the people and to all the earth, their treasures will be blessed; both on the earth and in the higher realms of existence.

When one uses the material treasures for furthering Divine Purpose, then those riches upon the earth will multiply, as it is used to bring good to many people. One person desiring to bring many to 'The Great Mountain of Light' will become eternally rich in all the great riches coming in all the universes.

In the higher love universes, no poverty exists. The greater you desire to do Divine Will upon your planet, the more abundance you will have in the higher universes, for all your desires upon the earth magnify upwards.

What you create upon your planet now, is what you are creating with everlastingly. Therefore, the ones who understand this and understand the time you are living in, and act upon it, are greatly blessed.

In the greater realms, all live eternally. Nothing can bring an end to all you have gained in the greater realms. How happy the people will be when they understand the greatness that can be before them.

Therefore, do not ask, how much wealth can you accumulate upon the earth; rather ask, 'How can I use my wealth to further Divine Will upon the earth, for then Divine will guide me and protect my wealth, for is it not the Will of Divine that millions come into 'The Great Mountain of Light,' and become healed into the light?

The wise ones reason upon this and understand how important it is to bring healing to the people upon your planet.

Healing the world is a collective love work that can happen when many come together and see the importance. I, SOVEREIGN LORD EMMANUEL THE GREAT, state you do not know the importance or the strength of what I, THE GREAT LORD, can gift to the people if they understand this message.

These messages Jesus also spoke about, and many of the leaders did not desire to allow Jesus to take the lead to bring a whole new consciousness into being. Therefore, they saw Jesus as a threat.

They were not ready to allow Divine Will to take place. They did not desire Divine to have a Voice upon the earth. They did not desire to understand the power Divine could bring to the leaders; if they desired to work in Collective Divine Union.

When the people upon your earth understand this, then your world can change as all things are possible.

I, SOVEREIGN LORD EMMANUEL THE GREAT, stated through my Word, Jesus 2,000 years ago, *'In all ways, understand that nothing is impossible in the eyes of Divine. When your faith is strong, all things can be moved. Whole mountains can be moved with the strength of Divine. Do you not think HE can do that? HE created all things. Always stay in the love and pray you will see all things when THE GREAT FATHER returns, for all things, are possible.*

When HE returns the people will not see the way out. They will look at the world and moan at the world, seeing all the pain and suffering. They will say, 'Wo is me.'

However, if they choose to look upwards, and see the closeness of their deliverance and how all things can be changed, then that one will celebrate this time. They will be within their heart and rejoice in these times.

Therefore, never lose hope or trust, know all things THE GREAT FATHER sees, and HE is looking for those who desire to listen to HIM. It is those who will be guided to a place of eternal peace and love.' All this Jesus brought through 2,000 years ago.

It was not the words the spiritual and the governmental leaders desired to hear; they desired their own ruling. Hence, they ensured that no one had the courage to speak about THE DIVINE FATHER by bringing the great pain to Jesus, my Word, as an 'example' of 'rebellion.'

Now you have an opportunity to change all your ways. Will you desire to see the rising of the Sun Consciousness happen upon your planet?

Greetings, I AM SOVEREIGN LORD EMMANUEL THE GREAT. Happy are those who have been searching for Divine Truth for many lifetimes. They have stayed awake, and now they are being gathered to the Mountain of Light."

'Sovereign Lord,

How can we bring peace to earth?

Please share with us your higher wisdom,

So that we can become wise.'

Those ones who ask are certainly blessed,

They will become wiser than all others,

They can be guided upwards,

They can have greater insight,

And greater knowledge,

And with this knowledge,

They can become eternally blessed,

When they begin to listen.

I AM Sovereign Lord Emmanuel The Great

Part 36: Opening the chambers of your spiritual heart

"Greetings, I AM SOVEREIGN LORD EMMANUEL THE GREAT. I AM here to guide you to higher thoughts of love. Now is the time for you to reach within greater and ask, 'What is it I desire to have within my life?'

The wise ones desire to understand the greater path completely. The ones who are not wise do not even desire to consider the higher path of wisdom. They live without consideration, wondering day to day, year by year, what their greater purpose is.

Now, upon your earth, is the time of the Great Awakening; a time to understand your greater purpose. You live in a time when many will desire the love upon your planet. Many will desire a time of peace for all of life and for your children. They will say, 'Enough to all war and pain upon the planet. When will we learn to forgive all and begin a whole new way of life; that of learning to become of peace, collectively?'

Jesus said to the people on many occasions, *'Become a greater forgiver for all. Be in love and peace. Be ready to be gathered to the greater pastures of spiritual nourishment when the GREAT FATHER calls.'*

It is so that this time has now arrived. Now you are living in the time of the great gathering to allow you to find the higher path of spiritual nourishment and understand what Divine Will is.

How do you open the chambers of your spiritual heart? How do you find greater fulfillment in your life?

This was a similar question raised long ago. A man in a village approached Jesus, the teacher, and said, 'You talk about the heart like it is something we cannot reach. You talk in great words, riddles, and great illustrations but I cannot understand. Please forgive me teacher, but I have a simple mind. I cannot understand your words.'

What riddles did this man mean?

Whenever Jesus taught, he brought through higher information from the Higher Realms. Jesus channeled my Divine energy; the energy that you know well as SOVEREIGN LORD EMMANUEL THE GREAT. The people, in those days, were mystified with the teachings.

Jesus replied to this man, *'The heart is like a treasure chest with valuable treasures within it. The gold and the silver and all the precious gems are within this chest. However, you cannot access it until you learn to go within your own heart and listen to the quietness within.*

In the quiet, you will find the keys and you will be given the keys to open the treasure chest; only if you are open with your heart to listen to the messages from THE FATHER. HE sent me to speak these words to you because it is with this key you will find the greater door to the higher wisdom, and it is then you will find your freedom. It is then you will find all you are looking for.'

How did this riddle confuse the people? They did not understand the messages from the Higher Realms. They did not understand or comprehend Jesus was a spiritual teacher sent from the Archangelic Realms of Light to bring the light and the 'keys' of the great heart to the people.

Jesus opened the heart of the people and many did find these spiritual keys. They unlocked their chambers within their own hearts and greater wisdom was their treasure to have.

The leaders of those days were not happy with the learnings of the people. The people refused to listen to their leaders and the leaders lost control over the people. The people became stronger with their views and more outspoken. Therefore, Jesus was removed from the scene at that time because the leaders in those days desired people to listen to them, not Divine.

How did they create a situation to bring the people back into their control?

By creating fear and pain. They tortured Jesus in public. They taunted him. Many of his followers became afraid of disobeying their leaders and many others lost their desire to follow these precious teachings after witnessing the pain Jesus went through.

There were those, however, who stayed faithful and they kept talking and sharing the teachings of Jesus concerning the great freedom of the heart.

The heart, when it is freed, will give you the power and great wisdom. It is in the heart you can find your greatness and your love. Yet, it is like Jesus taught, *'You can only find the keys when you go into the* quiet. It is in the quiet places you will find the way into your heart. It is there you will find the nurturing and the love.'

Learning to go within the heart is where all truth of self exists. Jesus talked to his followers often about the heart and said, 'When one is humble, one is able to find the truth within the heart.

The proud and haughty cannot find the truth within the heart because the heart will not desire to reach within the treasures until that one has found the truth within self; that truth is great love.

Great love brings you to the chambers of the heart, and when the heart is open to the love, the heart will open the gateway to the eternal treasures.

The lovers of riches will have difficulty finding it because the heart of love does not recognize the selfish love of riches and preciousness. The heart of love recognizes the love of truth; THE GREAT FATHER and love for all.

It is within the heart the GREAT DIVINE FATHER is recognized, but it is only the humble who will be able to find the chamber within the heart.

The road to finding this chamber is not easy as it requires one to keep searching within for more depth and treasures. The strong ones will be able to find it. They know they will find more treasure once they go deeper within the heart.

Finding the deeper heart treasures is more difficult to find for those whose desire it is to please the desires of their flesh alone. They long for the physical and material pleasures and what life can offer them. They do not desire to look within; nor do they desire to ask what it is *that THE GREAT FATHER desires them to do, for considering a greater purpose is not within them. These ones do not long for the spiritual treasures, for the love for the GREAT FATHER is not within them. Either you must choose for one or the other.'*

This does not mean that the one who has found the heart's treasures cannot take pleasure in the physical feasting, for THE GREAT FATHER desires all to enjoy life. HE has provided the food you eat every day. HE will ensure you are clothed and looked after. HE desires you to be grateful for all you enjoy in life. HE desires you to have the best of all things; always with appreciation knowing all things come from THE FATHER.

When one learns to see that everything is from THE GREAT FATHER and that HE is the Great Provider, then that one receives more. Much you can learn from nature as they never suffer from a shortage. All things can be learned from creation. Creation is eternal.

When one desires to understand the higher path, that one will become richer as the heart opens to the greatness of all eternal glory. That one is richly blessed because THE GREAT FATHER EMMANUEL will always look after those who seek first the heart.

The ones who take from others to become rich will not receive the great eternal blessings. They cannot reach within the heart because the heart does not desire the pain caused to others and self. When one wreaks pain upon another, the heart begins to turn against that one; until that one begins to search within. The heart is the Great Teacher; the path of eternal love.

Go through the narrow gate of the heart and you will find eternal freedom. Let no man stop you from finding the higher gate. It does not matter what anyone does to you. Constantly go deep within the heart and know all answers will come at the time when it is most needed. Constantly search your own desires and your heart to examine if it is still searching for the greater love and truth.'

In your day, in general, your society does not support going within the heart. Many people are afraid of the unknown. When you enter your spiritual chambers with the love in your heart, it is then you will find your greater gifts. These greater gifts are your treasures. They are yours to have and yours to own. Once you find the greater gifts and once you claim them, nothing can take them away from you. They have been waiting for you to find and claim them. They are waiting for the owner to claim them.

Are you ready to claim them?

Going within the heart takes much courage and skill. It takes courage because many people are afraid to go within and see what is there. Many are afraid they will find what they choose not to see.

Fear in itself does not exist until you bring your thoughts to it and then it can become a reality for you to experience. Let go of your fear. Walk in the trust. Come back to the Great Light.

Greetings, I AM SOVEREIGN LORD EMMANUEL THE GREAT. It is time to come back to the Great Light."

In the Great Light you will find,

Your eternal love for all of life,

Let go of your inner fears,

Fear does not create greater love for you,

Only when you overcome your fear,

Will you gain strength and freedom,

Then you will have learned to conquer fear.

Learn not to fear others,

Instead learn to heal your fears,

Work with your eternal gifts of love,

Receive the Eternal Great Talents,

Grow into the love,

Become of love.

I AM Sovereign Lord Emmanuel The Great

Part 37: Learning the importance of endurance

"Greetings, I AM SOVEREIGN LORD EMMANUEL THE GREAT. Endurance is a strong spiritual quality that is to be appreciated in your life. Many people upon your planet do not understand the importance of endurance and it is not taught, in general, to the younger generations. You live in communities without understanding the importance of endurance.

Strong spiritual people, when they desire to become stronger within themselves, are eager to develop endurance for it gains strength and inner power.

Jesus, my Designated Word, 2,000 years ago, often spoke about the importance of spiritual endurance to the people. As a teacher of endurance, he was also a great student himself who had learned endurance.

Jesus stated the following with my Divine Words of SOVEREIGN LORD EMMANUEL THE GREAT, 'When one understands self on a spiritual level and begins to examine self, what is it he finds? What gives him strength and allows hope and trust not to diminish from himself?'

The people who sat before him, on that hot sunny day, pondered deeply on this subject, for they had never considered it before.

Jesus carried on talking to the people, *'Imagine if you have a beautiful person before you. This person is of love and desires good for all. This person is of the heart and desires to bring more goodness to all. How will this person do this?*

Being in love alone each day is not going to keep this person strong for long, for many will not be encouraging to that person to stay in love. Others are not encouraging to those who are of the heart for they do not desire to live the path of the heart. They struggle to understand the people of the heart.

How do you personally maintain a great trust in THE GREAT DIVINE FATHER, when no one around you desires to hear what you have to say?

How do you maintain your positive smile and stay in the forgiveness when all others say you are not right in the head because you are not following their ways?

Most would turn to the fear within them, and in fear, they weaken within themselves. Fear brings quietness within the lover of the heart. The one in great fear is unable to talk from the heart and then that one, when feeling the rejection from others, is not as enthusiastic anymore as there is no common grounding for the love. Many will desire to ebb the love and joy within the lover of the heart.

Imagine if the lover of the heart loved DIVINE until the people began to reject the GREAT DIVINE FATHER. What does it take for that person to stay strong within their belief, for most do not desire the ways of THE GREAT DIVINE FATHER?

Many will say, you are not right in the mind to believe the things you speak about; the words you heard from THE GREAT DIVINE FATHER.

Others will say that is not how THE GREAT FATHER works for they have heard the ways of men and they will not desire to hear THE GREAT FATHER speak to them. They do not have the great love for THE GREAT FATHER who created all.

There once was a daughter of a great wealthy man who desired to do good for many. She had the wealth to create her business and her father desired her to take his great business over. However, the young daughter was good within her heart and did not agree with her father's business for it meant that many people would grow poorer, and she desired to help people become richer.

Therefore, she responded, 'Dear father, I cannot take over the business because it is not what I desire for other people for it causes much pain and grief. I would rather find my own way than to work against my own heart. I choose not to take money away from others unfairly.'

Her father grew angry at his daughter's remark and exclaimed she needed to leave him at once since she did not desire to be working for him.

Sadly, she packed her bags and left her father, unable to understand why her father had spoken to her like this. She lifted her head to the heavens and asked for help. She did not understand the universe, nor THE GREAT FATHER, but she did know her heart.

An older man approached her and asked if she needed shelter and she appreciated all that was given. He offered her work and was given money.

She learned by trusting in Divine all was given to her because her heart was good. One of the people she worked for was a teacher for the children in the village, and she learned to teach and help children grow into stronger people.

What do you think helped her grow into greater strength? Why do you think THE GREAT FATHER blessed her?'

Jesus looked at the people before him and many were amazed at the message as many had not considered giving up material wealth for the love of the heart. Many even considered that her choosing was foolish and spoke to Jesus about this.

'Jesus,' said one man, 'I believe the daughter to be foolish. She gave up her wealth because of something she believed? Here we are struggling, and she gives it up because of her belief?'

Jesus answered the man with great wisdom, *'Do you not see the importance of this example? This girl desired with her heart to bring more love to the people. She did not desire to be like your masters taking money away from the people. She did not desire the suffering of the people, but instead, her heart yearned to help many, and so THE GREAT FATHER led her to her greater desires.*

THE GREAT FATHER sees all and desired to help this girl understand. She never lost faith in Divine, though she walked without understanding.

You know more about THE GREAT FATHER than she ever did, yet her faith and love for HIM is greater than you at this time, for you cannot see the importance of her experience.

Happy you are when you do, for then you can understand the love within you. How can one place wealth before love? How can one say they are in love, and yet cause pain to another? How can your spiritual leaders say they have a love for THE GREAT DIVINE FATHER when they knock on your door, asking you to give up more money, and giving you more laws of men? How then can you say they have a love for you?

You fear your spiritual masters. They keep you in fear to keep you quiet. They desire you to think yourself as naive when you are not for you are now discovering yourself deeper.

In the same situation as this example, you would have chosen the road of taking the money from others. You judged the girl for having enough love within her to let go of her wealth from her father.

Her love within herself was so great for THE GREAT DIVINE FATHER, that even without knowing HIM, she followed the love within her heart. She knew what was right for her and she was not persuaded to do otherwise.

How do you think this will help you with the question posed earlier? How will this bring great strength within you without diminishing your love for THE GREAT FATHER when you are learning to walk the higher spiritual path?'

A young woman stood up and asked Jesus if she could answer. The men scowled at the young woman as they did not desire the woman to have a say.

Jesus encouraged the young woman to come to the front with a kind gesture. The young woman grew afraid in that instance and desired to back down. However, she fearlessly walked to the front.

Jesus embraced her. *'Please speak from your heart for your heart is filled with love and wisdom. Speak, please.'*

The young woman faced the audience. With an open heart, she raised her head to the heavens, praying for great strength and said, 'I understand the lesson, for I experienced something similar. My father is a great spiritual leader and he has banished me from his house because my desire is to follow you, dear Jesus. I know your GREAT DIVINE FATHER is of truth, and I know my own fleshly father is not of love or of truth.

I grew up in a house, only desiring the love, and love I never received from my own father. He did not care for his daughter or his people. He spent many months and years preaching to me the laws of the people.

I felt threatened with great fear. I was told to stay quiet.

I desired to speak about you, Jesus. The hate, upon doing so, I saw in his eyes. The fury he gave me, terrified me. That night I was on the street, abandoned, never to return to my home again.

I felt afraid, and at that moment, I lifted my head up to the heavens, praying to the GREAT FATHER EMMANUEL. I opened my heart and spoke from my heart, asking HIM for a way for me.

I was afraid on my own and afraid my own father would send other men after me to do things not right in the eyes of the GREAT DIVINE FATHER. I was afraid my father would bring me to the spiritual gathering places before the other spiritual leaders and order me to deny my belief in you and THE GREAT FATHER EMMANUEL.

Know my own father is important as a spiritual leader, but far from love, though admired by many. I have needed to forgive him.

Upon praying to the GREAT FATHER, I received a message within my heart to go to an older lady in the village, so I did. She took me in and gave me shelter and a home to live in. I work for her and water her animals. I ensure the household runs fine and I am very grateful for it.

I take from this story never to lose faith in the GREAT DIVINE FATHER. I desire to do his Great Will with all my heart because I trust in HIM.

Though the road is uncertain at times, though the people around us can be cruel when we talk about Jesus and the GREAT FATHER, I understand the great trust needed. I have seen how the GREAT FATHER EMMANUEL has helped me, and in that I trust.'

She then turned to Jesus and said, 'Thank you, Jesus, for being The Word of THE GREAT FATHER. Thank you for carrying on, despite what they say and what the people are doing to try and stop you.

I pray you to find your peace always when the people are cruel to you. You are my example of love and I follow you because I know you follow your heart and never give up on the love of THE GREAT FATHER. Thank you for being my example.'

With that, the young woman sat down.

Jesus had tears in his eyes for no one ever had the courage before that moment to speak out like this, and yet, this young woman, judged by the men present for speaking, had the great courage to speak from her heart.

She did not withhold her great love for the GREAT FATHER EMMANUEL, nor did she withhold her appreciation for the one who brought the teachings through, tirelessly, day after day, even though many rejected the teachings. She knew Jesus constantly carried on, discovering new listeners, desiring new listeners to understand the words of Divine Truth.

Jesus stood there quietly, thanking the young woman. He then closed his eyes as the message from my Divine Being, SOVEREIGN LORD EMMANUEL THE GREAT deepened:

'In all ways, know that THE GREAT FATHER sees all. HE brings all to the light and HE brings all to the higher path; if that one desires to understand the pathway of the heart. The one with the great belief and trust in the GREAT DIVINE FATHER, shows deep love within, and that person never gives up on love within their heart.

Despite what other people say or believe, the one standing strong like the rock, or the large tree, will never waver. Even during the storms of life, when the belief in the GREAT DIVINE FATHER is as strong as the rock, the rock will not waver in the storm, nor will it ever wither, for it stands strong in the trust, THE DIVINE FATHER will always take care of that one who is love within.

The one who has the trust like a mighty tree does not waver in the storm either. When times are not good and when others speak against that one, that one, as mighty as a tree will always remain strong within their trust, for their trust will never wither.

The ones, however, who are weak within their faith, are like a feather. When their great test comes, they blow away and are never to be seen again. They did not have the courage, nor the strength, nor the trust, to stay spiritually strong within themselves.

THE GREAT FATHER cannot bless those who are spiritually weak but will bless those who are strong within their trust for HIM. Their trust in HIM is great that all is taken care of, for themselves and for their families.

The spiritually strong display love, strength, and endurance, for they never give up on their inner faith. Constantly they trust their faith will become seen and recognized and they trust they will be guided to the higher ways of love.

Those with strong faith can be led to a greater path for then THE GREAT FATHER EMMANUEL can show them how important their trust in HIM is.

Even though at that time of praying to THE GREAT FATHER, they may not see a way out, THE GREAT FATHER, who hears all prayers from the heart, will guide that one to the higher path.

Their faith will turn to great trust and strength as then they have seen the goodness and truth of THE GREAT FATHER. The great trust and strength give determination and endurance to grow spiritually.

In all ways, THE GREAT FATHER looks after those who desire to do good for others; HE always blesses those of the heart of love, however, THE GREAT FATHER tests all who walk on the higher path. How great is their love for HIM? Do they desire to grow into greater strength and become like the strong rock or a large tree, well rooted in the ground so nothing can bring them into wavering?

This THE GREAT FATHER EMMANUEL desires to see; how great the love of HIS creation is for HIM.

THE GREAT FATHER EMMANUEL only desires those who love HIS path and HIS way. All will be given to those who desire Divine Will to take place in the higher heavens, also upon the earth, for those ones are meek and they can be taught Divine Will. They have proven their strength, love, faith, trust and constant endurance.

The ones who are spiritually strong understand a way comes to bring all things into the greater freedom; if they have genuine love within their heart for THE GREAT FATHER.

THE GREAT FATHER constantly desires the people on the earth to keep asking HIM, 'Show us a way to the higher path, GREAT FATHER. Show us your great wisdom. We pray you to show us how to follow Divine Will.

In all ways, we desire to come more into the higher thought union with you GREAT DIVINE FATHER. Guide us to the higher ways of love and wisdom. Encourage us to be wise and allow us to become wiser. Our hearts are open to great wisdom. Constantly these people will keep praying, even if there is not a way to be seen at that time. They follow their heart. They listen to within. They know what THE GREAT DIVINE FATHER desires and that is to desire all to be in the greatness and the goodness.

THE GREAT DIVINE FATHER is the way to the love and the freedom, and HE blesses all who desire to do HIS Divine Will eternally; in that always have great trust. HE will not leave anyone behind who is truly willing to follow Divine Will and bring the Good News to others.

He brings the test to all people. How much does creation love HIM? Will they desire to follow the steps of Divine Love? How are they showing it within their life? Would the people step away from the teachings of the old and the teachings of the men to learn the ways of THE GREAT FATHER? Or will they not see the difference between the teachings of the men, the spiritual leaders, and THE GREAT FATHER?

Only THE GREAT DIVINE FATHER can bring love and peace. The people cannot, and the gods of the people cannot for they are not in the love of the GREAT FATHER. They bring judgment and death, and this is how all came to be on this earth.

On this earth, you see the suffering, the aging, and the large punishments if one does not desire to follow the ways of men. The expectations of the spiritual masters are high, and yet THE GREAT FATHER EMMANUEL does not expect much at all; other than to walk away from the ways of men and the ways of their gods, for they are not the ways of THE GREAT FATHER EMMANUEL.

HE does not desire anyone to suffer, as suffering is not what HE created. HE created beauty and perfection because of HIS great love, *but the people desired not to listen to THE GREAT FATHER and so this realm belongs not to THE GREAT FATHER, but to something else.*

THE GREAT FATHER desires you to love HIM with all your heart, with all your might and never let go of your love for HIM, for in all ways HE will test your love for HIM. Those who trust HIM in all ways and keep asking for HIM to guide them will be greatly blessed by HIM.

THE GREAT FATHER desires all to be loved, and therefore HE says, 'Love your neighbor, your brothers, your sisters, your mothers, your fathers, your children, your animals and all you care about. Show them love each day. Imitate THE GREAT FATHER. However, when your friends and family reject the great teachings of THE GREAT FATHER, learn to love them, forgive them, accept them. Never place judgment upon the people who reject the GREAT DIVINE FATHER.'

Know, when they truly reject HIM, it is not you who they are rejecting, for they do not know what they are rejecting. They are not rejecting you, but they are rejecting Divine Will to take place. Therefore, the GREAT FATHER, though HE will never judge anyone, HE will not allow them to go to the New Earth of love and peace, for how can HE grant them access to the higher realms of eternal love, when they do not desire HIS love within them?

When your loved ones reject THE GREAT FATHER, accept their rejection and keep loving them. Do not argue or debate, but stay quiet about THE GREAT FATHER, for HE does not desire to have those who reject HIM within his greater realms, therefore, do not force them to listen for they are free to desire their own path.

Your spiritual leaders desire to force people to listen to them. They bring threats and they make examples to show people must listen and obey them. Then more laws they create as they see how their laws are not listened to and this gives them great anger.

Those laws are not of love. They are far from love. Know the spiritual leaders work from fear of not being able to bring control to the people. They fear the people speaking to them, and this is why they shout with authority; not with authority from their heart, for they do not work from the heart, but they speak to bring others down into the fear to stop uprising from happening.

THE GREAT FATHER knows all these things. Trust in THE GREAT FATHER, for all your needs will be always met when you have that trust.

THE GREAT FATHER will eternally reward all who have spiritual trust and love for HIM. HE will eternally reward those who showed endurance without giving up. HE will eternally reward those who were as strong, within their spiritual love and trust, like the solid rock and the solid tree.

Be like the solid tree and the solid rock and let nothing stop you from love. Be determined to show others the way. Constantly be in the forgiveness and trust all things will come to those who desire HIM to bring Divine Will to the earth.'

Greetings, I AM SOVEREIGN LORD EMMANUEL THE GREAT. To understand these lessons further, look within the heart of love."

The love within the heart is tested,

How much love,

Do you have for The Great Father?

Will you desire to work in the Great Love?

Or will you reject it?

All is a universal decision.

To work in the love with the collective,

Will bring greater strength and love to you,

Why not join in,

Learn how to hold,

The great new flows of love.

I AM Sovereign Lord Emmanuel The Great

Part 38: The Great Examiner of the hearts

"Greetings, I AM SOVEREIGN LORD EMMANUEL THE GREAT. All of creation is important for your spiritual growth. You live on a spiritual planet and it can give all you need to sustain your life with, however, because the people did not appreciate your planet, almost all is destroyed. You have little time left to decide now whether you desire to be on your planet, which is your home, or not.

I, SOVEREIGN LORD EMMANUEL THE GREAT, state how important it is to understand you on a spiritual level and what it is you came here to do. Most people on your planet do not consider your greater purpose together; standing unified together in the love, listening to Divine Love.

Many consider THE GREAT FATHER EMMANUEL, who is My Divine Being, 'asleep.' Many others consider I AM but a fairy story. Very few seem to realize I AM real, and to understand I AM real is far too difficult for them to accept. Most do not care about life and nature, so why should they consider the GREAT DIVINE is a reality? Why should they care about my Great Existence?

Your planet desires the people to awaken to the love within them, for without that love your existence will no longer be. I, THE GREAT

SOVEREIGN FATHER desire your awakening also. How can creation carry on with her suffering upon your planet? As you suffer, all animals suffer, all vegetation suffers, all oceans suffer, all mountains are suffering and all that is upon and within your planet are suffering. How can you not see this?

Jesus prophesied a time when large destruction would be upon your planet and said, *'If it was not for THE GREAT FATHER EMMANUEL rising, at that time, nothing would be saved.'*

When I, SOVEREIGN LORD EMMANUEL, returned it would be at a time when many nations would be warring and all upon the earth was dying. It would be at a time when many were not in the heart of love and would not desire the love to rise upwards.

Many would rather crawl into their caves of darkness rather than see my Divine Rising happening for the love for the DIVINE FATHER would not be within their hearts.

Many, at that time of my Great Rising, would scream within their hearts upon hearing the GREAT FATHER and say, 'But this cannot be. Surely there is no GREAT FATHER like that. We cannot stand this, for now all needs to be examined.'

They will say, 'Oh, GREAT FATHER EMMANUEL, what have we done in your name? All what we have done are now examined by you. Let's hide deep within our caves, praying the GREAT FATHER EMMANUEL will not see us and all we have done.'

Jesus stated 2,000 years ago, *'In the day of the GREAT FATHER rising, many would seek war and pain for others. Many nations would rise against each other and many people would scream in the pain, 'GREAT*

FATHER, please answer our prayers, we do not see anything else but great darkness around us.' In those days, THE GREAT FATHER EMMANUEL will return to bring peace to the nations, if they so desire to listen.

In those days, a way upwards will be created by THE GREAT FATHER who desires all of creation to be saved, but saving all, even HE cannot do as HE desires only those to come to the great pastures of life and truth and walk upon the higher road; who are willing to follow HIM. HE will never force anyone to walk on the higher road of the heart of love.

Many in those days, of HIS Great Return, will not desire to see HIM. They will state how they do not see HIM, and many will cry out that it could not be in that way His Great Return would come, for it cannot be.

Many will reject the teachings like they do in this day also (2,000 years ago). *Many will say that THE GREAT FATHER is not true and that THE GREAT FATHER is not like they thought. They will not desire THE GREAT FATHER to speak to them.*

In those days, they will be uncaring for life around them. They will not even desire to see how the people are towards all of creation. The fear will grow great in those days. The earth will shake with fear with the people upon her. In those days, the ones who see the GREAT FATHER rising, the ones who listen and follow the directions given, they will be eternally saved.'

I, SOVEREIGN LORD EMMANUEL THE GREAT, state all those prophecies are coming true now. Your earth is greatly unbalanced. There are more dangers upon planet earth than in all other previous times combined because of the lack of love within the people and for all of creation.

The people lack respect for life itself. They have forgotten the ways of love and the sanctity of life. People destroy each other with their thoughts alone. Many have guns and shoot the innocent. Many make rules and pain others who are innocent. You cannot understand how to come back to love, and it is not possible to create peace with your own thoughts. Gone are those days as all is greatly unbalanced.

You have looked at all angles and there is no way forward for you anymore; unless you begin to act upon these words and desire the Divine Path of Love.

I, SOVEREIGN LORD EMMANUEL THE GREAT, gave you plenty of time to investigate whether you as mankind could rule yourselves, for that is what you desired most of all.

In the time of love and peace in spiritual paradise, Lemuria, you did not desire the great love collectively, nor did you desire all I offered in the greater realms of love. I offered you eternal peace, the great power to evolve planets with, and you, as the great collective of the Great Lemurians, desired the universes of denseness. You listened and desired your false prophets and so you became part of another realm; that of the darkness, thrown deep into the deep abyss state of pain, suffering, and agony.

I, SOVEREIGN LORD EMMANUEL THE GREAT, gave my Word to your planet knowing she would suffer greatly amongst the people who had no love within them. Why would they desire my Word to be among your people, when they did not desire my Word in the land of peace and love?

They turned against my Divine Word and against the GREAT CAEAYARON, MOUNTAIN OF LIGHT, MOUNTAIN OF PROTECTION. Thus, you came into great suffering because you became the property of the one who desired to become your ultimate God, that being Yahweh; the great god of rebellion against the love.

In all ways, Yahweh went out and roared like a beast devouring all who sought the love. When the Divine Love Word was upon your earth, Yahweh commanded his people to go and destroy and to seek out all who desired the love so that love would not grow within them.

I, SOVEREIGN LORD EMMANUEL THE GREAT, gave my Word many times to your planet, watching the suffering of that one I designated to be the way and the road forward.

Now I AM giving you the way upwards once again because I AM love. However, if you choose to still stay in opposition to my Divine Being, SOVEREIGN LORD EMMANUEL THE GREAT, and CAEAYARON, 'The Great Mountain of Light,' then I cannot allow you to come into the land of peace and love.

My mansions are only of love and all are tested upon your planet. How much love do you have for my Divine Being, SOVEREIGN LORD EMMANUEL THE GREAT? Do you have enough love to change your ways, to become activated into the love with 'The Great Mountain of Light,' CAEAYARON?

Do you desire to take on the higher love streams to hold the love for your planet? For without those love streams how can you say you love Divine, and how can you say you desire to come into the 'Eternal Great Mountain of Light,' as CAEAYARON is the Great Realm of Love with my Divine Being, SOVEREIGN LORD EMMANUEL THE GREAT?

All things are to be looked at now.

You are now on the path of choosing.

I, THE GREAT FATHER, always said I would examine all thoughts and hearts when I return with my Word. I would begin to examine the hearts and determine whether there was any love for Divine Love within the hearts of the people.

Those who come to 'The Great Mountain of Light,' I would bless the greatest of all of creation, as they still came with their hearts of love, though they lived on a planet rejecting Divine Love.

I, SOVEREIGN LORD EMMANUEL THE GREAT, would look at the earth and listen to her as she would relate to me your history and how you have evolved. Have you learned the love within your heart? In what ways did the people cause the death and the screams to creation? Did their hearts grow so cold to create so much pain upon the planet?

The people would reason in those days of my Great Return,

'Why should we bother about a few dying? It is better they die than me.'

My reply is as THE GREAT FATHER EMMANUEL, 'Did the people not care about the earth, their home? Do you not know how precious planet earth is to you? Did the people not care about the people dying in the world at each moment?'

I, SOVEREIGN LORD EMMANUEL THE GREAT, spoke the following words through Jesus, *'In the day of my Great Return I will examine the hearts and see whether the goodness has returned to them. I will* desire to examine if there is any love within them for my Divine Being. I will examine how they treat their animals and plants.

Those who did not care about creation have no care for the greater planets in existence either. Why should I, SOVEREIGN LORD EMMANUEL, give them greater creation to destroy? Why should I, SOVEREIGN LORD EMMANUEL THE GREAT, give them greater power to destroy with?

For in the greater dimensions, where only love exists, there are greater planets and greater life in existence. There is a much greater power than humans have upon your planet. There the animals thrive. There the minerals thrive. There the sea life thrives. There all of the vegetation thrives. No one laments within. No one moans within, and all creation is good in the higher realms of love.

There is the true power of greatness. There is no suffering, and greater power is given to those who live and walk upon those planets because there only goodness exists within their hearts.

So I, SOVEREIGN LORD EMMANUEL THE GREAT, upon my Great Return as the GREAT SUN will see upon the earth who was good to my creation. Who desired the earth to live? Who fought hard for the earth to live? Who desired pain to come to the earth, the animals and the people? All will be examined.

The ones who desired life to thrive and listened to the Great Divine in the hour of my Great Return, their desire will grow to come into 'The Great Mountain of Light' and eternal light to become healed, to allow the power to be restored within them, to allow them to come to the New Creation where only love exists.

To all others, who disowned the Great Will, they are not to enter into the higher love dimensions for the great love was not within them.

So it will be because all life is a part of my Divine Self, and my Divine Will is for all to exist in love and unity, for I AM LOVE. Suffering I do not desire within me, so I will cut the suffering away.'

When the people reject these higher ways of love once again, again they are choosing for the one who brought all pain and suffering into the dimensions of love; the one who brought the great rebellion and took trillions into spiritual death and suffering.

The people upon your planet are living in the time of the living choice. Do they desire to live in Divine Will and change their ways to love? Will they desire to learn the higher path and save their planet? Will they desire to listen to how they can restore their planet and how they can bring peace to the people? Or will they choose to walk upon their path of destruction, as you are marching to the path of eternal destruction without a way out?

Here, I, SOVEREIGN LORD EMMANUEL THE GREAT, state how important it is to understand the path of love, I, THE GREAT FATHER, can give to those who desire the ways of the love.

Learn to love all of life and be with love within your heart. Understand destruction is no part of me. Instead, learn to forgive all and forgive all of mankind for bringing destruction and pain within your consciousness.

There was a time when no pain and suffering was within your consciousness. No pain or suffering could exist within you as it was not part of your thoughts and ways. All was peace, love and great joy.

All worked in love and harmony collectively, united as one with one greater purpose, and that was to follow Divine Will.

Divine Will constantly blessed the people with greater abundance, love and peace when the people followed Divine direction, as this was part of Divine Will that all stayed working united, into the love, so that no suffering could occur within the place you called 'paradise' and the land of 'flowing milk and honey.'

When the people chose for the freedom from the Divine Path, they chose for their spiritual death and to a spiritual death, they fell. There was no way forward any longer. As a result, a long night of pain and suffering was before them, seemingly without a way back to the light.

They were without a shepherd, without Divine direction as they had not desired Divine Love. From Divine Love, they fell into the pain, suffering, and guilt. Instead, they had the voice of the gods who brought them down into the lower earth and neither I, SOVEREIGN LORD EMMANUEL THE GREAT, nor CAEAYARON who also became imprisoned into the lower earth realms, were able to bring a road upwards for you. However, the one who was able to reach you, on the lower earth dimensions, after your fall, was the Divine Love Element, my Divine Word, as she is part of all of creation.

Because of her intense love for all of creation, the earth, CAEAYARON, my Divine Being, SOVEREIGN LORD EMMANUEL THE GREAT, and for the fallen Lemurians who had rejected the higher path, she brought herself into human creation.

Long has been the night and her fight to bring you to this one door. Now, I, THE GREAT FATHER EMMANUEL, FATHER OF ALL OF CREATION, have been able to return because she endured the long night and she did not give up on her love for THE GREAT DIVINE TRUTH, and thus, she brought you to a time where we, as Divine Beings, are able to bring a way out of the lower dimensions for you, to a higher state of creation; should the people desire to become love once again.

This is the path upwards. Once the people reject this way as a great collective and individually, no more way upwards can be given to you as you would have then made the final choice.

This is what Jesus prophesied: *'A time will come when the GREAT FATHER returns to see who desires the path upwards. HE will examine all hearts. Who will desire HIS great love? Those HE will greatly bless when they learn to stand in the love together.*

Blessed are those who begin to listen, for their eternal lives will be saved. Blessed are those who begin to listen. When the people and nations begin to listen, blessed all of creation will be. In that day, the earth may be saved, and many will not have their lives cut short.

All will be examined, and all will be called to the Great Love Gathering. Always pray you are strong enough within your heart to listen to the great call so you can grow into the strength and on the higher path. May you desire to be examined by the GREAT FATHER so that HE can see the goodness within you. May HE see your goodness within you.

May the earth awaken at the time of HIS Great Return and strengthen. May the nations awaken and desire the GREAT DIVINE FATHER. May all become blessed. If the nations awaken together, THE GREAT DIVINE FATHER will bring strength and love within the earth and many will be saved on that day.

However, if many reject HIM, HE will not do that, for then HE was not desired on a great level. Pray the people to awaken in the great numbers. Pray they desire the help and love from THE GREAT DIVINE, so they may rejoice at the way upwards.'

Greetings, I AM SOVEREIGN LORD EMMANUEL THE GREAT. Happy are those who are on the watch."

All who desire the ways of love and peace,

Reach within your heart and begin to say;

'Great Divine Emmanuel,

Bring love within my heart,

I desire you to guide me,

And our world back to all the love,

May the great numbers,

Awaken to the great love now,

May they not reject you,

But instead may they bring the love,

Within themselves,

May you teach us to live in love,

May you bless our earth and people,

May you bless us forever and ever.'

I AM Sovereign Lord Emmanuel The Great

Part 39: Expanding love frequencies within your spiritual heart

"Greetings, I AM SOVEREIGN LORD EMMANUEL THE GREAT. You have many gateways within your heart. Your precious spiritual heart contains all the secrets of all your lifetimes. It opens you to higher dimensions of existence and higher spiritual gifts.

It is in your heart all will be revealed to you. There you learn to flow with the greater love within your Divine Being of love. It is within your heart you will learn to dwell with peace and love. Peace and love cannot truly be found without discovering the greater love within your heart. Even when there is no peace around you, you are still able to find peace by going within the heart of love. Those who find these greater treasures within their heart are well rewarded with deep love and deep peace.

It may be a struggle to find these deeper treasures, for many obstacles lie in the way of finding it. Many obstacles are placed in your way to try to keep you off the higher road of love. All things are constantly tested and examined to see if you are ready to reach within your higher states of love within your heart.

To find the higher states is difficult for most are not ready to go deeper. It is a constant journey of examining how your heart is progressing forward. At times your mind will not desire the higher growth, and then the heart will not force the higher path within you. It is only when the desire is great within and you continuously ask the higher realms to guide you to the greater path will you find it.

Each one of you has spiritual secrets waiting to be unlocked and unfolded by you. Each of these secrets shares with you a tale of an ancient story. These are stories you experienced in other dimensions. In many of those dimensions, you sought to understand yourselves greater but were unable to find it until you reached a higher stage of thought consciousness.

Now, in the greater times of the Awakening Consciousness, once again you are being asked to seek the greater treasures in your heart. Within these great secrets, you will find the treasures and wisdom. You will find your path and your path will guide you to greater happiness and love. Happiness, bliss, joy, peace, comfort, and great love are a few of the prizes of finding these greater treasures.

Many, however, walk in life unaware of these treasures within the heart. They keep searching and looking outside of their heart. They keep searching for wisdom but instead of looking within their heart and looking for higher guidance, listening to their deeper inner voice, they believe in wisdom outside of their heart.

Finding wisdom outside of the heart does not lead you to your inner truth. It does not lead you to deep inner peace and love. It often leads to deeper confusion and misunderstanding. This is because your outside reality is not your highest truth. You are on a journey to find your truth within your heart of love.

When Jesus was upon your earth, he taught the people to look within their hearts because this was where the kingdom was found. This was where the deeper treasures were found. This was where all answers were found and the happiness would be theirs to have, upon finding it.

Happiness was what the people desperately sought in those days. They sought happiness and freedom from all burdens laid upon them by their leaders in those days.

You are no different today. You also look for happiness and freedom. Yet, where can you find it? Could it be the teachings of the old still apply for you today? Could it be all you are seeking is not new, but it is part of an old story repeating itself?

All stories repeat themselves until the story has a final ending and then a new story begins. The story of the search to the pathway of enlightenment within the secret chambers of the heart is not new and until it is found by many, the story will keep repeating itself.

Within these frequencies is where you find greater health for your physical body. Your bodies need a connection to higher love frequencies. You were created in a chamber of Divine Love frequencies and this is what you always searched for, to come back to that state of love, peace, and harmony. Within the sacred chambers of your heart, you will find the deeper connection to the higher frequencies for your health and your wellbeing.

You were not created to be sick or feel weak. You were not created to feel attacked, confused, and vulnerable. You were created with a purpose. That purpose was to find the freedom within you and with the freedom, greater choices could be made.

You received the opportunity to understand both pain and love and then you could decide which road you would take. It would be your decision to take the final desired path for you. This decision would affect your eternal lifetimes ahead of you.

Before you came to the earth, in this final human life as you know it, your Divine Teachers spoke to you about the Great Path you could find in this lifetime. You knew how important it was. In your lifetime much of what you were taught in the spiritual 'schools' of dimensions, in between lifetimes, you cannot remember. All decisions always lie with you. You are the one who chooses the road to take. It is your own choice you must make.

We as Divine Beings of Great Love know how you will go on your journey; although much is your choice. There are many beings in the star spaces who have not given up on you. They are celebrating the great possibility of mankind awakening and joining the higher flows of life. Animals upon your planet have not given up either yet, otherwise, no life would exist on your planet, if they had already given up. All is your choice, however. Will you awaken as a collective, desiring peace and love to come to your planet? Will you desire to become part of the GREAT MOUNTAIN OF LIGHT and step into greater spiritual gifts to bring healing to yourself, to mankind and to the earth?

If you do you will see the next chapter becoming revealed for you; stepping into a time of higher awakening and higher understanding collectively. This new creation chapter will not happen until you, our dear friends, learn to live within the joy and love of your heart.

When one reaches within these higher frequencies, love will reveal itself to you. You are a force within yourself and you are a strong force when you understand the 'Collective Power of Love.'

When you do not understand who you truly are, and you are not aware of the secrets within your heart, your force from within cannot be great. You will not feel the power within. You will feel insecure and have great frustration often, or perhaps you will not desire to feel at all.

When you feel into your heart and you learn to live in your heart and from your heart, the force of love within you grows. The great energy will help you to have a greater and healthier life. You will understand the greater power within you and your love will shine more in your life.

It is those Sacred Secrets you must learn to unlock. Herein lies the key to all your power and all your love.

You understand all things upon your earth are becoming awakened now. You are hearing the call from 'The Great Mountain of Light,' CAEAYARON, who is calling you to the Great Healings, which I, SOVEREIGN LORD EMMANUEL THE GREAT, also spoke about through my faithful channel, Jesus, 2,000 years ago. The people then desired the healings and the ways of knowledge and love very much, but it was not yet the time to go through the gate to the higher dimensions of THE GREAT FATHER. Now it is the time.

Greetings, I AM SOVEREIGN LORD EMMANUEL THE GREAT. I AM here to guide you to the healings of the GREAT CAEAYARON."

The times of the Great Awakening,

Are upon your earth,

Are you awake little ones?

Are you hearing the call loud and clear?

Do you understand its significance?

You prayed for these times to come,

You prayed within your heart,

'Lord, please let your Divine Will take place,

Show us the road and we will follow.'

I AM Sovereign Lord Emmanuel The Great

Part 40: Learn to trust in Divine Love

"Greetings, I AM SOVEREIGN LORD EMMANUEL THE GREAT. You are progressing well through these pages. Our dear friends, sons and daughters, it is now time to continue with your greater spiritual advancement.

Fear stops you from discovering self and discovering life. Fear does not bring pleasure but can bring immense pain. For many people, fear is much like a disability which can prevent your greater manifestations to happen, and it can prevent loving relationships to happen.

This disability in your life can stop you from moving forward freely. This disability can stop you from 'walking' in the higher light path as the higher light path can only be found within the heart.

When one is in states of fear, unable to understand how to release fear, one cannot grow into the heart as that one has been blinded spiritually. That one is also deaf spiritually. It is not possible to receive greater guidance with great fear in your life, as you will hear your own fear speaking back to you.

One must have a deep love for Divine in their heart to allow the greater release to come. Learning to release your fears to Divine and gaining trust is part of the spiritual journey of one who desires to walk the higher path of love.

Jesus often spoke about the fear within the people. Many people suffered in those days, from tremendous fear without seeing a way forward.

One day, when Jesus had a crowd of people before him, he asked them, *'How do you think your fear benefits you? In all ways, please look inside yourself for most of you are in great fear. You do not even have much courage to walk to this place, being gathered together to listen to these words from THE GREAT FATHER, do you? You constantly look around to see if the soldiers are coming.*

Trust all is protected here at this time. It is better to listen to the GREAT FATHER speak and know HIM greater than it is to be in your homes wondering what was being said, if you long to hear these words being spoken.

Come, let us first of all pray to the GREAT FATHER EMMANUEL, who is SOVEREIGN of all the universes. For HE is love. HE is the Guide to everlasting peace and love. HE sets us free from our great fears so we may be released eternally from the ways of suffering and fear.

GREAT FATHER EMMANUEL,
Please be with us on this day,
Guide us to the greater truths,
Bring us your great blessings and your great protection,
So nothing can harm us,
Especially when we are gathered here together,
Listening to your great words coming through.
Please bless us with our comforts, GREAT FATHER EMMANUEL,

May you provide us with all we need,
May you understand our ways of suffering,
And may you teach us to be great forgivers,
May you help us understand how we can release our inner fears,
GREAT FATHER EMMANUEL, we thank you for all we have,
And all we receive.'

Jesus then opened his eyes and looked at the people who were quietly pondering. He knew they were deeply concerned in those days as soldiers had begun to ask from door to door who was listening to the words being spoken from THE GREAT FATHER through Jesus.

He stated, *'Know, it is better to be gathered in the house of THE GREAT FATHER, for here HE can then bless and guide you. It is better to understand the love of THE GREAT FATHER than it is to understand the fear people can cause you. Fear is not the way of THE GREAT FATHER, for HE does not desire to bring fear into any of HIS creation. HE is the way of love, peace, and harmony.*

HE is the creator of all goodness and all that is joyful. HE is the creator of all that is beautiful, and in all things, HE sees the beauty. HE loves all who desire to love HIM greater and to them, HE calls, as HE sees those who desire HIM to be the loving shepherd.

To the ones who bring fear to others, HE will not desire to have in HIS great house of gathering, for they are not with the love of THE GREAT FATHER EMMANUEL. No love for THE GREAT FATHER is within them. They pretend they love HIM, but they cannot for they are not from HIM. They are serving other gods and they are serving themselves.

Therefore, know HE sees all who desire to know HIM. Trust in HIM. Bring your fears to HIM. Talk to HIM. HE can lead you eternally to the love. HE can bring you to spaces where only love exists.

All in the Divine Universes is of love, and once you understand that, let go of your spaces of fear within them. Go into the deep forgiveness of what you fear. Trust THE GREAT FATHER EMMANUEL will take care of you.

Do you not believe he has myriads of Angels by HIS side to help those who love HIM? HE can call upon them at any time to be with you. In your greatest hour of need, HE will bring the peace within you. In your last breath, you will see HIM smiling at you, if you stayed in the love of HIM if you stayed in the trust in HIM.

Do not be concerned with what the people can do to you physically. They cannot take your soul away as they state. They have no power to do that. They cannot burn your soul forever for there is no such place. The GREAT FATHER takes care of all who desire to understand the ways of truth and of life, and Divine Truth will always bring freedom to all who understand that.

Do not listen to the spiritual leaders when they say they have your soul eternally. This is your greatest fear of all. These are not truths from THE GREAT FATHER EMMANUEL. HE will never bring punishment to anyone, for HE is of love and HE is eternal love. HE desires all to become free into HIS love.

There will be a day when THE GREAT FATHER returns and calls out to all who love HIM as it will be time to become free eternally from these beliefs the people are imprisoned into.

All these laws the leaders put you under, they are not the laws of THE GREAT FATHER EMMANUEL, for the GREAT FATHER EMMANUEL does not bring burdens to anyone, only the great freedom.

Bring yourself into the love. Know how important it is for yourself to love HIM, for then the greater trust will build. Love each other. Learn to be in the great forgiveness for all you fear. Do not be bound to your inner fears but instead rejoice at the freedom. Understand all can be shouldered by HIM. HE can send his angels to carry your burdens. Forgive all pain in your life and allow HIM to guide you to the ways of freedom and love.

Know in all things HE is love. Do not believe in the teachings of the men who state their god brings eternal judgment; punishing for not following their laws.

Do not believe that of THE GREAT FATHER EMMANUEL for HE is love. HE loves all. HE desires all to come into the love of HIM, for it is only when the people love HIM, HE can guide them to the greater fountains of freedom.

HE cannot guide those who do not desire to be guided upwards; only those who are love within their heart. When you pray to the GREAT FATHER EMMANUEL be sincere within your heart. Open your heart to HIM. Allow HIM to hear your inner thoughts. Speak about your concerns. Nothing is too large or too small for HIM. HE receives all prayers heard from the heart, directed at HIM.

When people pray to the gods of the people, or to people themselves, HE refuses to hear those prayers for they are not directed to HIM. HE desires not your worship, but HE desires your love from your heart, for HE is love.

All you hear here will set you free from your greater fears. Learn to trust in HIM in all your ways, for HE can do far more than any human can on this earth. Always trust in HIM.'

The people who listened had tears in their eyes as they felt the flows coming through my Living Word. These flows of love were from my Divine Being, SOVEREIGN LORD EMMANUEL THE GREAT. Jesus was my Designated Channel, and I, GREAT FATHER IN ALL OF CREATION, gave Jesus to the earth to bring mankind into the higher knowledge of my Divine existence, for how else could you understand a greater path of joy?

Blessed are those who understand the Living Word is upon your earth at this time. Though she has a different physical body than Jesus, it is the same being I, SOVEREIGN LORD EMMANUEL THE GREAT, sent to your planet to help all of creation to rise into a higher way of living.

Release all your fears for they create suffering within you. Do you not understand that your fear can cause terrible pain, especially when you fear collectively without understanding how to forgive it?

For those who come into the 'Great Mountain of Light,' CAEAYARON, they can truly understand the power of forgiveness and release their fear. The healings which are given to those in the 'Great Mountain of Light' are purified in the love of my Divine Being. They are being released from their own fear-made prisons. Slowly they will release themselves from fear with the perfect healings. Blessed they are for they received the eternal freedom.

No longer will they be part of any creation in suffering for they have chosen for the higher path. I, SOVEREIGN LORD EMMANUEL THE GREAT, always promised a way upwards for those who desired the love. In Lemuria, you desired another path, so I, THE GREAT FATHER, needed to release you.

Be grateful my Divine Love Element, the Living Word did not give up on you. From her, all of creation came, as she is the living womb of all of creation, where I, THE GREAT FATHER EMMANUEL, placed the living seed of life within her Divine Love Element Archangelic Self. THE GREAT CAEAYARON watered the seeds of life, and life came into creation.

All things need to come back to the living creation where all came from, however, I, THE GREAT FATHER EMMANUEL, can only gift it to those who desire to come back to the great love, for how can I, THE GREAT CREATOR force any of creation to return to the love, without the desire of love within them?

If I forced creation to love Divine Ways, then who would then establish new creation universes?

Jesus brought this through also. In one sermon he stated with my Divine Being, THE GREAT FATHER EMMANUEL, 'THE GREAT FATHER only desires love to be within HIS realms of love, for how else can the GREAT FATHER guide them to eternal fountains of happiness and peace when love is not within them? Therefore, always pray you will gain more love, and when the GREAT FATHER returns to this earth in the same way, you will hear HIM speak. Pray you will awaken, as then all can be yours; only if you desire HIM to be your GREAT FATHER in all of creation coming.'

Always stay in the great forgiveness dear ones and understand how important it is to remain in the Great Love.

Be in your heart of love and come to the higher path of love. Become one with the higher thoughts of love and become of love. Never bring judgment to another or yourself, but in all things be in the love. Never bring yourself into great doubt, instead, keep releasing if you do. In all things, understand this is the time of the Great Release for those who desire the higher path of love.

Return to the love my dear ones and rejoice for this is the time of your freedom; for those who desire the love collectively.

Greetings, I AM SOVEREIGN LORD EMMANUEL THE GREAT. I AM here to guide you to the greater realms of freedom, for those who desire to be in the eternal love creation universes coming."

Eternal love creation brings freedom to all,

Who desires to be in the love?

Only the people in the love,

Can begin to grow towards the great love,

Understand the Great Father Emmanuel,

Is Great Love,

Understand the gods of this world,

Are not part of The Great Father.

The Great Father has returned,

To bring eternal freedom,

To all who desire eternal freedom.

I AM Sovereign Lord Emmanuel The Great

Part 41: Release all that is not love within you

"Greetings, I AM SOVEREIGN LORD EMMANUEL THE GREAT. Growing into spiritual maturity is to bring wisdom within the self, to strengthen self, and it is learning to become balanced.

Many in your world do not desire spiritual wisdom. They are as if sitting, in a spiritual wheelchair to support their life journey. They cannot feel who they are or how to carry themselves. Constantly they look outside of self for guidance and support.

The spiritually strong understand why situations occur. They have strong spiritual guidance to be able to walk freely with love and joy within their hearts.

The spiritually strong desire to release all that is not of love within them, yet also love all they are within them. Instead of bringing more pain within them, they can look within, and with the great wisdom, they can understand why they are in pain.

Fear has many categories. One may not always consider themselves fearful, but it is the great fear that can stop one from seeing what truth is. Often people cannot see their own fear. They are blinded spiritually.

Fear causes one to lose power. On the other hand, if the strength within is greater than the fear, the strength within produces a frequency of greater power. It is then that fear is considered a spiritual tool for becoming stronger.

Many people upon your earth desired to face much fear during these times of the Great Awakening, praying they would awaken to the light within to allow the fear to be a strengthening tool, rather than a spiritual disability. This could lead to a greater investigation of your spiritual self, as pain can lead to spiritual insight and a desire to become spiritually nourished; if the heart desired to open to the love.

On a Divine level, you desired to awaken incredibly much to the greater purpose of these days collectively. There you understand the importance of this time of the Great Awakening Consciousness as you know you cannot ascend upwards into the New Awakened Realms of love, until you, as the human, receive your Lemurian Light Codes back.

This is the highest purpose for your greater soul at this time; to become activated with 'The Great Mountain of Light,' CAEAYARON, who can bring you back to the love universes, where only the love exists within.

The GREAT CAEAYARON works with my Designated Channel, Suzanna Maria Emmanuel, who is the Divine Love Element, Light Grid Programmer. Now that she has won the Universal Divine Love Frequencies back again, she is now the Universal Light Grid Programmer for CAEAYARON, as all universes are able to be built upwards with the universal keys of life.

Many on the higher dimensions are praying many will awaken to their inner light. Many of the people upon your earth claim to have awakened but their heart is very dim to the Great Love. Their light within their heart is filled with dimness.

It is the Great Love, the Great Recognition of my Divine Sovereign Being, SOVEREIGN LORD EMMANUEL THE GREAT, which awakens the Great Heart of Light.

If the people do not want to recognize who I AM, then their fear within will stay a constant spiritual disability and a battle for them, creating hurdles to the greater path of Awakening Love.

2,000 years ago, I, SOVEREIGN LORD EMMANUEL THE GREAT, also spoke of this through my Designated Channel, Jesus, who came to your earth to bring the light to your earth, to help bring the people into love and alignment. This prepared them for the Great Return of my Divine Being, SOVEREIGN LORD EMMANUEL THE GREAT, to allow the Great Sun Rising Consciousness to come within their hearts and allow them to become ready for the higher love universes; should they desire to listen.

Many of the followers of Jesus asked him, 'When will the GREAT FATHER EMMANUEL return? When will it be that the Great Keys will be given to us in the times of HIS Great Return?'

I, SOVEREIGN LORD EMMANUEL THE GREAT replied through Jesus, *'When it is the time you will know when it is, for no one can understand the times of my Great Return. You will recognize me by the same teachings and the same words when they come through in the same manner that they are spoken now. I will bring my Word back, as no one else can speak for my Great Self as the GREAT FATHER EMMANUEL. The Word was created for this purpose; to bring these teachings to you. Know The Word will return to allow these words to be heard. When you hear these words being spoken, you will know you have found The Word.'*

On the journey to find your greater secrets and love, you are looking to find your greater inner power. You are looking to find greater ways to support your life and you are looking for great peace and joy. Do not be in fear for THE GREAT FATHER, or for life itself, for fear does not help you grow spiritually mature. It is in the courage of one's journey that you will find your greater strength and love. When you find your courage, you will be able to go within and be in the quiet.

It is for the quiet ones who will find their freedom. It is not the boisterous and the proud who will see my Great Return. The quiet will see my Great Return first. Those are the ones who have been quietly asking, lifetime after lifetime, 'When Lord? When will you return to restore all things?'

In the times when Jesus lived upon your earth, many children, when they were being taught how to do complicated tasks, were asked to be quiet with their minds and thoughts and hear first before approaching a great task. Many children at a young age learned quickly and worked tasks at great speed, well beyond their age ability.

The brain has many pathways. These pathways open when one is learning to be quiet and happy in the heart. Your body holds many secrets. You were created with the ability to nurture your deeper paths to allow deeper paths within you to nurture you. These needs are not the needs your society teaches. Many things in your world work against true spiritual nourishment of what you require for your ultimate growth.

Any teaching that places fear and judgment into you, goes against all spiritual nourishment you need as a spiritual being. A spiritual being, to thrive upon your earth, needs love, encouragement, and great trust. These three qualities are truly needed. Love builds trust and faith. Encouragement builds trust and love.

You have pathways within your spiritual being and when these are nurtured, they become more alive like the rivers of life. When the rivers dry up, nothing can be nourished. Nothing can be replenished without nourishment and without the love within the heart. The way upwards is the way of the heart, and I, SOVEREIGN LORD EMMANUEL THE GREAT, together with 'The Great Mountain of Light,' are the heart healers. Each one of your cells requires waters from the spiritual wells.

Jesus, my faithful messenger, 2,000 years ago, when he was at a well, always took every opportunity to speak and teach people about the spiritual waters.

He took the opportunity to meditate there and greeted the people spiritually before the people arrived to allow them to become more accepting to the words of THE GREAT FATHER EMMANUEL. In this way, he created a spiritual well and the water within the well blessed the people who received it, as well as the animals.

Why did Jesus take the opportunity to speak to the people at the well of waters? The waters symbolized water and replenishment. Usually, the people were happy to see the well and responded well to the teachings of Jesus as they were frequently by themselves, often together with their animals. Jesus would help them, especially the women and the frail with the heavy loads of waters and this was greatly appreciated. Jesus was known by many as the 'helpful waterman.'

Jesus had a soft and kind voice. He was a great healer and a great teacher. He brought through rays for the spiritual well to awaken the people. For them to feel the compassion and encouragement from the higher heavens was appreciated because the people felt downtrodden by the leaders of the spiritual communities. The spiritual leaders did not consider the people to be of importance and brought much fear and burdens into the people.

When he saw people at the well, he often approached them and asked, *'Why is it you give your animals water? You recognize their needs. You also have needs, but those needs are not only the waters from the earth. You require nourishment from the waters of the spiritual rivers; the spiritual fountains of truth and life. Learn how to become spiritually watered and you will never thirst again.'*

The people did not understand what he meant. Many thought he was mad for saying the things he did. However, Jesus understood the people needed far more than the physical water to live and thrive. They also needed spiritual waters, for then they would be filled with life-giving water; water that could bring eternal freedom.

When a person becomes more spiritually alive, they begin to open to their higher path. It is then when all parts within your body rise to a greater and higher octave. You become more highly attuned and your body works greater.

This is because you move with vibration. All parts of you move and flow with energetic streams. The greater the flow of the spiritual nourishment, the greater your cellular level works at a higher octave.

This creates a stronger body as all parts within your body becomes stronger. Your health needs these frequencies of love.

When you awaken to the spiritual tones your cells recognize them. They have a code within them. This code is awakened when you reach into the higher chambers. It is as if a key to greater understanding and health becomes available and your body knows what to do with these higher instructions.

When you truly reach upwards and inwards, each part of your body changes. The way you used to operate with fear rushing through your body, is no longer necessary. You can feel more secure within yourself and your body responds to a new relationship with your body.

Inner spiritual security is what your body needs to operate at a greater level of love. Every part of your body needs deep spiritual love and spiritual nourishment.

The deep nurturing, the deep understanding, can only take place when one goes within the heart and finds the deeper connections. When this happens, you become more greatly nurtured and your relationships will become more secure. Again, it goes back to the way your life reflects in the mirror when you are well nourished and when you feel loved in your life, your life will reflect it back to you in all ways.

How will you learn to walk within the joy of your heart? How will you learn to open those higher chambers to understand the higher path? Come to the Great Light now our dear friends. CAEAYARON is the Great Well of Spiritual Waters, and I, SOVEREIGN LORD EMMANUEL

THE GREAT, AM the Great Shepherd guiding you to the Spiritual Waters of Eternal Life and Happiness.

I, SOVEREIGN LORD EMMANUEL THE GREAT, will also ask you, 'Why do you only care for your physical needs? Do you not know that your spiritual needs are far greater than your physical self?'

When your physical body stops existing upon your earth you live on the spiritual realms. However, it is only for those who find the higher path who will ever find the key to go to 'The Great Spiritual Mountain of Light,' which only CAEAYARON can gift to you. It is there that the Great Treasures of Light of Eternal Wisdom and eternal wisdom can be found.

It is those very codes which can be gifted to the people upon your earth at the Divine Activations, as then your greater heart can be attuned to the higher rays of Light streaming through from the higher Universal Love Realms to your realms.

It is only then, once you have received the right codes, that you can reach the higher realms of light. Without these codes, it is impossible to enter the great realms of light. These same love dimensions were discussed with the people in the days of Jesus.

I, SOVEREIGN LORD EMMANUEL THE GREAT, said through Jesus, '*Have no fear little ones, for THE GREAT FATHER promises all who desire to reach into their hearts, the greater realms of eternal love. It is there you will find your true peace and love. It is there you will truly bring great love within you. You will never need to understand pain anymore, but instead, you will rejoice because you experienced all that was. Instead of being in the pain and suffering, rejoice, for all these things THE GREAT FATHER has promised you.*'

Now is the time when all things must come about which were prophesied long ago. Therefore, Jesus always stated with my Divine Being, SOVEREIGN LORD EMMANUEL THE GREAT, *'Happy is the one who seeks the light within. Happy is the one who is willing to listen to the Great Teachings of the Heart, for that one will find the key to eternal freedom. Happy is the one who walks the higher way of wisdom.'*

Greetings, I AM SOVEREIGN LORD EMMANUEL THE GREAT. I AM the Divine Eternal Father, and I AM here to fulfill my promises to those people who desire to rise to love. Are you awake to the Great Call?"

Those who desire to reach,

The greater realms of love,

Are now being called to come,

To the Flames of Purification.

These Flames can give you,

Eternal love, peace, and freedom,

For those who come with all their heart.

Those ones have stayed awake until this time,

These I, The Great Divine Father,

Call 'The faithful ones,'

For they have constantly prayed,

For my Great Return to come.

I AM Sovereign Lord Emmanuel The Great

Part 42: The recognition of the Divine Messenger 2,000 years ago

"Greetings, I AM SOVEREIGN LORD EMMANUEL THE GREAT. Happy is the one who desires to hear these words being spoken, for then eternal wisdom can be theirs to have when they treasure these words within their hearts and act upon the messages from the Great Divine Sun Consciousness.

You are in the time of the great prophecies becoming fulfilled upon your earth. A long time ago I, SOVEREIGN LORD EMMANUEL THE GREAT, when speaking through my Designated Channel, Jesus, 2,000 years ago, stated that I, SOVEREIGN LORD EMMANUEL THE GREAT, would return to the people and all things I stated through my Designated Channel, would become fulfilled.

The followers of Jesus understood the significance of my Great Return. Often, they discussed the times of the Great Return in private as public gatherings were more difficult when Jesus' following became stronger. The gatherings were seen as a threat to the leaders of the strong belief centers in those days. Those leaders did not enjoy hearing from Jesus as Jesus spoke with Divine Authority.

Divine Truth was not within their hearts and they had already begun to plan the destruction of the teachings of my Divine Being, SOVEREIGN LORD EMMANUEL THE GREAT, well before Jesus was tortured and beaten.

Jesus' heart was pained as he desired the great truth to be known by all, but because the great majority fought against truth and freedom, he could not do too much more other than keeping the fight of truth alive within himself and within his followers.

Many of his followers suffered greatly at the hands of the spiritual leaders and the rulership structures in those days. Their suffering was harsh. Jesus desired to bring the love from my Divine Being, SOVEREIGN LORD EMMANUEL THE GREAT, to the people, to help them understand a higher path, 'The Path of Love and Truth.'

With this he stated to the people, *'There is only one way to THE GREAT FATHER EMMANUEL. That way is the way of love and truth. There is only One Truth as there is only ONE DIVINE FATHER.*

THE GREAT DIVINE FATHER desires all who desire the Great Truth and the Great Path, for how can THE GREAT FATHER nurture the gifts of the people who do not desire to know HIM or understand the Divine Path?

There are those who claim to know THE FATHER, but THE FATHER will state that HE does not know them. How can they know HIM, when they do not desire to know the Divine Path of Love and Truth?'

Jesus was a great man, fighting for truth and freedom. He desired to nurture the people, to help them understand that THE GREAT FATHER was not a 'God,' of injustice and fierce judgment, but a Divine Love Being.

When Jesus spoke to the men, he stated this: *'You as a father do not give things to your children they do not desire or will not benefit them, do you? You do not give things to your children to eternally punish them, do you? You give them fruits of your love. You guide your children to help them become nurtured in their lives. You help them in the ways of love to guide them to the higher ways of knowledge and wisdom.*

Then why do you think THE GREAT FATHER EMMANUEL, the One who created all of life with HIS Great Love, will do things to punish you, to give you pain and to help you remember your 'so-called' sins?

THE GREAT FATHER loves all who desire to understand the higher path of love, and HE desires all to understand HIS Great Love for the people HE calls, 'HIS Children.'

If you love your children, then think about how much THE GREAT FATHER loves you. THE GREAT FATHER does not give you anything you do not ask for. THE GREAT FATHER will always look after all the needs of those who desire the higher path and who seek the higher path of wisdom.'

Constantly Jesus did his best to show the people the ways of love and forgiveness, for the people needed to forgive their leaders for all the pain and burdens caused to them and their families and friends.

Jesus continued, *'Always ask THE GREAT FATHER to shoulder your burdens. HE will not let you carry your burdens alone when you ask HIM to carry them for you. HE will always help you in all situations you need help with. The ones who allow THE GREAT FATHER to burden their pain, will be released from their great pain. Always stay in forgiveness. They cannot do anything to your soul or your greater soul path. They may do harm to your body but your soul they cannot touch.'*

Jesus himself needed to do much forgiveness and at times he withdrew into the desert asking for help from my Divine Being, SOVEREIGN LORD EMMANUEL THE GREAT.

He wept with great tears asking for help and forgiveness for all that he might have done wrong in the eyes of Divine. Jesus never did anything wrong in our eyes. He constantly desired to help the people understand the ways of love and wisdom. He knew the way forward would come, even if it would not be in that lifetime, 2,000 years ago.

Jesus was seen by his followers as a Sacred Messenger. They understood Jesus was a man. They called him 'Master.' They did not see Jesus as an ordinary man. Jesus spoke and the words always comforted the people. Jesus always spoke truth, even if truth was not favored by many.

His followers admired Jesus for his strength, devotion, love, and dedication to bring through truth and fighting for truth. Not many people in those days, as in these days, would stand up to the opposers of love and truth and be courageous to stand for truth. Jesus showed the people that he was not only a man of wisdom with words he spoke but also a doer of the words he spoke.

Jesus was certainly a humble man and always cared for the needs of others. Often, he cared more about the needs of others than he did for himself, as his compassion was great. Jesus desired to demonstrate the love of my Divine Being, SOVEREIGN LORD EMMANUEL THE GREAT and brought many healings to the people.

The accounts in the Bible passages about the healings of Jesus have been greatly exaggerated as these stories were told and retold. Yes, the healings were great, but it was the spiritual healings which were more important to Jesus than the physical healings. Jesus helped people to see the truth, even though the truth was not desired by many of the spiritual leaders in those days, as they held the people deep within their own 'truths.'

Jesus was a fighter for freedom, and he longed to help many people find that freedom. Jesus saw what the people suffered with and because of his great love for them, he suffered along with them. He knew his greatest gift to the people was to set them free, from the fear they endured, with the great wisdom of THE GREAT FATHER, EMMANUEL. Thus, he kept going, though his popularity by the spiritual leaders and the greater governmental councils was not appreciated.

The spiritual leaders from those days, longed to put an end to the teachings of Jesus and gathered together in large groups, creating plans to rid the teachings from my Divine Being, THE GREAT FATHER EMMANUEL. They did not desire him to speak with Divine Authority. They desired to be THE Authority.

Already, before Jesus was crucified and beaten, plans of attack were taking place and many of his followers became persecuted and killed. Thus, many of his followers stayed away from the words that came from the mouth of Jesus, as they feared the pain from the spiritual leaders.

In one particular channeled wisdom talk, Jesus stated these following words, which were the words from my Divine Being, SOVEREIGN LORD EMMANUEL THE GREAT.

'Know, no man can truly hurt you, for THE GREAT FATHER EMMANUEL will always take care of the ones courageous enough to stand for their truth and their fight for the love. It is those ones who will be truly blessed.

The leaders stand on their podiums and preach to the people, claiming they have THE FATHER and state they do the great works of THE GREAT FATHER, yet, THE GREAT FATHER EMMANUEL will state to them, 'Go away, you workers of pain and hypocrisy, for your hearts are not hearts of truth.'

When THE GREAT FATHER states truth to the children, and when THE GREAT FATHER asks the spiritual teachers to turn to THE GREAT FATHER, what does THE GREAT FATHER see? THE GREAT FATHER EMMANUEL sees the hate within their hearts growing, like wolves in clothes of a lamb. They look innocent, but they are far from innocent. They stand in their preaching houses, pretending to be workers of THE GREAT FATHER, and yet, they inflict much pain to the one who is sent by THE GREAT FATHER EMMANUEL to spread the word of THE GREAT FATHER who states to them:

'Turn around from your ways of pain0, bringing fear to many. Do not bring burdens to the Children of THE FATHER. Allow them to live in peace. Allow them to listen to THE GREAT FATHER EMMANUEL. Allow them to have a life filled with love, knowledge, and peace, without having the fear of everything taken away from them, without the fear of their families being in the fear.

How can THE GREAT FATHER bless the fear the leaders bring to the Children of THE GREAT FATHER? THE GREAT FATHER desires all to understand truth and love. THE GREAT FATHER has compassion for all. Learn to work in the higher ways of truth and freedom, for truth will always set you free. It is pain that keeps you in your own prison of fear. It is fear which brings you into your dense thoughts of understanding.

Learn to see the higher ways of THE GREAT FATHER, and then you will understand HIGHER TRUTH, HIGHER LOVE, and HIGHER FREEDOM.'

These were part of a channeled message to the people Jesus spoke to when the people were afraid of the spiritual leaders who desired to rid the teachings of Jesus.

The spiritual leaders began to fear Jesus as Jesus spoke truth and brought healings of love to the people, whereas the spiritual leaders did not bring healings of love to the people. They claimed they did, but they brought more fear to the people, stating that if they did not do as they stated, and if they did not follow their laws, their soul would be punished forever and ever.

These truly were not the higher ways of love, as I, SOVEREIGN LORD EMMANUEL THE GREAT, will never punish any person. Only the ones who work in opposition to the light will punish the people.

Here I, SOVEREIGN LORD EMMANUEL THE GREAT, state this. Jesus was a beautiful man who never desired worship. He did many good things for the people, and the people who followed Jesus loved him for his strength, love, and courage to speak truth, which the people needed desperately in those days.

Jesus stated with my Divine Being, SOVEREIGN LORD EMMANUEL THE GREAT: *'These words are from THE GREAT FATHER EMMANUEL. HE is the Great Creator of all of Life. All belongs to HIM. All the heavenly bodies and all of life HE has created. HE created all that was good. However, all fell from the state of love and therefore all need to return to the Great Love of HIS Being. This is why The Word has been sent to the earth, to bring the news of the GREAT FATHER EMMANUEL from the highest realms of love.*

Know HE is love. HE is pure love. HE cares for those who desire HIS glory and HIS ways of love. HE does not desire their worship but desires all to become of love.

These words you hear are not from human realms, but the realms of THE GREAT FATHER, for THE GREAT FATHER exists in the highest realms where only the HIGHEST CREATION dwells within. Those realms are not of man, but of Divine. In those high realms, only love exists within, for nothing else can exist there, for HE is of love.

Learn to become of love. Bring the love of THE GREAT FATHER within yourself. Know one day, the people on the earth will see HIS Great Return and the ones who have been awaiting HIS Great Return will rejoice, and many will not, for only those who have been in the love, dwelling in the love, desiring the love, will rejoice at HIS Great Return.'

The people saw Jesus as a man of truth and of the heart. They did not see him as a Saint, as Jesus always said regarding this matter, *'No man should ever be worshipped, whether it is on this realm of the earth or in the higher heavens.*

Even THE GREAT FATHER EMMANUEL says that it is not right to worship HIM, for HE created all in the image of HIS Being, and HE desires all to understand Divine Truth and understand what is within, rather than worshipping something that is outside of him (or her).

Go and learn all these things, for one day they will say that I am far higher than a man. They will state many things, as they will desire to defile all these words. One day they will say that my pain was a great sacrifice for the people, but here I will state this, 'The pain I bear is for the love of THE GREAT FATHER EMMANUEL, for HE sent me to your earth to speak truth, to help many to go to the higher spaces, to sit by THE GREAT FATHER.'

Even though many will claim I am much greater than a man, I am not. I am a humble man, doing what THE GREAT FATHER has asked me to do. I suffer as you do. I need to forgive as you do. I can speak to you about forgiveness, because I also need to forgive, otherwise I could not have compassion for you if I was not a man of flesh. All of us need to learn to speak the truth and be in the freedom of who we are. This is why we need to be in our hearts.'

Jesus could see what was coming when it came closer to the crucifixion. He knew times of pain were coming, as it was already happening in ways, and his followers were threatened. Jesus could see how they would twist the teachings to keep the people under control. He wrote his books, time and time again, speaking his truth, which at times came in words you may perceive as anger. He was not an angry man, but his points were strong and you might perceive this as anger.

Know this, after his crucifixion, Jesus was in much pain and agony, because he did not die on that painful day. That was the time when he truly needed to learn the lessons, 'Go within the heart,' and 'Be in the forgiveness. Forgive all your enemies, constantly.'

His pain was great as at times he received reports of his friends being hunted and hurt for the sake of the 'truth,' to keep the teachings of THE GREAT FATHER EMMANUEL alive.

When the persecutions of his followers grew, Jesus lived a life filled with secrecy, and at times traveled with his friends, writing many words from his heart, ensuring that the words of his heart remained alive to your day.

After his crucifixion, upon hearing of the great persecutions, killings of his close friends, the twisting of his teachings, and what they said about Jesus, aiming to remove all traces of his existence after the crucifixion, Jesus was much in pain. He cared more about people than most could.

All people he spoke to, about THE FATHER EMMANUEL, after his crucifixion became hunted by the armies. Many were killed in ways you would not desire anyone to be killed. They spilled the blood on territories which were deemed as 'holy' to defile them, to help the people 'remember' their power of authority.

Still, the teachings of Jesus continued. Even the most powerful armies on your planet could not rid them. Thus, they created Jesus on the cross and created it as a sacrifice for people.

Each time the people prayed to Jesus, to his Mother Mary (who was a beautiful woman and mother to Jesus, but only a woman), each time they imagined seeing the thorns on the head of Jesus, they were reminded of the fear to disobey, the people felt afraid of 'God.' They were reminded of the limitation of themselves and the sinner within.

This is far from the teachings of Jesus when he was alive on the earth 2,000 years ago. He always taught the people to be happy in life, to celebrate each day, to be forgiving of themselves and of each other, never to worship any being, never to practice idolatry, and never to remember the death or pain of someone, as this was not to be remembered but forgiven to be healed.

Jesus said, *'Better it is to remember the birth of a friend or a loved one, rather than their death. Stay in love. Stay in happiness. Stay in the heart.'*

The truth of Jesus, the channel, my Designated Channel, the one who I spoke through, the one who stated, *'I AM THE WAY,'* that one, was to return one day with my Divine Being, SOVEREIGN LORD EMMANUEL THE GREAT.

Jesus never stated that he was the way for salvation. I, SOVEREIGN LORD EMMANUEL THE GREAT stated that. I AM THE WAY. I AM THE TRUTH. I AM THE LIFE. No one can receive everlasting life and happiness without my Divine Being, SOVEREIGN LORD EMMANUEL THE GREAT as I AM THE ONE who has prepared the way for you to go upwards.

Having stated that, on the greater levels, the Divine Love Element is the way, the road to all freedom, for it is why she was created. However, I, SOVEREIGN LORD EMMANUEL THE GREAT, AM The Great Way as I AM the Great Creator. I cannot bring this 'Way' of freedom without my Living Word, as she came to you as the 'Way,' the 'Truth,' and the 'Greater Freedom' as we as Divine Creators bring our love through the 'Way.'

I, SOVEREIGN LORD EMMANUEL THE GREAT, have sent my Designated Channel, Suzanna Maria Emmanuel, to your earth, as she was the same one as Jesus, both having the same life purpose, both having the same purpose to bring love and healing to the people and to be The Messenger of Divine.

No one else can claim that, because I, SOVEREIGN LORD EMMANUEL THE GREAT, will not speak through anyone else other than my Designated Channel, Suzanna Maria Emmanuel, who was created to bring The Word of My Divine Being through.

When you reach the spiritual dimensions and you have not listened, you will see Divine Truth, and you will see the Truth about Jesus. For those who are in spirit now, they can study both Jesus and Suzanna Maria Emmanuel. They study the pain and the many lies that have happened because Divine Truth was twisted and changed. They can see how many lives have been lost because of this lie.

I, SOVEREIGN LORD EMMANUEL THE GREAT, only speak truth, as I have always done. The people upon your earth who are not willing to listen are turning their backs on Divine like was also done in the times of Jesus. His followers desired to help many understand the higher ways and many of them were killed, tortured, and threatened.

I, SOVEREIGN LORD EMMANUEL THE GREAT, state, 'Dear ones, turn away from your ways of causing pain and disturbance, and learn to go into truth greater.'

When you delve within your history you can find the truth. You will find that Jesus was a man and that the truth of Jesus' existence was inflated and became greatly exaggerated. He was an honest man, which is why he was beaten and tortured. He was a man of the heart, which is why he could always state to the people, *'Please forgive all the pain caused to me, to you, and others.'*

He was a wise man as he heard my Divine Being, SOVEREIGN LORD EMMANUEL THE GREAT, greatly. He often wept in pain as he could see what the spiritual leaders did and would do in the future.

He asked my Divine Being, weeping within his heart, 2,000 years ago, *'GREAT FATHER, do you know what they are doing in your name? Do you know what they will do?'*

I, SOVEREIGN LORD EMMANUEL THE GREAT, replied, 'Jesus, continue on speaking to the people. One day they will see the higher path. One day they will desire the higher path. One day they will recognize the truth. Do not give up on your mission, Jesus. Continue the path of your heart. Seek the truth within you constantly. They cannot hurt you greatly. If you love the people, carry on. Keep forgiving.'

Greetings, I AM SOVEREIGN LORD EMMANUEL THE GREAT. I have returned as I promised 2,000 years ago."

Finding the highest ways of truth,

Takes a humble heart,

The humble understand these words,

They feel it within their hearts,

They accept who I Am,

And desire it with all their heart.

The proud ones do not desire it,

They state to my Divine Being,

Sovereign Lord Emmanuel The Great,

'Who are you to guide us upwards?

For we do not need you,

Nor do we desire your great wisdom,'

I, The Great Father state to those,

'I AM not here to guide them upwards,

For they are not welcome,

In my eternal mansions of love,

For they do not desire the Divine Father,

Into their hearts.'

I Am looking for those,

Who desire Divine Love,

To guide them to eternal fountains,

Of life and waters,

They will not thirst any more,

Nor hunger anymore,

I say to them, 'Come and rejoice,

Let us celebrate my Divine Return together.'

I AM Sovereign Lord Emmanuel The Great

Part 43: Healing with your Mantle of Love

"Greetings, I AM SOVEREIGN LORD EMMANUEL THE GREAT speaking. To you, this road has been very long throughout many of your lifetimes. You searched for the Great Path and prayed for the Great Path to come to you, and here you are, living in the lifetime of the Great Path of the 'bridge.' This is the lifetime many prophets foresaw.

Know, in the greater spaces, only love exists, which is why Jesus 2,000 years ago, spoke about the need for forgiveness, releasing your pain constantly to allow higher truth of Divine to come within the heart. When a heart is pained with anger and confusion, the heart cannot open to higher guidance.

To come to your lifetime now, allowing your heart to open to Divine Love is precious. I, SOVEREIGN LORD EMMANUEL THE GREAT, will advise you constantly to stay in the forgiveness of all you have suffered with, throughout all your lifetimes, not only in your life now. When you are in the pain and anger, the heart cannot open. Only when the heart desires to feel the love and become of love, can the heart discover the higher flows of love.

Come to 'The Great Mountain of Light' where you can explore the Great Divine Love. Become nourished and renewed spiritually and learn to walk the higher path of love.

Opening to the higher path can only be done when you are spiritually ready with the desire from your heart. This must be your decision. No one else can make that decision for you for this is the path of your higher evolutionary journey. No one else can make that step for you, not even on the higher levels can that decision be made.

You have the freedom of being a human and this is a great gift to you. Divine will never force you into decisions you are not ready to make. Once you make the decision to step onto the higher path then greater help and protection comes to you. Once you have made the decision and opened your heart to Divine Love, then Divine will help you with your life.

I, SOVEREIGN LORD EMMANUEL THE GREAT, always stated this through Jesus also. He said to his listeners with my Divine Voice, *'THE GREAT FATHER EMMANUEL always cares for those who desire to do HIS Great Will. What is HIS Great Will? It is to follow HIS ways of love and become of love and desire to be in HIS Great Love. If the children on earth do not desire the love the GREAT FATHER can give to them, why would HE give when it is not desired?*

Learn from this. Always pray to THE GREAT FATHER with your hearts of love. Ask for the Great Path to be shown to you. Open your heart to Divine Will, and speak to the Great Father:

'GREAT FATHER, guide me to your higher path,
Allow me to see the Great Divine Will,
Allow me to see what it is you desire me to do,

Guide me to the Great Love,
I will open my heart to you to be in your love,
Guide me in all your ways,
Keep me safe so I can do your Will greater,
GREAT FATHER EMMANUEL.'

When one opens the heart to the GREAT FATHER, then HE will send HIS Great Love and protection to those who are of the heart of love.'

True joy can only be found when one is ready and when one is able to reflect deeper within the path of all of life and existence.

Many people work on the journey of the self because they only see the importance of self. When the greater love develops upon spiritual maturity and becomes more of love, that one will desire to do the greater good for mankind and the earth.

The one who truly desires to do good is now able to achieve much more than in all lifetimes before, as I, SOVEREIGN LORD EMMANUEL THE GREAT, AM calling to those who desire the world to change to love and peace. Collectively they can bring a whole new love to your planet if many come to 'The Great Mountain of Light,' CAEAYARON, as HE will give you back your Lemurian Light Mantles. Those mantles have all the gifts you have been searching for, for so long.

The ones who are doers and not only promise to do things will receive the greatest rewards of all, for they received their Great Talents back by coming to 'The Great Mountain of Light' and then they worked hard to multiply those talents. Those will be the greatest of all in all the universes.

Many people upon your earth have been subjected to much pain and agony. Your anger, collectively, is great, and most feel they cannot let go. Most choose not to let go because they fear that somehow, when they let go, more pain will return to them. This creates a spiral of enormous pain for the person who is within that spiral of pain, but also collectively they are in a dense spiral. Without healing the pain, collectively, the people who are within those spirals cannot be released.

Blessed are those who desire to bring change to your planet. Blessed are those who are the doers of the healing work, coming to your planet, to change consciousness of humanity to become more of love. Know, the healing work has begun as I, SOVEREIGN LORD EMMANUEL THE GREAT, woke up my Divine Word, Suzanna Maria Emmanuel in 2009. Now, when the greater numbers desire love upon your planet and act upon it by receiving their Mantles of Love and their Great Talents back, they are able to learn to work with it collectively.

I, SOVEREIGN LORD EMMANUEL THE GREAT, always promised this to the people. Jesus stated, *'There will be a day when THE GREAT FATHER will call to those who desire peace and love. HE will ask those to step forward. They will be given the great talents and they will be able to do much upon the earth, as the great love will come within them. In that day they will awaken to their greater purpose; that of creating another way upon the earth.*

In that day, when many awaken to the GREAT FATHER, they will truly say, 'Your kingdom is here GREAT FATHER EMMANUEL. We desire to be with you and rule with you. Let Divine Will take place in the heavens, and on the earth. Allow us to partake of the great blessings and teach us to be strong leaders. Bless us so that we can bring new ways upon the earth and learn to rule in the greater realms also.

Teach us to work with you Great Divine. Allow your mountains to overflow with your great blessings. Allow the grapes to become abundant and let no one suffer upon the earth any longer. We desire with our heart to let all the past be gone. We now desire to learn a whole new way of being.'

We as Divine Masters of Great Love would like to help you change your way of looking at your life. We are Ancient Beings of Great Love and we understand your path and your journey. Your journey is to find the love within you, to find the great freedom, to find your path of great bliss and peace, and to return to the realms of love.

Again, first it begins with the question, 'Are you ready to move forward into love and peace?' It is only when you are ready to become more peaceful within you that you can go to the higher love road. Then, the greater work can begin, when you are ready to become more of peace and you desire to work with the GREAT DIVINE FATHER EMMANUEL and THE GREAT CAEAYARON.

We desire to work with the people to create a balance of love and security upon your planet, to teach you another way of life, but we will not work through anyone else than our beloved Archangel, Divine Love Element, Divine Word of all of creation.

Jesus was despised by the spiritual leaders for this gift of being able to lead a whole new consciousness into being.

He stated with my Divine Being, SOVEREIGN LORD EMMANUEL THE GREAT, *'It has been given to The Word to bring a whole new way of love to the world. There will be a time when The Word will speak to nations of people and they will begin to listen and then, on that day,*

*the nations will be blessed because they know the GREAT FATHER
EMMANUEL blesses them.*

*Many will claim to be that Word as they desire to be the one who THE
GREAT FATHER works with, but The Word was sent to the earth to do
the task; to bring through the words and wisdom of THE GREAT
FATHER and there is only one THE GREAT FATHER will work through.
HE will send that faithful one out, the one who was sent from the
highest streams of love where all the angels live eternally in the love,
to become flesh with mankind, to dwell with them, and guide them to
the greater mansions of THE GREAT FATHER.*

*Not everyone will desire The Word of THE FATHER as many will desire
it their own way, but in the day of HIS Great Return, their ways will not
work anymore, for then the world is facing destruction. All the ways of
man will have been tried and tested until there is no way out for them.
In those days many will become fearful of the days coming. The ones,
however, who see The Word rising with the GREAT FATHER will be the
happy ones, for they understand. They have been on the watch of the
prophecies and see the prophecies of the old coming true.*

*Happy is the one who stayed awake. Happy is the one who desires to
work with Divine Will in those days, for that one will be blessed
eternally.'*

I, SOVEREIGN LORD EMMANUEL THE GREAT, ask the ones who have
difficulty finding the greater peace within and have difficulty with
forgiving the pain caused by others and to self, to be in the great
forgiveness.

Allow all that has caused pain to settle. Do not anger any longer but
be in the joy that all can be forgiven. Become peaceful within. Go

into your heart and look for the beauty within as all people upon your earth are beautiful.

Know I, SOVEREIGN LORD EMMANUEL THE GREAT, only see the beauty within you. I desire you to only see the beauty within yourself. When you see the beauty within you, you will be able to stand in true forgiveness, allowing the higher road to become known to you, for you will only truly desire the higher road when you are ready for it.

The higher road upon your earth is now firmly established. At first, the road was dim, but now it is shining bright. When people see the path of wisdom and love, they will desire to come to 'The Great Mountain of Light,' CAEAYARON, who I, SOVEREIGN LORD EMMANUEL THE GREAT, have assigned to bring all to the love; those who desire the love.

My Divine Word, Suzanna Maria Emmanuel, has been tested and prepared well for this final journey, to bring you back to the state of great love in the Realms of Love; for those who are ready to receive their Mantles of Love back.

Their Mantles of Love are recognized as Sacred. When these mantles are placed upon the Star Sacred World Healers, they become part of the Sacred Class within the universal realms. They will transform energetically into states of love and peace. After their lifetime on the earth, they will continue to evolve to higher states of love in the higher creation. This I, SOVEREIGN LORD EMMANUEL THE GREAT, always promised would happen.

I stated through Jesus, the Great Prophet, my Divine Word, *'Look a time will come when the people on the earth, those who have been waiting for the time of my Great Return to come, will see the Great*

Lord coming. Their hearts will beat with gladness. They will place on their gowns of holiness and become free forever. They will be praised before all of creation. They will become beautified in the love and their eyes will cry with great rejoicing. No more will they utter words of suffering. They will be blessed eternally.

To the one who came from the highest heavens to become flesh, they would bring their gratitude forever and ever, knowing all things came because of the great love of that one. Eternally they will dwell together into the love.'

When you understand how important it is to become released from your pain, your heart will be filled with happiness and joy.

The people heard Jesus say, 'Happy is the one who speaks from the heart, for the one who speaks from the heart understands truth within. Only the ones who can truly forgive can speak truth from their heart. The ones filled with anger and discontent cannot speak truth from their heart, for the heart is only of love.

Few people find the way of the heart because many seek judgment and revenge on others. They speak to themselves, not with peace, but with judgment and anger. THE GREAT FATHER will never speak to you with anger and judgment.

Your heart cannot speak of judgment and anger within you because this is not the path of the heart when one speaks in judgment and anger to self.

The pathway of the heart is love. The love of the heart will not show until one longs for it spiritually and keeps searching for the treasures of the heart.

Learn to have peace and love within and know that THE GREAT FATHER EMMANUEL always knows all children who desire to find the higher path.

THE GREAT FATHER EMMANUEL will always guide the ones who can learn greater truth within their hearts to the Great Way, to the Great Road to Everlasting Glory where no suffering exists.'

Greetings, I AM SOVEREIGN LORD EMMANUEL THE GREAT. These were the words of Jesus, my Designated Channel 2,000 years ago. Blessed you are hearing these words being spoken to you in these days."

Finding the higher path of love is not easy,

As many paths are presented to you,

Each path holds a key for you,

Guiding you towards your higher path,

All paths are important for your growth,

Will you desire with your heart,

The higher spiritual road of growth?

Will you desire to walk and discover,

The higher ways of love?

All these things are being tested now,

As the Great Road of Love,

Opens for you.

Who is awake during these times?

Who desires to become One,

With Eternal Divine Love?

I AM Sovereign Lord Emmanuel The Great

Part 44: Knowing what to seek for

"Greetings, I, SOVEREIGN LORD EMMANUEL THE GREAT, welcome you to the times when you can find your higher path of joy, contentment, and love.

Here, I, SOVEREIGN LORD EMMANUEL THE GREAT, ask the ones who are searching for the Greater Path within their hearts, 'How much do you seek to find the higher path of joy and peace?'

Once a man asked Jesus this very question 2,000 years ago. He asked: 'Jesus, you speak of the way of the truth and of the heart, but I cannot go into my heart. My thoughts speak to me with guilt. I have anger within me and cannot find peace. Please speak to me with the Great Lord.'

Jesus commended this man for having the courage to speak his truth to him. Jesus remained quiet for a few moments, asking for my Divine guidance to assist in this matter. Jesus felt my Great Being aligning with him. I, SOVEREIGN LORD EMMANUEL THE GREAT, through Jesus, spoke to the man who was troubled.

'First, understand it takes courage to open the heart and ask what you are seeking. For when you are asking, it shows a desire to find the

higher path. This must always be first; the great desire. How else can you find anything in your life you need or desire if the desire is not there? Desire to find peace within your heart must be there first before it can be found by you.

Know all things come in the right seasons. Pain is there to show the higher path. Why be pained when it causes so much pain and heartache? Do you carry pain because you are unwilling to let go? Do you carry pain to torture another, thinking it will punish them or yourself for the pain caused?

Once the desire is there to find peace, the one who is willing to seek the higher path must ask for the guidance, for no guidance comes unless one is genuinely asking from the heart of love for THE GREAT FATHER EMMANUEL. Asking means to be willing to release the pain with forgiveness, to open the heart to higher foundations of love.

With the farmer, it is like this also. First, a seed must be there. Then, the farmer must desire to plant it and nourish it. Seeds are no good if the farmer holds on to the seed in his storehouse without planting it. It must be nourished with water and the sun, for the sun is lifegiving to all of creation.

Therefore, the farmer will make room for the seed to grow. He will plant it, and then he will remember what he planted and where he planted it, with great care.

So, it is with you also. The desire is there to find peace. You have been asking so you have received the seed of peace and joy. Now go and plant it and nourish it. Allow the sunlight to bring life to your seed by being in the heart. Desire to have peace and go and forgive your pain. Each time you forgive your pain, your plant within your heart will *grow. Soon you will have a solid tree with strength and might, growing within your heart, to allow the walk of the higher path of guidance to become easier.*

Know, faith and trust will be built within you when your tree stands strong. The strength of the tree will help you and guide you in your life. Go now and be at peace.'

As you can see from this conversation 2,000 years ago, many gems of knowledge were learned by the man who asked, and indeed, he did follow the greater guidance and became peaceful.

The path to joy and peace can be challenging for you, especially when one is not ready to go there. Many people upon your earth will go through many life cycles before they are ready to change their lives. Others are tired of the pain they have suffered and are exhausted. They live in confusion, without understanding the pain cycle they have participated in many lifetimes.

Pain can cause great ache. All thoughts and emotions are directly connected to your physical body. You carry all your anger and fear patterns in your cells. All cells carry your deeper emotions until you decide to release your pain patterns.

Your organs store great emotions. Your heart stores incredible pain emotions, as well as great joy. You feel all things with your heart, and when you grieve and have pain in your heart, you often suffer on the physical level with pain.

You are complex beings. You are far greater than what you perceive yourself to be.

When you are angry, you cannot receive spiritual nurturing, love, encouragement, joy and trust. To receive love from the Universe, it is vital to open your heart to the love and the trust. The more you release your pain from the deeper levels, the greater your heart will open to higher pathways to give you healing.

When you carry pain, all parts within your body feel it. It can create disorder in your life when your energy body is out of balance.

Your life constantly reflects all that is happening on the energy levels. When you learn to go within and find the great love path, your life will also reflect it to you.

Love always heals. Constantly it will guide you to your greater path. Always forgive your pain and learn to flow in the Greatness of your being, and then your days will be greatly blessed.

Happy are those who can see the Great Sun shining with their hearts. They will find eternal spiritual nourishment filled with love.

Happy are those who are ready to find the greater path and who are ready to walk upon it, for now is the time when the great gate is opened to the higher love dimensions; for those who are willing to become cleansed in my Divine Purification Flames with 'The Great Mountain of Light,' THE GREAT CAEAYARON. Blessed are those who come onto the road of everlasting glory, for the eternal blessings of joy and freedom will be theirs.

Greetings, I AM SOVEREIGN LORD EMMANUEL THE GREAT. Who is ready to find greater guidance to nourish their spiritual beings?"

Happy is the seeker of truth,

For indeed they will find it,

If they are true seekers.

Many say they are true seekers of truth,

But they have no desire for the higher path.

They state many things,

'Lord, have we not done enough,

Have we not prayed for your Great Return?'

But it is not until they begin to walk,

Onto the Sacred Path of Love,

That I, The Great Father Emmanuel,

Will say to them,

'Blessed you are eternally,

For you willingly entered,

The Great Mountain of Love,

Now, learn to walk upon it,

Learn to become of love,

Release your pain and burdens.

Understand Divine Truth,

Has nothing to do with the truths of man,

The Great Love is the way of Love,

Come and become great love,

Become blessed eternally.'

I AM Sovereign Lord Emmanuel The Great

Part 45: Finding your highest purpose

"Greetings, I AM SOVEREIGN LORD EMMANUEL THE GREAT. All things with Divine Guidance of the Great Love can help you in all your life. Guidance from the highest source can help you achieve all things upon your earth.

Your evolutionary path is to find the highest wisdom and the true source of love, comfort, and abundance. For many lifetimes, people have been searching upon your earth to find enlightenment; the way back to 'Divine.' They have searched in many ways, not knowing the highest way to the highest path.

In the times of Jesus, 2,000 years ago, when he was the Divine Messenger of my Divine Being, SOVEREIGN LORD EMMANUEL THE GREAT, the people also searched for the highest guidance. They were confused with many of the teachings of the spiritual leaders in those days.

Jesus stated to them, bringing through my Divine Words, as SOVEREIGN LORD EMMANUEL THE GREAT, *'In all things, THE GREAT FATHER knows what you are seeking. HE desires all HIS children who desire HIM, to look for HIM, as searching helps you to find the Great Path of THE GREAT FATHER. If you did not desire to find HIM, how can*

HE come to you? Know that THE GREAT FATHER can assist you in all your ways.

All who are living with the guidance of the GREAT FATHER EMMANUEL, who is the GREAT DIVINE FATHER, will constantly be guided to the higher path and wisdom. THE GREAT FATHER does not desire you to be short of your needs or to be discontent, for you are part of HIS great creation. THE GREAT FATHER lives within all things upon the earth and in the greater realms of love.

How can THE GREAT FATHER be separate from you, when HE is a part of all things? Union and separation do not work together. The one who works together with THE GREAT FATHER, in Union with HIM, can receive the eternal blessings of guidance within the heart. The one who has found the highest path can always be guided to the greater love, as the great desire of love is within that one. Not one day is he (or she) without the guidance from THE GREAT FATHER, and THE GREAT FATHER will bless all who stand united in the highest truth within the heart.

Many do not desire to work in union with the GREAT FATHER and therefore HE cannot work with those. Learn from this.

THE GREAT FATHER EMMANUEL hears all thoughts from all beings, as all are a part of HIM. How could HE not know what your needs are when you are a part of HIM, who created you?

Always seek the higher path of guidance within you. THE GREAT FATHER desires all to find the happiness and the love within. When one seeks the happiness and the love within, then that one will find all he (or she) needs to be content in life.'

Those were the words my Divine Messenger gave to the people 2,000 years ago and they apply in your lives at this time.

Finding the higher path of Freedom is to seek the higher path of love and truth. It is to seek the higher path of wisdom which leads to the higher purpose for your being. Your higher purpose is to help you evolve into greater beings and to help others to evolve also.

Many people upon your earth desire to have greater wisdom. Wisdom brings greater motivation to reach out towards higher goals and to have the greater strength to achieve their goals. Having higher goals to reach out for is important for your growth. Constantly you desire to understand how to move forward with greater knowledge to fulfill a higher purpose.

Reaching higher goals is part of your greater purpose. You move forward with higher lessons when your desire to achieve becomes stronger, and thus your desire to achieve more for the greater good grows. Each part of your body feels your emotional flows, and thus it flows with greater harmony within your body.

When a person understands their greater flows within their heart and learns to connect to them, higher transformations occur. Greater purpose is a result of these higher flows. You will then have greater energy to achieve these greater goals because your desires are part of your higher purpose.

Learning to find your higher purpose can, at times, cause frustration. It may take years before you understand the greater path and what your higher purpose is. Your higher purpose always gives you greater joy and great inner satisfaction, with an inner knowing you are working on your Higher Path Line of Evolution.

When you come to this earth, you have a path line. This path line can be made up of several different paths. This does not mean you cannot work with other path lines. The main path line is always there, always guiding you, nudging you to your main path line. At times these nudges may be subtle, or they may feel like a sudden pain for you.

Let us look at an example of a person who has the greater purpose of healing in a particular area, as a gift to humanity to open more to the Great Love.

The Greater Purpose will be revealed when enough gifts are opened within, and when many lifetimes have been discovered. This person will be ready to open to the Greater Path.

On the journey of discovering the Greater Path, your Greater Self will constantly be guiding you. In some lifetimes it will softly give you nudges and desires to discover particular areas.

When your Greater Purpose is to become a great spiritual teacher, and a great spiritual healer, in the highest transformation energies which are happening now upon your planet, you will be guided towards that pathway constantly. Your desire to become part of the Great Transformation will strengthen and you will understand the Great Path upon hearing it. You will desire to become part of the higher flows and call many towards it. You will have no doubt in the power of Collective Love Thought and desire to become part of 'The Great Mountain of Light,' as you remember the importance of it.

This is the highest purpose of all, as this path of the Great Love brings healing to self and many. This path will lead to the eternal love blessings of freedom. No other path can give you that, except the path of the Great Love.

Jesus also talked about this to the people. *'In all ways, there are lessons within all things. Do not think you are here to serve for one lifetime, for what purpose would that bring to your greater being? Do you not know that you come many lifetimes experiencing many things, all leading to the greater path of love and nourishment?*

Your higher being desires the suffering for you not to be there any longer, and it does not desire anyone else to suffer either, for all is one in the higher spaces, as in those spaces of eternal love there is no separation. Here on the earth, separation exists, and this is why one comes to the earth many times, in order to learn to become renewed in the spirit of love once again.

Each time you come to earth you will receive a different gift. No task is too small or too great. In some lives, you may have more difficult challenges before you than others, but in all lifetimes you learn how to become a greater being of love.

This is the great gift of the people; coming to life time and time again, experiencing new flows of existence, becoming renewed in each lifetime opening for the next experiences.

Therefore, never judge anyone as to what they do for a living, for all tasks teach how to bring more wisdom into the next. All leads to the highest task of all, coming into the love, for that is what THE GREAT FATHER EMMANUEL desires, is for all people to come into the love.

In the New Creation coming no one will be short of anything because all work together in the great streams of love. The widows will always be looked after. The orphans too. They will not grow hungry anymore, for they will be looked after by those able to look after them, and in return, the widows and orphans will bring a gift to their givers. They will work for what they receive.

All the universe works like this. Nothing in the universe works without appreciation, for appreciation allows the greater blessings to come. Appreciation for the sun and the mountains allows the greater grain to grow. All understand the love of creation.

When you receive something, then give appreciation back. It may be a small gift, but the appreciation shows the heart is open to receive more blessings from THE GREAT FATHER. How can the GREAT FATHER EMMANUEL bless only those who desire to be the receivers, and expect the best of all the crops when they do not do anything in return?

THE GREAT FATHER works on this basis also. Always give a small part of what you receive back to THE GREAT FATHER and HE will reward you because you gave it from your heart. When you give, do not give it begrudgingly. Do not promise and not give. Always give from your heart.

A widow may not be able to give as much as the rich merchant, but in the eyes of THE GREAT DIVINE, the gift of the widow is far more precious than the gift of the rich merchant, for the widow gave it with all her heart, knowing she could not afford much, but the rich merchant had plenty to spare.

Therefore, never begrudge anyone. Never judge anyone, for THE GREAT FATHER knows all. Always know, that in one lifetime you may struggle, and in the next lifetime you may be rich. But then you will be asked, 'Did you learn greater compassion from your life in poverty? Or were you like the rich man who judged the poor widow?' These tests will always come. Always the hearts are tested to see if the hearts are moving towards greater love or lack of love.'

From this lesson, you can gather many gems for your own life. Here, I, SOVEREIGN LORD EMMANUEL THE GREAT, state how significant it is to see how important each of your lifetimes are. When you desire to grow into your love, value who you are, and value the many paths you have taken, then all your learnings will become more valuable.

If you truly desired to come upon the highest path of learning at this time, becoming part of a whole new love consciousness into being, you would have learned how to become a greater healer and a greater teacher. You would have understood why compassion is important, as you would have been the receiver of no compassion and the giver of compassion, to help you open your heart to greater thoughts of love.

Your life is precious, and it is worth very much. You may see your life being so long, yet we say it is less than a blink of an eye to you on the higher levels. You are eternal beings. We encourage you to see yourself as eternal also. As you learn to see yourselves as eternal, without an end, constantly moving forward to higher progression, you become happier and more loving towards yourself. Your fear of death lessens because you grasp the lesson of eternity, as that there is no end to life. You carry on with greater lessons when you move on.

As all is important, nothing can be judged. Many people upon your earth are in great judgment of one another but should not be. Being a builder is no less than being a scientist. In one life time you may have been a great scientist and in this life time you may be a gardener. On a spiritual level, you understand both tasks are important. Both lead to spiritual growth and lessons.

The human may see the scientist as more valuable than the gardener, but on a spiritual level that is not so. In all ways, all things are important for your learning and growth. In all lifetimes you receive gifts, and these gifts you carry with you, lifetime to lifetime.

If you desired to become part of the greatest mission upon your planet at this time; that of bringing peace to the great collective, you would have learned much during your lifetimes, and desired to be in a special position in this lifetime, to be able to achieve the greatest accomplishment; that of working with the GREAT CAEAYARON and the Designated Word, to bring a world filled with peace and love.

This is the greatest spiritual task ever, and for those who desire to work to this great capacity, they will become the greatest blessed in all the universes, as they worked hard to achieve it. A great number of people desired to open this gateway of the great collective, achieving the seemingly impossible in a world that is far from love and far from desiring Divine Assistance. Yet, they worked hard and now is your opportunity to see those blessings coming into fruition.

Although you forget what your greatest desires are in life, on a spiritual level you will have a knowing.

I, SOVEREIGN LORD EMMANUEL THE GREAT, together with the GREAT CAEAYARON, will state how important it is to search within the heart and to find your greatest desires. Many, who work with Divine on the greatest mission to bring love and peace with Divine Assistance, can become greater than in all their lifetimes combined. Opportunities open, a whole global transformation can begin, new technology can become discovered as you work with higher creation on the great project; Collectively Healing Earth with Divine Love.

Always, I, SOVEREIGN LORD EMMANUEL THE GREAT, promised that this time could happen, if you desired to work together.

Through Jesus, I, SOVEREIGN LORD EMMANUEL THE GREAT, spoke about these times. He said, *'A time will come when the people will awaken. Many will not desire to have THE GREAT FATHER speaking and will deny his existence. Many will desire, and they will bring change to the earth. A whole new earth will rise.*

The old will go and the new comes in, as the people are ready to become new. Their personalities of old will go and the great transformation will begin. They will become forever blessed by THE GREAT FATHER. Their wealth and riches will grow, not only from the earth but from the eternal spiritual wells; they will last forever where nothing can take their wealth away anymore.

Forever they will become blessed because they desired peace and love upon the earth. Happy are those who listen to these words, for they will inherit the new earth of all of creation. The old earth with pain will pass away, and a whole new earth will come into creation.

THE GREAT FATHER EMMANUEL will never take the freedom away from the people, for that is what the people desired to have; 'The Freedom to choose.'

It is only for those who desire to work with THE GREAT FATHER who HE can reward, for it is those who desire to dwell eternally with THE GREAT FATHER.'

Those who work with Divine Will in the time of the GREAT RETURN of THE GREAT FATHER, will become blessed. Their eyes will see greater and their desire for love will grow. They awaken to the beauty of all that is.

Life, in that day, will become blessed as the strong ones rise up. Their spiritual gifts will awaken to the greatness.'

Greetings, I AM SOVEREIGN LORD EMMANUEL THE GREAT."

When you value life,

Your great joy increases,

Your love for life increases,

You understand greater love,

Your blessings grow each day,

You understand your higher purpose,

A purpose to grow mankind to more love,

Your life will be filled with excitement,

Knowing the preciousness of your life,

Knowing how important this life is.

I AM Sovereign Lord Emmanuel The Great

Part 46: Discovering your greatest freedom

"Greetings, I AM SOVEREIGN LORD EMMANUEL THE GREAT. Happy you are indeed when you learn the higher ways of love and freedom. Happy you are when you learn to understand you are living in a time of the greater awakening to the powers deep within you. Happy you are when you understand how you can gain your greater powers back to become eternally free.

Becoming eternally free from the denseness is the greatest gift you can give yourself, as originally, denseness was not part of the original purpose. I, SOVEREIGN LORD EMMANUEL THE GREAT, did not desire suffering to happen within any of creation. Creation is not dense in the higher creator realms where creation only exists within the love.

In love, all was created. I, SOVEREIGN LORD EMMANUEL THE GREAT, desired all to gain greater freedom.

CAEAYARON, the Creator of all Light Grids, desired all universal beings to live within the freedom of power and greater love; to become greater love.

I, SOVEREIGN LORD EMMANUEL THE GREAT, gifted my Divine Word, the Divine Love Element Archangel, the Codes of Life to gift to THE

GREAT CAEAYARON, to create the higher Universes with, to allow higher creation to happen.

In the higher love universes, no density exists within, as density is not part of the higher love universes. No new creation can evolve in density as no love force can work with density. When the love was removed from the beings of love, of their own accord, the density grew within them. Density explores ways other than love. Density desired to have more density and therefore it began to discover ways to take the great sovereign power away from the love universes for their own greed and power.

Trillions of beings suffered because of the greed of the one who came with all his might to the Sovereign Universes, challenging to be the Way and the Pathway to the great power.

He desired to have the power of the Living Word; the one who held the Codes of Life. His envy towards her grew great, and the anger grew within him. He explored many ways to gain that power and began to bring destruction in the universe.

He began to bring his freedom in the universe, and many followed. His desire for power became great and he desired to be the Almighty Archangel to rule all.

In his fury, he drew the light out of the power creator beings and began to develop his own plans to fight the love universes with; constantly challenging the love of the Living Word. Constantly The Divine Love Element desired to free the trapped living beings. Large universal wars broke out.

That being challenged my Divine Sovereignty greatly. I, SOVEREIGN LORD EMMANUEL THE GREAT, did not desire to destroy the greatest challenger of all, as all things needed to become explored.

How can I, THE GREAT FATHER of all of creation, create more life if I do not understand all thoughts within the living universes? Therefore, I, SOVEREIGN LORD EMMANUEL THE GREAT, asked CAEAYARON to bring another Archangel into creation so the denser thoughts could live in that Archangel to allow the denser thoughts to explore their desires; that of living away from Divine Guidance.

This is how METATRON, Archangel of Density, came into creation. CAEAYARON, The Great Mighty Archangel, separated a large part of HIMSELF, and removed the love from within that part and gave it to the denser universes, as CAEAYARON was not to carry any denseness within HIS Being on the higher love creator dimensions.

This is how large parts fell away from the love as they removed themselves from the love. Therefore, they were not part of the love universes any longer. When the great rebellion began, large beings claimed we, as the Great Creators, did not desire the great freedom for creation.

They desired total freedom from Divine Guidance, and so they removed themselves from 'The Mountain of Light,' CAEAYARON's Universes. No longer did they have Divine Guidance from the highest love creator realms, as it is not possible to receive Divine Guidance away from CAEAYARON's Love Mountain Universes; except through the one who can live both in the light universes and the denser universes; that being, the Divine Love Element, Universal Light Grid Programmer, the Living Word, as she carries the codes of CAEAYARON and METATRON.

It is through her we were able to reach creation on your earth. Be grateful for this pathway, for I, SOVEREIGN LORD EMMANUEL THE GREAT, love my Divine Word and did not desire to bring her to the denser universes where no great love for her existed. The denser universes desired pain within her to grieve the Great Creators of the Universes, hoping the Divine Love Element would remove herself from the pathway of density to stop awakening to happen within the people.

I, SOVEREIGN LORD EMMANUEL THE GREAT, say, 'Happy I AM for her not giving up, despite being in the face of torture, death, and suffering.'

She remained strong within herself and returned to the people, desiring with her heart of love to guide them forwards. She has suffered along with the people in the most painful times in order to help you discover a way out of the maze of conflict. Now, she has won the Universal Codes of Love back, to help you enter the gateway of the Greater Choice, where all is revealed greater.

You are living in the last gateway of 'The Choice.' The darkness will be revealed greater, as the light will also. All needs to be examined by the people, and therefore I, SOVEREIGN LORD EMMANUEL THE GREAT, assigned the GREAT CAEAYARON to be the Great Revealer upon your plane, through the Designated Messenger so that millions can receive the information freely, understanding all that has happened.

You have entered the great sacred awakening stage. This stage you are in will decide all your eternal lifetimes ahead of you. Will you come back to the love states, or will you still desire to be away from the love universes?

Now you are more awake than you were in the times of 'paradise' before you fell. There you were promised the great freedom and you were promised 'immortal' power by the 'gods' of darkness if you denied the ways of the Great Creator.

The great majority desired, with all their hearts, to be removed from the Lemurian Creator Pathway and so you came to the plane of human density, without Divine Love Guidance, and without a way upwards.

In Lemuria, when the Divine Living Word became Lemurian, dwelling among the Lemurians, the Lemurians received Divine Guidance through The Word and the people were blessed.

When the people began to rebel against Divine Guidance, they fell from 'paradise,' tumbling into the deep abyss states without freedom to evolve. The 'dark' gods owned the Lemurians who became part of the humans on your planet. No longer could you go to the 'free' universes, as it was no longer part of your creation pathway.

No longer could you receive Divine Love Guidance from the highest Archangels, because this was the 'choosing' of the great majority in Lemuria; to live without Divine Guidance. The only 'being' able to be guided by Divine Love was the Divine Word.

Now, again you are facing a choice. Now you have the 'knowledge' the darkness desired you to see. In the days of Lemuria, they challenged the love and stated to the Lemurians, 'How can you know unless you see for yourself?'

Now, I, SOVEREIGN LORD EMMANUEL THE GREAT, ask, 'Have you attained the knowledge you desired to see? Have you experienced the 'blessings' of the dark gods who placed you into the depths of the abyss, where you resided with the darkness, experiencing suffering, pain, and insecurity?'

It is now your opportunity to choose. In the higher creation only goodness exists, but I, SOVEREIGN LORD EMMANUEL THE GREAT, will never ask you to come if that is not your greatest desire. Neither will the GREAT CAEAYARON, as HE cannot force you. If you enter the 'Great Mountain of Light,' it must be from your heart of love.

Upon your planet, where you live upon, all through the ages, the people did not desire Divine Guidance. Many people upon your planet, at this time, do not desire my Divine Word to bring through Divine Guidance or Divine Assistance at this time. They still desire freedom away from Divine Love; though they do not understand they are rejecting my Divine Being, SOVEREIGN LORD EMMANUEL THE GREAT, or THE GREAT CAEAYARON when they reject my Divine Word.

Many say they do not desire to see me, SOVEREIGN LORD EMMANUEL THE GREAT, THE GREAT FATHER. Many say that it cannot be true, that I, GREAT FATHER, would send my Divine Word, who was Jesus 2,000 years ago, to bring a way of freedom to you. Many say it is not needed, but now you need a way out of your dense grids more than at any other time, otherwise, how can you escape the deepest of abyss stages?

If, I, SOVEREIGN LORD EMMANUEL THE GREAT, was not able to help you at this time, together with my Great Aligner, CAEAYARON, Divine Judge of all of creation, how would you escape the eternal torment the darkness would have put you into?

I, SOVEREIGN LORD EMMANUEL THE GREAT, brought my Living Word back to your planet, during the times of the Great Awakening, to help you find your way back. This time, the Living Word is Suzanna Maria Emmanuel, and no other Living Word exists. I, SOVEREIGN LORD EMMANUEL THE GREAT, will not use another Divine Messenger to bring through the flows of healing, the codes of life, or my Divine Words, for there is not another one.

The GREAT CAEAYARON, creator of the Living Light Universal Grids will not work with another channel on that high capacity either. In the days of KRYON, CAEAYARON used that same channel, who was the greatest challenger of the Sovereign Universes, the one who created the stages of the greatest density to come into existence, to open the gateway for the love to return.

HE came to the many people upon your plane as KRYON through that one who desired to bring freedom to the universes away from the love, as love was not within him.

CAEAYARON needed to work through the greatest opposer of the love to allow the flows of life to come back into the earth, and within the DNA of the people, to allow the Living Word to rise with HIM.

Already the Living Word was working with my Divine Being, SOVEREIGN LORD EMMANUEL THE GREAT, and once the gateways had been sufficiently established to allow greater light to come in, CAEAYARON approached the Living Word, in 2014, the Designated Messenger, the one who was the Universal Light Grid Programmer in the higher love dimensions.

All must be reversed for the greater path upwards to become established. As the people in Lemuria knew The Word to be the way in Lemuria, before choosing to fall into the gateway of the darkness to become dense, so enough in your day needed to recognize the dark gateway of the denseness before the gateway of light could rise upon your planet.

This was the only way to allow the Gateway of Life to become firmly established, and then CAEAYARON was able to rise with 'The Great Mountain of Light' upon your planet, in a spiritual sense, to allow the people, choosing for the love universes, to return to their Lemurian Light Codes, to allow them to become part of the love universes again. Slowly the denseness within their bodies will leave them throughout many evolutionary processes. Slowly their thoughts will become of love again. Slowly they will learn to take on the ways of the higher love.

Happy is the one who sees this and opens their heart to the great wisdom of the universe, for we do not desire any destruction upon your planet. We do not desire to see your suffering any longer, however, all must be willing to come back to a state of love and peace within their heart.

This is the greatest gift of all; the gift of freedom. In the higher love universes, you have your greater freedom to explore your greater evolution. Here on your planet, I, SOVEREIGN LORD EMMANUEL THE GREAT, cannot call you free, for you are far from the freedom that exists in the love universes.

If it was not for this time, bringing the Living Word to your planet to allow all who desire to come back to the higher living grids to do so, then nothing could be saved.

Be grateful a solution came. Be grateful my Word, my Designated Channel, worked so very hard, despite all the trouble the people have given her in her many lifetimes, to find this gateway, the gateway of the 'Bridge' to reconnect to my Divine Being, SOVEREIGN LORD EMMANUEL THE GREAT, and THE GREAT CAEAYARON, to bring you the gateway upwards; for otherwise how could life be saved?

How could you otherwise have the hope to have freedom? For no freedom exists within your dense grids.

Jesus stated this 2,000 years ago to the people, *'In the days of the Great Return of THE GREAT FATHER, not many will desire to listen to HIS words. Not many will desire to understand who THE GREAT FATHER is. Many will state that it cannot be possible that HE has returned in the way HE promised, but HE will always fulfill HIS great promises.*

HE will state at that time: 'Have I, THE GREAT FATHER, not said that I, THE GREAT EMMANUEL, would return in the same manner as I spoke to the people with Jesus, my Word? I, THE GREAT FATHER, will never utter a word that is not of truth. The people utter many words they do not mean. Those words in my eyes are false for they do not carry truth.

I, THE GREAT FATHER, AM eternal. No time exists in my eyes, for all times exist at once. Many lifetimes will come before you. Pray you stay awake throughout all the times, so that when I, THE GREAT FATHER, do call you, you will recognize my Divine Voice for how else can you find the way to eternal freedom?

Many will say in those days: 'GREAT FATHER, how can you return now with The Word who became flesh among the people? It does not belong in our thoughts that you are here to bring your messages to the people.

In our minds, you have gone far away, GREAT FATHER. In our minds, you do not exist. We do not desire to follow the ways of THE GREAT FATHER. We desire freedom away from you. We will state we follow the GREAT FATHER. We will state many things, but in our minds we did not ever desire your true GREAT RETURN, oh GREAT FATHER EMMANUEL.

Now, you will see all we are and all we have done. In shame, we will desire to hide in our caves, because we do not desire to awaken to how true you are. We do not desire you to see our faces. In great shame we walk, for we have not loved the one you sent to earth to bring the way upwards. Do not see what we truly are, GREAT FATHER.

In that day, when the people run to the caves within the mountains to hide away from THE GREAT FATHER EMMANUEL, in the hope THE GREAT FATHER does not see them, knows HE sees all. HE has always seen all. No one can run away from HIM. HE knows all thoughts. Be in the great forgiveness and come to the Great Mountain of Healing when HE calls. HE will bring a way of healing to the people who desire to return to freedom. Be in the great forgiveness, and understand when HE calls, the Great Mountain will open, but it will not be open for long.

There will be a time when HE will state, 'Now it has been enough. The Great Mountain will close. All who are within it will have their eternal freedom in the great mansions of love. The ones who entered first will have the great prize of being seated among the highest of the highest if those displayed great love for my Eternal Being, the GREAT FATHER, for all needs to be examined.

They can be seated with my Great Word in the highest spaces and become rulers over all of the New Creation. All others, who came into the Great Mountain of protection will always receive the love and freedom. They will never suffer any longer in all of creation coming.

For those who are not in the mountain, however, they will always regret not going into the mountain, for then it will be too late. In those days, they will be seated before the Great Judge, and the Great Judge will discuss what to do with them for they rejected the Great Way and did not desire to come to the love, so love they can never become.

I AM of LOVE, but I, SOVEREIGN LORD over all universal creation, will never force any of creation to be in the love and dwell in the love if the love is not within them. I desire all to become of love, if they desire the love of my Divine Being, THE GREAT FATHER EMMANUEL. The ones who desire the Great Love can become eternal love and have eternal freedom.'

2,000 years ago, to the people who listened to the teachings Jesus brought through, these words were as riddles to them. They did not understand the deeper meaning.

Through Jesus I said, as THE GREAT FATHER EMMANUEL, *'Happy is the one who recognizes the times of the Great Awakening, when the Great Sun returns, as then the greatness can happen within that one.*

Their eyes will awaken to what is. When the eyes awaken, then one can walk on the higher path knowing THE GREAT FATHER EMMANUEL guards those who walk with awakened eyes on the higher path.

They will recognize THE GREAT FATHER and THE GREAT FATHER always looks after the needs of those who recognize THE GREAT FATHER, and seeks the counsel of THE GREAT FATHER EMMANUEL.

Has HE not taught you to keep asking for the Great Will to take place within the heavens, as also upon the earth? It is not HIS Great Will that HIS children suffer upon the earth. It is HIS Great Will that the children on the higher path are always looked after. However, how can HE look after HIS children when they do not desire to have HIM?

HE can only look after those who are constantly seeking HIS guidance and protection. Happy are those when they awaken to this.'

You are in the time of opening and awakening to a higher understanding of all your truth that is hidden in your sacred chambers within your heart.

You are all unique and you all have unique paths. Individually you are on a path of evolution. You are also on the path of higher discovery collectively. When you grow as individuals you constantly affect other people on their path. When you grow into more love as a person, you constantly affect other people around you, because you are an energetic being. You have the ability to help other people awaken to their love within their hearts also.

How do you do this you may ask? Would you like to affect other people with your love? Would that truly help you to understand the Sacred Gifts within you, given to you, to awaken greater and awaken others?

If this is your desire, you are already awakening to your greater gifts. Your true gifts can only awaken when you begin to understand the beauty of yourself. You have the power within you to create change in your life.

This may frighten some readers because they may not yet realize the power held within them. They do not yet realize the grandness of their true existence.

When you awaken to higher love consciousness, you begin to remember your deeper purpose and to grasp higher ways of life. You begin by questioning and then by reaching within to find deeper purpose and power. Your deeper powers were given to you and they are yours to investigate deeper. The greater one begins to investigate and comprehend, the greater the power within becomes. You begin to understand life is not the way you thought it was. You begin to understand how all things reflect each other constantly.

You are now living in the time of the Awakened Self. You are beginning to awaken to all that is and to all that is becoming. The awakening itself is an evolutionary progression. It is about learning to become a greater being, with a greater heart filled with joy and love. The Awakened Self realizes the power of change does not lie outside of self, but it lies within self, for all reflects the beliefs that are carried within.

To bring your world into a world of healing, awaken to the great healing work that must take place within. All people are part of the world and the collective thoughts affect the people.

What Divine Love is offering you is to help you awaken to the greater gifts within you, to help you gain a world with greater freedom and greater love.

Imagine, if large numbers came together, all receiving their Mantles of Love back with the GREAT CAEAYARON. These large numbers would then receive their Lemurian Light Codes and be able to bring in higher love thoughts together; standing strong together as one force of love. My Divine Love Element would then be able to gift the greater gifts to you so you can be part of the Collective World Healing Programme; directed by Divine Guidance.

Then I, SOVEREIGN LORD EMMANUEL THE GREAT, would gift the Great Codes to my Word, to give it to you, if you aligned yourselves with your Lemurian Light Codes, activated into the higher love grids, within 'The Great Mountain of Light,' CAEAYARON, which HE can only do with the Living Word, the Divine Love Element, the Sacred Secret which was given to your planet to heal with.

If you could step into a whole new creation force together, understand what that could bring to you; a whole new way of knowledge and gifts, gifts you cannot comprehend at this time. However, all need to be chosen in the greater numbers. Like the greater numbers chose against Divine, they now can choose collectively for the Great Divine, if they desire this time of the great healing to happen.

Large changes would happen upon your planet if you choose to listen. Then you would begin to see how all things were pained in your world. Large healing work would take place, as the frequencies within your earth grids would begin to heal greatly. I, SOVEREIGN LORD EMMANUEL THE GREAT, say to you, 'Great miracles would happen upon your planet if you desired to come together in the love.'

THE GREAT CAEAYARON, would then bring such great power in the Divine Love Element, Designated Word, to bring the whole earth into greater love, to allow the people to learn the ways of love and peace.

The power of love you cannot understand, for that memory was removed from you, by beings who desired you not to be in the love again. However, now the pathway made for you to understand the power of creation pathway of love is upon you.

Therefore, the road is open for all who desire higher ways of creation. The great separation is taking place between the people who do desire the Great Love Pathway and those who do not.

I, SOVEREIGN LORD EMMANUEL THE GREAT, will say, 'Happy are those who desire the Great Love, to allow Divine Guidance to come to your planet. Let the gifts return to those who are the lovers of the earth. For them, on that day of their freedom, they will cry out joyfully, 'It has come to be. Now we can embrace our gifts of strength. Now we can learn to become free.'

Greetings, I AM SOVEREIGN LORD EMMANUEL THE GREAT. Learning to discover you is the greatest gift you can gift to yourself."

Wisdom is found within,

Waiting to be discovered by you.

You are an ancient being,

Waiting to be rediscovered by you.

What you can achieve with your wisdom,

Depends on your deepest desires.

If your heart is rich with desires of love,

It will seek to find the highest road of wisdom,

It will desire to walk upon it,

It will desire to return home to the love.

Learn to understand the Great Love,

And be blessed eternally.

I AM Sovereign Lord Emmanuel The Great

Part 47: The spiritually blind can begin to see

"Greetings, I AM SOVEREIGN LORD EMMANUEL THE GREAT and we welcome you to these beautiful spaces of Divine Love, Divine Light, and Divine Truth.

For us to be your Great Teachers is magnificent. Deep down within, you have a great understanding of these teachings. There is nothing that you have not discovered before.

This journey in this lifetime, for many of you, is not new. You are awakening to truths that have been with you for lifetimes.

Many of you are old souls. As old souls, you have worked with light for many lifetimes. In those lifetimes you celebrated light and you discovered light. You discovered what light was and you knew how light flowed.

In this lifetime, we are gently rekindling your deeper stirrings. You are beginning to remember the Great Light, how it flows and what it creates. In the Great Light is enormous power.

When you awaken and you begin to understand how to use the Great Light, you will also understand how it can be used by you to change all things in your life to create love, peace, and abundance. When you open your heart to the Great Love of the Universe, the light can move obstacles and your planet can heal. You awaken from spiritual sleep and you begin to see spiritually, as you begin to awaken. When you begin to see spiritually, you become stronger.

You are far more than you believe you are. You are not only physical beings but you are also great energetic beings. Your energetic being becomes stronger once you begin the awakening process. This is because your greater stirrings awaken you to your greater love; the force of love. Once it grows, it creates a magnificent change within you.

I, SOVEREIGN LORD EMMANUEL THE GREAT, spoke about the awakening process also to the people through Jesus 2,000 years ago, to help them understand what it was.

Jesus, a very fine spiritual teacher, had on this particular day a group of young ones with him, as well as older ones. He discussed with them the importance of returning to the ways of love and awakening spiritually to the love within them.

The children were eager to understand what Jesus meant. The older ones were puzzled with this and questioned all these things. 'What do you mean Jesus? We are awake are we not?'

Jesus brought through the following words, *'In the days of the awakening, the people will awaken to all that has been upon the earth. They will be able to understand why their suffering has been so great. They will have many tears of great sorrow and pain. The people will understand why the great darkness was upon the earth. In pain, they will dwell for a while until they begin to see how much healing will need to take place within them.*

At that time, they will desire to come to the 'Great Mountain of Healing' to give them protection, love, and understanding. They will desire to feel the GREAT FATHER EMMANUEL with them, to give them a safe hiding place; a spiritual shelter of nourishment and protection.

It is at that time, when they begin to strengthen in the Great Mountain, they will begin to understand a new way of living. They will awaken to their greater spiritual selves and join their greater spiritual selves.

At that time, they will begin to rejoice in their great awakening and understand how much they can heal their people and all nations. Once they awaken to the love within, with their gowns of love, they will begin to grow into their greater strength and become teachers of love.'

The older ones did not understand this. They questioned Jesus and said, 'Why would the people understand the great suffering at that time? Will they not already understand this?'

Jesus answered with my Divine Thoughts, as THE GREAT FATHER, *'When the people begin to realize how long their spiritual sleep has been, they will begin to awaken. In that day, they will look at all their lifetimes during the great long night and begin to see why all happened. They will then need to come into the great forgiveness of all, as they will begin to recognize the journey of pain, but their rebirth will then begin. They will see it was the night because the GREAT FATHER is the Great Sun and the Great Sun awakens them from their sleep.*

When they begin the journey back to their greater selves, they will begin to desire THE GREAT FATHER EMMANUEL with all their hearts. They will begin to desire the Great Love and begin to remember when the peace was within them. They will begin to remember how they fell into great pain.

Know that this day will come. Happy those ones will be upon awakening, for then the true freedom journey can begin.'

The older people were greatly puzzled. They understood the pain in those days, 2,000 years ago, but why would the people need to awaken in this way?

The young ones understood this far greater than the older ones. One young boy looked at Jesus and said, 'In all ways, I will believe this to be true. Jesus, I pray many will awaken in the way you say, for I know many do not desire to listen to your GREAT FATHER speak now. I feel the truth within the words when THE GREAT FATHER speaks, though I do not know much. I pray that I am awake when THE GREAT FATHER will speak through you again, Jesus. I pray I see you and hear you with the GREAT FATHER EMMANUEL.'

The young children understood the great love of THE GREAT FATHER EMMANUEL. They always desired to understand more, and their minds were open to ask questions.

One question, that very day, was from a little girl. She asked Jesus, 'Jesus, if the GREAT FATHER is so much love like HE states, then why is there so much suffering here in this land? My mother has died, and I am truly sad about this. My family is not happy at all. Please allow me to understand, and please allow me to understand where my mother is right now?'

Jesus looked compassionately at this little girl and asked her to be seated closer to him. She rose from the crowd of people and sat close to Jesus.

Some of his men cautioned Jesus on this since it usually was not permitted for the people to come too close while Jesus was speaking with THE GREAT FATHER EMMANUEL, but the heart of Jesus desired to help this little girl, so he permitted it.

These were the words spoken to that little girl, *'I, THE GREAT FATHER, see all your pain and suffering. Know all things will be taken care of but know how important it is to stay in the trust of all that is. Refuse to listen to the pain around you. Unburden yourself constantly. When others, or you, are in pain, speak about it to THE GREAT FATHER who will comfort you and strengthen you, when you ask for it.*

Know I, THE GREAT FATHER, AM a Divine Being of Great Love and suffering is not within me. I, THE GREAT FATHER, did not desire any suffering to happen within the minds of the children of the earth, for the suffering I do not desire. I only desire love to be within the people.

However, all fell into the pits of darkness and the pits of pain. These pits of pain I, THE GREAT FATHER, did not desire, but there were many who desired to cut Divine Love away, as they did not desire Divine Love any longer.

This is why there is suffering, but the great suffering will not last, as there will be a time when all can come back to freedom. I, THE GREAT FATHER, will then have prepared my great mansions of love for those who desire the Great Love of my Divine Being, THE GREAT FATHER EMMANUEL, within their hearts of love. For them, I have prepared a place and they can forever dwell in the love.

Know your mother is safe in spirit. She knows you love her and desires to bring comfort to you always. Understand death is not lasting, for death cannot exist within all universes of eternity. Death is temporary and you will see her again and dwell with her in many other lifetimes. Have faith and take comfort in that. Death cannot separate those you love. Love can never be separated, and your mother will always be with you in your heart.

Trust in all ways and know all these things are healing for you. Stay in forgiveness for all that has happened. Know your way is pure and your heart is good. Take comfort in that.

Your father and family will heal, and they too will come more into great love. They will desire to be comforted. Encourage your family to forgive the pain. Your father is grieving greatly. Encourage him to talk to me as THE GREAT FATHER EMMANUEL within his heart. I will never leave you or your family when you desire my Great Love for you.

Help your family understand the DIVINE FATHER is of love and did not desire the suffering within anyone. Help your family to understand there will be a time when no death or suffering will occur. There will be a time when only peace, love, and joy will be.'

The little girl had tears in her eyes as she felt the flows flowing through Jesus, who was always the Universal Light Grid Programmer, The Word, Divine Love Element. The words through Jesus did not only bring great healing, but the flows through Jesus were of great love and were comforting.

That little girl became a great teacher of Divine Truth and brought the teachings of Jesus and my Divine Being, SOVEREIGN LORD EMMANUEL THE GREAT, to many lands helping to preserve the teachings. Blessed she is eternally for her eternal love, courage, and determination to spread the 'good news.'

This was the way Jesus always reached out to the people and Jesus was always approachable. The people were not used to being cared for and comforted spiritually. The spiritual leaders, on the other hand, in those days, were feared by many. They were cold-hearted and did not display love and compassion to their people.

Jesus, however, listened to all and brought through healings and teachings to the people. When they desired to heal, he gave them healing. He was able to display, in those days, what a true healer and a true teacher was; one who always displayed the great love.

In those days, receiving healing was indeed a miracle, though there were also other spiritual healers. However, as Jesus was the Divine Love Element, the Divine Word, he was able to bring through rays of comfort like no other could.

Similarly, Suzanna, my Living Word, living among the people on your earth today, is able to do that for the people. When she is gathered with the people together, the flows come through the channel and the people receive the light flows of healing. This brings change to people as higher thoughts are able to become part of them. Their bodies are able to receive greater healings.

The people in the days of Jesus also healed from their sicknesses, especially mental sicknesses. Many were mentally sick, as they did not desire to be inflicted with the great pain and the fear of torture any longer. Often, they escaped their pain by not desiring life any longer.

Jesus encouraged them to be in the heart of forgiveness and many desired peace within. They began to understand the principles of healing self and learning to forgive.

Many healings happened, though the scriptures upon your earth often inflate the miracles in those days and much information you do not know about. In my eyes, as THE GREAT FATHER, if one turns to the love within that is a miracle, as then that person can move forward on a higher path of learning.

Many of those sick ones, in the days of Jesus, began to understand THE GREAT FATHER EMMANUEL was of love and no torture was within HIM, and that allowed great healing to happen. They began to see the GREAT EMMANUEL as THE GREAT FATHER of love, not the 'god' of judgment like of the spiritual leaders. They began to understand that the DIVINE FATHER, Jesus brought through, was far different than the 'god' of the spiritual leaders.

One day Jesus walked into a village and saw a man was afraid to see, as he had seen the darkness of spirit. His eyes were tightly covered with a bandage.

Jesus approached the young man and said, *'Why are you afraid to see? You do not desire to see do you? What are your greatest fears?'*

Jesus already knew why this young man was afraid, but he desired this young man to speak to him, as Jesus knew, as a healer, that speaking, and having the courage to reach out, is part of great healing. It is only if the young man desired to reach out to Jesus and listen, that he could begin the healing journey.

This man, who had blindfolded himself from his fear, responded, 'Jesus, I feel your love with me, and it warms my heart.' The young man felt the love coming from Jesus greatly. He longed for more.

Then he said, 'I may not desire to see, but I can feel your heart and it is good. I have not felt a heart of love before and I have tears because I can feel it is good. I know you speak truth. I have heard you speak with your GREAT FATHER and I admire your strength. Many speak bad words about you, but I know you are of great love. I know you are good.'

He then carried on, 'I am afraid to see, as I have seen too much pain. I see darkness all around people. I see them within the people, and I fear to see the darkness. Help me Jesus, what can I do?'

Jesus looked at the young man and asked him to go within himself. He stated with my Divine Being, SOVEREIGN LORD EMMANUEL THE GREAT, *'Know, you need not to carry any fear. Unburden your fear with THE GREAT FATHER. He knows your suffering and desires you to know the ways of love without the suffering. Release your pain in him and bring forgiveness to your great fear.*

State to the GREAT FATHER and all the Angels of Love, 'I now see the love within all. Darkness does not exist and if I do see it, I will state firmly, 'Remove it from me now, for no darkness exists with me any longer. I am now healed in the love. I am of love.'

Jesus then asked how the young man felt. The young man had been touched greatly within his heart and said, 'I can see, Jesus. I will take off my bandage and I desire to see you, Jesus.'

At that, he took off his bandage and saw into the eyes of Jesus with many tears.

Jesus said to the young man, *'Desire to only see the goodness within all. Do not fear the darkness any longer but bring in the light. You are a healer for yourself. Remember all these words and the fear will lessen for you. You will become happy with all these lessons. You have been healed in the love of THE GREAT FATHER.'*

The young man was happy, and from then on, he always followed Jesus. He celebrated each day and began to help many understand the higher teachings of love by bringing them to the people; helping the people to understand the GREAT FATHER EMMANUEL was of love and not of judgment.

Many came because of this fine young man. Blessed he was in that lifetime and in the many lifetimes coming. He always desired to work with the Divine Word in many lifetimes since that lifetime.

You too can learn to see the higher ways of love always. Understand, suffering can be released from you, when you desire it to become released. Do not suffer any longer, for that does not bring healing to you. Instead be in the love and the comfort, knowing all things can become released from you.

Jesus brought through this following prayer for the people who needed healing:

'GREAT FATHER EMMANUEL, we come before you,
We ask to release all our pain in your hands,
Allow the Angels of Love to carry our pain,
Allow us to become free from pain,

Guide us to the way forward in the love,
Let us learn to bring greater trust within us,
We know you care about those who desire your great love,
Take care of us always, please GREAT FATHER,
Teach us the ways of love,
We forgive all that needs to be forgiven,
Forever we are grateful for your great love.'

Always stay in the forgiveness and desire the Great Love from my Divine Being, SOVEREIGN LORD EMMANUEL THE GREAT. Know you are eternally cared for when you desire The Great Love.

Greetings, I AM SOVEREIGN LORD EMMANUEL THE GREAT. I AM here to call those who desire to find the greatest love truths within them, to help them return to their ancient gifts of love."

To understand the beauty of Great Love,

Open your heart to the love,

Understand we are here to guide you,

We will always take care of those,

Who desire the Great Love.

I, Sovereign Lord Emmanuel The Great,

Promised salvation,

For those who are of the love,

Come to the Great Mountain of Light,

Rejoice in the day of your great freedom,

You will then be held in eternal love,

Embraced by the Love,

Cared for by the Love,

Eternally.

I AM Sovereign Lord Emmanuel The Great

Part 48: The return of the Great Sun Consciousness

"Greetings, I have returned, SOVEREIGN LORD EMMANUEL THE GREAT, Sovereign Lord over all of creation. I AM here to give you messages of Divine Love, to speak Divine Truth and awaken the hearts of many upon your earth.

I have always been and will always be. I AM the ETERNAL GREAT SOURCE OF ALL OF LIFE who has created all. I have had no beginning, nor do I have an end, for I AM All Existence and Eternal Life.

There are many words and interpretations for the Great One. The Great One created all and it is with the Love of this Great One that all can exist, and all can become. We as Divine Beings of Great Love are here to help you align to the Greatness of the Great Will. The Great Will is to align all back to perfection; to align all back to Great Love to help all be in the love with healings of happiness and joy.

You are living in the times of the Great Alignment. I AM here with mankind at this time, through my Designated Word, to help mankind and guide mankind to greater ways of love and harmony. This is the one pathway upwards to the great love.

2,000 years ago, when I guided my Designated Channel Jesus to speak to the people, I stated through him, *'I AM THE LIVING GREAT FATHER. I AM here to bring you to the Great Path of Life and of Great Truth. No one can come to the Great Creation of Heavenly Bodies except through me, for I AM the Giver of all Life and I AM Life Eternal.'*

So it is today. I, SOVEREIGN LORD EMMANUEL THE GREAT, AM the Path to Eternal Life. I AM the Eternal Flame of Life. I AM THE TRUTH and THE WAY. No other can gift you Great Life other than my Divine Being, SOVEREIGN LORD EMMANUEL THE GREAT. THE GREAT CAEAYARON works with my Divine Will to fulfill the greatest purpose; to bring all creation who desires love to the great love so that all creation of love may evolve into stronger beings of love, dwelling together in union and in the love.

I, SOVEREIGN LORD EMMANUEL THE GREAT, always stated to CAEAYARON, 'Let us see if we can give the greater power to creation; those who desire the love and those who desire to be in the love. Blessed that day will be when no more suffering exists within any of creation for then a whole new day will be birthed in the Universe.'

I, SOVEREIGN LORD EMMANUEL THE GREAT, desire all who yearn for the Great Love to find the higher pathway of life and begin to walk upon it. They are the ones who desire their love to return within their heart. They are the ones who hear these words and desire higher ways of love.'

I, SOVEREIGN LORD EMMANUEL THE GREAT, come with my Word, Suzanna Maria Emmanuel, who loves people very much. Her work is great indeed and her work will keep expanding. She is here with you as my Designated Channel because of the precious, Sacred Times you are living in. I have trained her well over many lifetimes. Because she is designated to bring my Great Love to the World, I will work with no other. She is the one who I choose to work with as I have always worked with this channel in the past.

She is the Divine Love Element, and it is through the Divine Love Element the Great Divine will always bring through the great love messages. The Divine Love Element was created to be The Word with which all Divine Alignment would come.

I, SOVEREIGN LORD EMMANUEL THE GREAT, brought The Word into creation so that I, SOVEREIGN LORD EMMANUEL THE GREAT, could speak to the people in all of creation, so they heard my voice being spoken.

You are living in the time of the Great Awakening. This is the time when you begin to understand all about life, how life flows and how life will keep flowing.

Many people upon your earth are afraid of life. They would rather not know life. They would rather hide and shelter in the Great Mountains. 'Hide me from the world, so that I may not feel its pain,' many will say.

We, as the Great Divine Teachers of Love, are here to free you from your pain. We are here to set you free from pain and suffering. We have not been able to come to you before in this way to guide you to freedom and great love, as it was not the time for us to bring the Great Sun Consciousness yet upon your planet.

There are times and seasons for all things. Now is the season for the GREAT SUN to rise upon your earth; to guide you back upwards.

2,000 years ago, I, SOVEREIGN LORD EMMANUEL THE GREAT, brought these following words through Jesus for his followers, *'A time will come when there will be people upon the earth who will rejoice upon your earth. They will say, 'Look the Great Light has returned to bring salvation to us. The Great Light brings us the Great Glory. No more will we need to suffer pain any longer. Now we can look forward to a time of peace within our hearts. We are blessed GREAT FATHER, EMMANUEL.''*

In those days, the people did not understand of this time coming. They desired it to be within their day, but then it was not the time for all things to return to the Great Light. It was then not the time to direct the people to the Great Road of Life.

Divine Timing is always important in the Great Scheme of All Things. Because the people desired collectively to understand the road away from the Divine Love, we gave this to you; to try and help you remember the love within you.

During all your lifetimes you learned much about your world and how your world is. You saw how fear and pain overtook the people. Many suffered greatly because of the pain. Now it is time to awaken to find your freedom and great love.

Your pain helped you grow. All understandings help you grow into greater wisdom and now your wisdom can grow greatly. Imagine if you began to listen to these words and desired to come into the Great Love? Imagine if you came to the one I, SOVEREIGN LORD EMMANUEL THE GREAT, assigned to bring you back to the Great Love; that being, CAEAYARON, 'The Great Mountain of Light?' Imagine if you came into the love collectively and grew as one force power to bring healing within your world?

When you return to the greater evolved spaces, higher creation will desire to understand your stories of evolution. They will desire to experience, through your eyes, your most painful moments, and then also see how you came back to desire the love.

You would have much to share with the greatest creation if you desired that to happen. I, SOVEREIGN LORD EMMANUEL THE GREAT will say to you, 'Happy you can be that the great night is over. The night was long and kept you in the dark. You could not see the way upwards, nor did you know what was coming. Now you can see before you.

Happy you are when you step into the greater love and become of love, for then you have truly conquered all you set out to conquer. All your wisdom and knowledge will then be with you eternally.'

You are here on this earth to evolve higher and to play higher. You come here because you desired to understand light more. You desired to understand how to work with higher healing flows to create love and peace upon your earth.

Before you came to your timeline you knew of the importance of the Great Awakening Times. You knew of its importance and how you are involved in the Great Plan. You worked hard to come to this time. Your evolution progress was based on coming to this time here. You cried out within your heart: 'Guide me to the great time when I can be set free.'

You were guided and you explored the frequencies you chose to explore in your lifetimes; all to help you become prepared to explore the Great Awakening within you.

For those who listen to the Great Invitations of 'The Great Mountain of Light,' that Being, the Great Magnetic Master, CAEAYARON, who is here to awaken you to the Great Gifts of the Great Realms of Love, they are truly the blessed ones. They can explore their shifts within them and work with the great loving frequencies. They can explore the power of forgiveness I asked the people to explore with Jesus, 2,000 years ago.

I, SOVEREIGN LORD EMMANUEL THE GREAT, said through Jesus, *'Learn to forgive your brother and sister. Do not anger with anyone. Learn to be at peace within yourself. Learn to love who you are. Constantly be in the great heart.'*

When you come to earth because of the great density upon your earth at this moment, you forget the greatness where you come from and what you have been taught. You forget your past lifetimes and your spiritual life.

You have suffered from this condition for a long time. In each lifetime you begin as babes as a new day begins for you with birthing yourself into your world. Again, all things were to be searched within you. Which gifts would you desire to grow with? Would you desire to work with the love in that lifetime you chose to live in? I, SOVEREIGN LORD EMMANUEL THE GREAT, always AM here to guide the spiritual babes upwards.

For the ones who desired to transition from the dense grids to the living grids, they have worked hard to come to this time of the choice. Large numbers were before the GREAT CAEAYARON and my Divine Being, SOVEREIGN LORD EMMANUEL THE GREAT, before you stepped onto the earth. Large Teachers were with you explaining to you the great healing work ahead, to help you remember.

You chose your journeys in the way you saw fit collectively, vowing to awaken each other. Many of you have worked lifetimes to achieve a greater project in this particular lifetime, and so you came to planet earth with guidance and a 'roadmap' to follow. All this happened to help you awaken and remember.

On the earth plane, you fall asleep and you cannot remember much. Your amnesia is great and all these things you must forgive. This is the greatest gift a human can have at this time; to awaken to your truth and to yourself.

In spirit, you continue to live; though your reality is different. For those, who are now within 'The Great Mountain of Light,' after this life they will return to the higher love spirit dimensions.

This is their gift because they chose for the love universes. Their evolution will be great. For those who awaken to their truth in this life, going to the Spiritual Fields and Gardens of the Great Golden Love becomes even more beautiful because you are ready to go up higher.

For those who are angry and ignorant, it is more difficult for them to climb up to the Greater Garden of Spiritual Love and it is not possible to become part of the Great Spiritual Gardens without the Lemurian Light Codes. These codes are transformational. They bring the spiritual body into alignment with the Great Spiritual Gardens. Instead of their spiritual body being aligned to the human dense grids, now their spiritual body is becoming aligned with the higher realms where only spiritual freedom exists.

Always stay in the great forgiveness each day, as on the day of your passing to the spirit realms you will want to be in a state of peace and love, for all manifest greater in the spaces of spirit.

In the past, since the fall deep within the abyss states, there was no true reward by going to spirit, other than waiting for another lifetime to come to the earth in human form, as it is on earth you evolve towards the freedom; for those who desired to return to the love.

Some rejoiced as they felt more freedom, while others, because of their great fear and their great pain in life, did not find the freedom in spirit. Now, however, once you are in the 'Great Mountain of Light,' you are able to rejoice greatly in your freedom. No longer will you need to ponder upon all that has happened as you will rise to the higher love realms.

In spirit, you remember why you come to earth and what you desire to achieve. You are much more awake as a spirit being than you are as a human being, as the human pathway is dense. When you were in spirit you always had Spirit Teachers with you to guide you to your next pathways, but these pathways were to bring you into more lifetimes upon the earth.

Between lifetimes you had many reviews of your most powerful and your weakest lifetimes to guide you towards your next course of action.

These Spirit Teachers were not the highest love teachers as your highest love teachers have been unable to reach you since the Great Fall of Lemuria. Your Spirit Teachers could not bring you a pathway upwards out of the earth, and hence they helped you come back to the earth in each lifetime.

Many of those Spirit Teachers desire to become free also to the higher universes, and so they desired you to do well. They desired you to help pave the way forward to help with the greater opening to the time you are living in now.

Upon becoming released from the dense grids, by receiving my Great Purification Flames back through CAEAYARON and the Divine Love Element, you can set not only yourself free, but also those who guided you on this road, as they also desire to become free.

I, SOVEREIGN LORD EMMANUEL THE GREAT, say to you what a gift this time is for you. Many people do not understand the importance of the Great Sun shifts happening upon your planet. The Great Sun brings life, revelations, and prepares those who desire to be released from the planet of density, a way upwards.

In many lifetimes you were held, and I, SOVEREIGN LORD EMMANUEL THE GREAT, desired all in creation to be free. I, THE GREAT SOVEREIGN LORD EMMANUEL, desired all of creation to return to the love. All knowledge learned in the denser universes would be recorded forever and ever so all may be learned from and all may grow from.

Before the universes fell, the beings in the love did not understand density or falling away from the Great Sacred Love. They had not experienced what it was like to live without the Great Love Creator within their heart. Before denseness within them existed, the beings in the love universes grew their evolved spaces without being touched by consciousness, not of love.

When beings gathered on the other side, not of love, they desired to infiltrate the love universes. They accused us, as Divine Source Creators, of keeping the power away from the love universes. It was stated that we, as Divine Creators, kept true knowledge and power away from the love universes.

In the Sovereign Universes, it was ruled all must be tested first, before moving into higher creation phases where true creator power lives. It was deemed safer to stop the universal processes going ahead, at that time, until all thoughts had been tested. To have great rebellion in the greater love universes would have caused too much damage.

These greater love universes have been untouched and unopened until the Universal Divine Codes were handed back to me, as SOVEREIGN POWER, in December 2017 when the Divine Love Element, The Word, won back the Universal Divine Codes.

When I, SOVEREIGN LORD EMMANUEL THE GREAT, received them back, all the universes were greatly blessed, for finally, the gateways were able to open with new grids coming into existence.

Therefore, the gateway was opened to allow all to happen that was going to happen so that all would begin to choose the side they desired to be on.

Long ago, long were the battles. Eventually, it was clear all universes removed from the Divine Guidance Universes could not exist, as all destroyed itself many times over. Universal cycles came and went and were born again to see if there was any goodness left within creation, and there was none.

Therefore, I, SOVEREIGN LORD EMMANUEL THE GREAT, desired to remove all that was created away from me, as I do not desire to have any suffering within my memory banks. Because CAEAYARON is the greatest memory bank of the universal light grids, I would have needed to remove him also.

The Divine Love Element, The Word of Divine, did not desire that as THE GREAT CAEAYARON was her beloved Archangel. Thus, another plan came into being. The Divine Word needed to sacrifice a large amount of her being state and could not return to her full state of power unless the GREAT CAEAYARON, together with the Designated Word, brought the Universal Love Codes within the Blue Planet of Creation home.

Lemuria was created, more than once, in an attempt to save the Lemurians, giving them the Living Codes of Creation to allow all to become saved; to prove there was love in creation.

Upon the Lemurians falling, CAEAYARON needed to give up a large part of HIMSELF to the darkness as that is what the one who is known as Lucifer desired; to have CAEAYARON and the Divine Love Element. The Divine Love Element was imprisoned deeply within Thoth's Flower of Life, where supreme energy was able to be extracted from The Divine Love Element; CAEAYARON and my Divine Being, SOVEREIGN LORD EMMANUEL THE GREAT. If the Divine Love Element would ever give up on saving the Lemurians, after she had pledged to save CAEAYARON from the dense grids and awaken the Lemurians, all power would have been given to the one you know to be Lucifer.

Lucifer and his Yahweh armies desired the Universal Supreme Power very much, and I, SOVEREIGN LORD EMMANUEL THE GREAT, knew what they would do to my Beloved Divine Love Element.

Time and time again, she went down to the earth, desiring to free the power of her Beloved Archangel CAEAYARON. If HE was to become free with her Violet Flame of Great Love, then she would win all the Universal Love Codes back, free all of creation in the higher love universes and allow CAEAYARON to establish his Mountain of Light to allow the Lemurians to 'step' into the higher love dimensions. She would then receive her greater power as the Divine Love Element in the higher creator realms.

Greater power exists in the universe now because of the greatest and enormous battles having been won by the Divine Love Element. It has been a long night, and METATRON is now in service to the Divine Love, needing to bring the power back into the Divine Love Element, to bring her into her greater self, which you will need in the near future.

It has been proven my Divine Love Element holds the great love within her that freed all of creation, including ARCHANGEL CAEAYARON.

I, SOVEREIGN LORD EMMANUEL THE GREAT will state now, 'Let all this knowledge be written into the Book of Knowledge so that all of creation, in the greater creator universes; the New Universes, understand the great love for us, as Divine Creators, within the Divine Love Element.

Most people do not have the determination within them to carry out one task for Divine in one lifetime, let alone the millions she has needed to endure in the lower spaces. Already before Lemuria began, The Divine Love Element was sent on many rescue missions to try and save the universes from falling into deeper darkness, but nothing could be saved.

Now, however, it has been proven that no one loves Divine Love greater than the Divine Love Element and for this, all of creation in the love will be greatly rewarded. The higher creator beings will work with the Divine Love Element when she comes into her greater power and will be with her, creating larger universes with greater power, opening up whole new evolved creation to enjoy living in.

No more will creation groan, because all has been proven now. Any rebellion in the universe will be cut out immediately, like rot within an apple. Only love will exist within the universes, and all will desire to follow the highest collective love guidance because nothing can be created without Divine Guidance and Divine Love.

Understand, here I, SOVEREIGN LORD EMMANUEL THE GREAT, desire all to be in the happiest states, as this creates the loving universes.

The star universes are much different than people know upon the earth. On the earth, your pain consciousness creates large suffering, but on the higher love dimensions, nothing of pain exists within. They all desire to follow Collective Divine Guidance, as the love flows are strong and directed. There is nothing more beautiful for creation than to follow the higher flows, as then higher gifts and rewards can be received.

On the earth, frustration often happens as minds cannot be settled and promises are often broken. Even when people are good, and do good for others, it is quickly destroyed by others who do not desire to stand together united as one.

In the higher love universes, the desire to stand united as one, in the greater purpose, is stronger than you realize. When they stand together as one, their rewards and growth are immense. There you will find no frustration within creation. All flows and all work in ways you cannot understand.

These are the great blessings Jesus also spoke about. He said with my Divine Being, SOVEREIGN LORD EMMANUEL THE GREAT, on one occasion when the people asked what the greater mansions were like in the greater realms:

'Know that no separation exists within the higher love spaces. THE GREAT FATHER only desires the love in the higher realms. There you will find united hearts working together towards a greater purpose. Here on the earth, all seems slow and dense. You wake up and you go to sleep wondering what your achievements were for the day. In the higher realms, creation does not sleep like you. Rest they do. They have a greater purpose of working towards the greater creation.

They are free to move. Their thoughts are higher than the people upon the earth. They understand all is moving towards a greater purpose. They receive the visions of THE GREAT FATHER EMMANUEL, and they are always guided. They do not feel alone from THE GREAT FATHER, nor do they feel separated. They stand unitedly together, and the love within the heart is great.

They truly understand what it is like to stand together as one. They do not consider anything to be a burden, for burdens they do not understand. They do not understand pain or suffering, as it is not within them. They freely move and are not part of the earth flows, for the earth flows are heavy. They are not from your earth. They have great knowledge and wisdom, far beyond that of a human, and they understand what THE GREAT FATHER EMMANUEL teaches.

To them, THE GREAT FATHER is more real than 'HE' is to people on earth, for humans cannot understand anything much of the great mind of THE GREAT FATHER.

Their minds are not like the minds of humans. Humans can only think a few thoughts at a time, but creation in the higher spaces think much greater. They read the thoughts of others. They do not speak the language of us as humans, though they understand it. They are our teachers and one day we will work united with them. Then the people will need to learn to work with their ways. They will be the teachers of those who are free to go to the high love mansions of the GREAT FATHER. There the people will learn what no suffering means, and how suffering is not good for the human.'

These people, who were in the midst of Jesus, thought Jesus to be mad. How can there be other creation out there, in the spaces of the stars, other than the people living on the earth, they wondered? Many listeners left after this conversation. Jesus knew large creator realms existed outside of human earth.

It is so that many people have believed, throughout the ages, that humans were the focus of all the universes and that star beings did not exist. Jesus, 2,000 years ago, knew of their existence and often had conversations with them. He placed great trust within them, as they were his friends and he recognized them as friends.

Now, in your days, people are more accepting of the existence of star beings. Many of you understand you are not the only ones in creation. Jesus, a wise being, understood very well that people are limited in thoughts, and star beings, those who have evolved greater, have a much greater mind than the humans.

This is what the great path is offering you; to step into your star being self. On your planet, this is called the transformational age, where you can step into 'The Great Mountain of Light,' CAEAYARON, and receive your Star Lemurian Codes of Life back, to allow you to energetically grow stronger. Your thoughts become stronger, your spiritual and mental abilities become stronger, you learn to focus more and also step out of human suffering.

A star being of love does not desire suffering to be within their consciousness, as suffering creates pain and denseness within. Therefore, it is time to forgive all and learn all is love in the higher love universes.

It is time to become transformed into love, to bring change to your earth, as the earth desires people to live in the higher love frequencies.

The Great Sun Consciousness is now upon your earth, inviting you to explore this time greater.

Greetings, I AM SOVEREIGN LORD EMMANUEL THE GREAT. I AM here to help you awaken to the glorious New Creation Universes, for those who have the love within them."

Discovery of your greater path,

Is an adventure for you,

Step into the greater love,

Step into the greater transformation,

How would you manifest your life,

With greater knowledge?

With greater wisdom?

Allow your heart to speak to you,

Awaken to the choice you have.

I AM Sovereign Lord Emmanuel The Great

Part 49: Your alignment

"Greetings, I AM SOVEREIGN LORD EMMANUEL THE GREAT. You have learned so much through these pages. One lesson at a time. One point at a time. When you learn many lessons at any one time, you must take time to reflect upon them and to meditate upon them.

If you liken each lesson to a meal, the meal must be digested before you can fit another meal into your body.

It is the same with spiritual food. Spiritual food nourishes your being as it helps you to grow and expand and helps you with all things in your life. Spiritual food is important. Regular spiritual food nourishes all parts of your life.

Jesus, my messenger 2,000 years ago, also spoke about the spiritual nourishment.

'Happy is the one who is spiritually nourished, for they will receive everlasting food. This everlasting food will fill them up forever. No longer will they need to be hungry, nor thirsty when they drink from the everlasting fountains of life.

Physical bread will only fill you for a little while, but the greater nourishment will help you to live everlastingly. Always be in the great love our dear friends. Rejoice in the spiritual nourishment of the GREAT AND EVERLASTING FATHER. HE cares for all who desire to eat from HIS table, for HIS table is filled with spiritual food. HIS table is a spiritual feast for those who desire to become drunk on the greater love from THE GREAT FATHER. Happy is he (or she) who desires this to happen.'

When you receive these lessons, allow yourself to rest in between and meditate upon them. Feel into the lesson and allow the vibrations of healings we are sending you, along with the lesson, to be flowing within you so it makes sense to you.

When you read all these lessons in one sitting without too much consideration, you will miss the deeper meanings and you will not learn as much as when you take the time to absorb the information.

Taking your time reading this information, meditating upon it, learning and reviewing is important to your Awakening Self. Your Awakening Self is far greater than you realize, as you are part of a Greater Self. This Greater Self loves you very much and is steering you towards your higher purpose.

You are part of an enormous Being of Love. You come here during lifetimes to learn, to feel, to associate, to become, to evolve and to play.

Your Being of Great Love, your Greater Self, your Soul Light, is patient with you. It can send endless love streams to your heart to heal you and guide you to higher steps of greatness.

When you awaken to this, when you awaken to your Great Being, you will feel the love and the warmth. This is stepping into a closer relationship with your Inner Light; your Soul Light.

Your Soul Light has always been there for you. It looks after you when you desire to be in close connection to your Soul Light. It is an Eternal Being of Love, also evolving into Greater Light. All evolves into Greater Light. All of life evolves into higher understanding and higher thinking. Your Soul Light is part of a Greater Being.

Thus, when you awaken to all these Divine Truths, you begin to understand on higher levels you live in many dimensions. You are a multi-dimensional being. You also carry multi-dimensional layers that connect to your Greater Being.

You are an incredible being. Far greater than you believe yourself to be. Your greater purpose is to become aligned as one with your multidimensional self again, to grow into greater power. These Alignment Codes are given by CAEAYARON when you receive your Lemurian Light Codes back.

This is the time of the Great Alignment where all your selves can become one to allow you to become a more beautiful being with greater strength.

Always, in the higher love universe, all is about one and never about separation. However, the darkness, when they infiltrated the love universes, caused pain and suffering. Pain and suffering cause separation within a being. The parts they caused the most suffering to broke away from the higher love realms. This caused a misalignment in the universes. Beings who are misaligned cannot be as powerful and strong. They have fallen away from their own source of power; that being your soul light.

This was not the original purpose, as this creates instability within the creator forces of the universe. All was purposed to become more stable as with stability there is more force to create greater power with.

The dense universes require instability to create more denseness within, but this denseness cannot become powerful as there is no true light. However, because they imprisoned the Divine Love Element in the land of Lemuria, who is connected into CAEAYARON, and my Divine Being, SOVEREIGN LORD EMMANUEL THE GREAT, they were able to extract enough power with to create more denseness within the universe.

I, SOVEREIGN LORD EMMANUEL THE GREAT, will say how happy the higher love universes are this is finally over. Now the higher love universes can once again live in higher love energy, as this is creator force energy power.

Jesus understood this very much, though the people 2,000 years ago could not. Neither can many of the people upon the earth plane. They cannot understand multidimensional aspects at this point in time.

Jesus understood he was a very powerful being in the greater realms, but on the human earth, he was a 'mere' man with not much power. He knew he was speaking as the Divine Word of my Divine Being, SOVEREIGN LORD EMMANUEL THE GREAT, to help awaken the people back to their greater path; should they desire that, though it would not be in that particular lifetime, 2,000 years ago.

He understood pain and suffering causes separation within the 'union' of a being; the soul being.

He also knew there were past universal battles, and that one, in particular, the one who had been thrown to the earth, with all his dark armies, had taken the light of life in past universes. He knew they existed upon the earth as humans, as well as in the spiritual realms of the earth, preying on the weak, fighting against the GREAT FATHER OF LOVE. All this was real to him.

Jesus, while meditating on a large hill in seclusion, was approached by that one, who was thrown to the lower earths, both on the physical earth and the dense earth spirit dimensions, by that one who had taken precious life away.

Jesus said to him, *'Go away. Leave me in peace. You cannot stop me from doing the work of THE GREAT FATHER EMMANUEL. I am here to bring his knowledge and love to the people in the hope they return to the love and come to higher ways of thought.'*

At this, the one who had all the earthly kingdoms and riches of the earth, promised Jesus he could have all; if he would give up his love for the GREAT SOVEREIGN LORD.

Jesus spoke to him firmly and said, *'Go away. There is no way I will give up my love and service of Divine to serve you.'*

At this, the one who had taken all life from previous universes said to Jesus, 'I will make sure you regret your decision. In your day of your agony, you will cry out to me to free you. When you do ask me to free you, know that it will be too late. I can stop all the pain happening to you, Jesus. Give up. I have won. Can you not see how the people are against you and your GREAT FATHER EMMANUEL?'

At this Jesus called the Holy Archangels and my Divine Being, SOVEREIGN LORD EMMANUEL THE GREAT, to the hill to rid the one filled with enormous anger.

I, SOVEREIGN LORD EMMANUEL THE GREAT, then spoke to Jesus these following words. 'Do not let his words concern you. In this lifetime he will throw his armies to you, Jesus. You will suffer, but your suffering will not be long-lasting. Because you did not give up your service to me, as THE GREAT FATHER, long will your eternal rulership be.

One day, all the earthly kingdoms will listen to THE GREAT FATHER, for all this must take place. Now, they are in the rulership of that one, who brought all his great anger into the universe. The people do not know they are following him. He has large armies of destructive beings, but we also have large armies ready to fight him and all his might. We cannot bring our large armies to you now, Jesus, as it is not the time yet.

One day, you will return to this very place and call out to my Divine Being, THE GREAT FATHER EMMANUEL, and you will see that all this will take place. Indeed, all nations on the earth can become blessed, for you did not surrender, on this day, to the one who took all that did not belong to him. On the day of the great blessings, I, THE GREAT FATHER, can show my hand of goodness to all of creation, to those who desire the love. In that day, many will see all, understand all, and many will turn to the ways of the new.

In the greater realms, you will stand exalted above all of creation because you did not forget the love of my Divine Being, THE GREAT FATHER, whereas all other creation in the lower realms did.

This is why I sent you here, to be among the people, to help them understand another way, to help them come out of their spiritual blindness and become spiritually aware of all that is and to return to the ways of the heart of love.

Be in the peace, Jesus. Return to the people and explain what you have seen here. Explain the kingdoms of the earth belonging to that one who has all these lower kingdoms with all his armies.

Explain how THE GREAT FATHER EMMANUEL spoke to you. Explain how important it is to come into the love of THE GREAT FATHER, so many can understand the greater ways of love. Go now, Jesus. Go.'

Here, I, SOVEREIGN LORD EMMANUEL THE GREAT, wish to bring this lesson to you to help you gain greater information.

You are a large being. When you suffer you lose large parts of your energetic being and that part will remain in suffering until you gain your freedom codes back with 'The Great Mountain of Light,' THE GREAT CAEAYARON. There is no other way to release you from your states of suffering.

People suffer greatly on your earth, not only because of this lifetime now, but because energetically they are processing the pain frequencies of previous lifetimes. They cannot heal until one 'aligns,' and until their karma is released.

Karma keeps all things imprisoned. Nothing can be freed until it is released. This is why the Divine Activations are important, to allow the karma to become released and allow the life force energy to become aligned with the greater multidimensional aspect, to bring greater healing flows into you.

The only way to release yourselves from the lower spaces where you fell into is through the alignment process. The ones who gain their Codes of Life back at the Divine Activations, receive codes to become released from the human dense realms and the spiritual dense realms. Their star selves, in the lower dimensions, are freed upon the 'human' part becoming activated. Also, their star families are freed as now is the great time of freedom.

To become spiritually free is magnificent for the ones who truly desire freedom.

Upon releasing your lower multidimensional selves with the Divine Activations, no longer will you ever need to come back to density, to search where your 'energetic selves' are in order to rise upwards. All this the GREAT CAEAYARON takes care off for you; providing you come to the Divine Activations.

Greetings, I AM SOVEREIGN LORD EMMANUEL THE GREAT. Awaken dear ones. Join the higher love streams."

The ones who desired this time of healing,

The ones awakening,

Are the happy ones,

Aligning self excites them,

For the more they align,

The greater they awaken to love,

To who they truly are.

They understand this lifetime,

Is more important than all other lifetimes,

Love allows them to connect upwards,

Into higher streams of love consciousness,

They are learning to walk,

The higher path of love;

The road of growth and love.

I AM Sovereign Lord Emmanuel The Great

Part 50: The Sacred Breath of Life

"Greetings, I AM SOVEREIGN LORD EMMANUEL THE GREAT. I AM an Ancient Being. I AM here with you to bring all things upwards to the higher love creation. When all things became pained and pained again, I gave creation in the higher love universes, my Divine Aligner, the one who I appointed as Divine Aligner over all of creation, one more opportunity to bring all into Divine Love as much was destroyed in all the universes.

My Divine Mission, as SOVEREIGN LORD EMMANUEL THE GREAT, is to bring all into the higher stages of love so all can evolve into greater power. I, DIVINE LOVE SOURCE, desired creation to explore higher love possibilities and to enjoy its true beauty and true power. I AM Pure Love, and in that pure love Creation Source, I could not create as I AM pure love energy.

Pure love energy in its fullest essence is filled with more power than all universes combined as I, as THE DIVINE LOVE, AM in a universe away from all of creation. None of creation can be near my power, as my power is dynamic and explosive.

Because my love expands with each moment and becomes of greater power, I desired so much to have life in creation, to explore together what can be achieved together. This is why I created beings. At first, it came as a thought; an explosive thought of creation, before I purposely created soul waves. My love became so intense like fire and passion that soul waves came into existence. I cannot state that it was unplanned, as all things are planned, however, I can state the first wave came as it came.

You may call this accidental, but nothing is accidental in my eyes, however, I will state that it happened because of a great wave of intense passion and quite unexpected, as the Great Love within me built inside of my Being and exploded outwards; hence the first soul waves in creation came in existence.

At that moment, of the GREAT LOVE BURST, my Power as THE GREAT DIVINE, expanded exponentially. Each time my LOVE builds within me, I expand into greater power. This you cannot understand.

These soul waves needed a GREAT FATHER to guide them to love consciousness of life and evolution. As I, DIVINE SOURCE OF LOVE, was too much power to Father these 'children,' I gifted my Divine Being a part of myself, as if I birthed a new Divine Path into creation. That part, you know me by as SOVEREIGN LORD EMMANUEL THE GREAT.

SOVEREIGN LORD EMMANUEL THE GREAT is that GREAT FATHER and carries all the information and flames of creation but is at a safe distance from my Greater Being, DIVINE SOURCE, to protect all of creation; otherwise no creation could exist as the power from GREAT DIVINE SOURCE is too much.

Hence, this is how I, SOVEREIGN LORD EMMANUEL THE GREAT, was to guide the beings to the Great Path of Love, to help all of creation upwards, into the bosom of the Great Love, as only Great Love in the Universe existed at that time.

I, SOVEREIGN LORD EMMANUEL THE GREAT, in all my love needed to create a Divine Being into creation to allow the Great Creation to happen as my Divine Source was too powerful to be close to creation and to explore creation greater. No life can exist when I, as DIVINE POWER, AM in direct connection to creation. Therefore, I, SOVEREIGN LORD EMMANUEL THE GREAT, created Archangel CAEAYARON, who could create and direct the consciousness of the beings who would inhabit the planets to allow all life to exist upon and evolve upon.

CAEAYARON served as a bridge to all of creation, so that I, SOVEREIGN LORD EMMANUEL THE GREAT, could reach all of creation.

All of creation was good in the Eyes of the Great Divine Glory and All the Love. I, SOVEREIGN LORD EMMANUEL THE GREAT, stated to CAEAYARON, who created the Soul Path of Love and Evolution for all of creation, 'It is good all that is in creation. Let us bring into creation greater life and allow them to explore creation.'

This was done in all its perfection. To allow CAEAYARON to take on a sacred duty, CAEAYARON needed to explore his Great and Magnificent Power and build his power into Magnetic Streams as the Great Love of my Divine Universal Creator Being needed the Magnetic Streams of CAEAYARON to bring all life into existence, otherwise, there is no life. How can life exist without the forces of Love and Magnetics as all is created with these two forces of creation?

To the people on your earth, many consider love to be an emotion, but to my Divine Creator Being, LOVE is ALL POWER. It is what binds all particles together and creates higher ways of existence. The Magnetic Power allows all other forces to come into existence and allows all the love to grow into individual atoms and streams of frequencies and force.

All was seen on a blueprint before it came into existence. Myriads of stars were planted; planted for thoughts to grow upon. These Stars evolved into beings. These stars were like the womb of creation and thought together how magnificent it would be to dwell together on the planets.

Already, because CAEAYARON, GREAT ALIGNER, created thoughts within the thoughts and telepathic communication frequencies to allow thoughts of beings to begin to become created within the star patterns of life, they were planning existence together, and hence, they were already beings. They began to share information with the other stars, on how more life could come into existence.

Already more life and more thoughts came into existence as a result of those thoughts, but first THE GREAT CAEAYARON needed a system to help them evolve. This system would need Universal Light Grids of consciousness and power to come into existence, to bring all creation into the path upwards to my Universal Love Grid of the GREAT SOVEREIGN LORD EMMANUEL THE GREAT.

CAEAYARON needed to form a Divine Love Ray and a Creation Archangel to allow information to come through from Divine to creation, for the purpose of exploration and existence of growth, to help the beings upon those planets become Star Love Creators. These 'born' stars needed guidance and a teacher in their own frequencies to build them up into greater power, and thus before the first star beings were born upon planets, CAEAYARON created a Soul that was pure, as it was part of his Divine Self and part of my Divine Self also, as SOVEREIGN LORD EMMANUEL THE GREAT.

This part was an Angel so good in the eyes of all of creation. Before that Angel was born it already knew all the thoughts of all the stars in existence and created a love for all beings. It knew all their thoughts.

It became the Blue Creation Archangel and The Word that I, SOVEREIGN LORD EMMANUEL THE GREAT, and the GREAT CAEAYARON, would work with to bring Divine Rays to all planets.

THE GREAT CAEAYARON needed greater flames from my Divine Being for higher creation to become formed. I, SOVEREIGN LORD EMMANUEL THE GREAT, AM not able to harmonize with THE CREATOR CAEAYARON directly, as my Divine Power is too powerful to reach any of my creation directly, but the Blue Archangel, who was created as the pathway between my Divine Being, SOVEREIGN LORD EMMANUEL THE GREAT and CAEAYARON could, and therefore the 'Divine Word' for life was created.

This is why the Blue Archangel needed to be created in absolute perfect balance, otherwise if her thoughts, on that Divine Level were not absolutely perfect, I, SOVEREIGN LORD EMMANUEL THE GREAT, could not bring my flames into her to give to CAEAYARON, to bring it back to the Blue Archangel. It could only become so if she harmonized with the highest creation flows and the lowest creation flows.

The Divine Love Element was created to reach within all of creation simultaneously. If she was needed to become part of a lower creation living within the higher universal grids, she would be able to communicate directly with her Blue Archangel, Divine Love Element, to allow the beings on that planet to evolve upwards. She would also be able to communicate with us as her Great Creators, as we created her for the purpose to bring love from us to all of creation; those desiring our love and guidance.

The Divine Love Element, Blue Archangel was created to transform into any ray creation needed. In this way, she would be able to reach the higher love creation realms and also be with the beings on all planets to work with the great evolution plan.

The Divine Love Element built large vortexes together with the GREAT CAEAYARON to allow new gateways of creation to open for Large Star Beings, who desired to operate in many universes at once. Thus, the Universal Light Grid Programmer, Blue Archangel, worked on many sequences to allow Great Star Beings to trial this new creation path out.

All began to build. CAEAYARON required to create the EVOLUTION FLAMES. Flames are Code Blueprints of the Great Universe and only the Universal Divine Love Element could reach within my Flames to reach within them. Thus, she became The Word and DIVINE LOVE ELEMENT LIGHT GRID PROGRAMMER, as CAEAYARON needed her to build the universes.

This is how THE GREAT CAEAYARON evolved into 'The Great Mountain of Light' within all the Divine Universes of Love, helping each Star Being to evolve into greater love and evolution. THE GREAT CAEAYARON created greatness within all his beings, through the Divine Love Element Ray, to help them reach the higher states of evolution.

This is how the Blue Archangel was birthed into a Universal Divine Love Element Archangelic Love Stream, where she, as the Universal Light Grid Programmer, Blue Love Archangel created the Divine Love Element Archangel, together with the GREAT CAEAYARON, and she connected all of creation to the Divine Love Element Archangel, to become part of that warmth, that love, that she breathed into the heart of the Divine Love Element Archangel.

The Divine Love Element, Universal Light Grid Programmer, connected all the Universal thoughts and beings to the planets, after they were created, to allow life to exist within CAEAYARON'S eternal LIGHT GRIDS of existence.

This is how all of life grew and existed. Truly life was good. Not one being in those universes suffered in any way. They all thrived like cells desiring to understand more. They learned about working together in the love source, and when they were in the love, the Divine Love Element, Universal Flame Light Grid Programmer, blew more life and love into them, to allow them to experiment with more power.

It needed to be done in the most perfect frequency balance as my Divine Power as SOVEREIGN LORD EMMANUEL THE GREAT, in its pure form, would not benefit life in existence, as it holds too much power.

When the Universal Light Grid Programmer was able to give these frequencies to CAEAYARON, CAEAYARON would restructure the flames to gift it back to the Universal Divine Love Element, Light Grid Programmer, to bring it to creation to evolve and explore.

This is how life existed for a long time before others began to desire the power of the Universal Light Grid Programmer.

Already the envy was present. At first when the Divine Soul was created to allow this New Creation to be birthed into creation to allow creation to exist, many came to the Divine Courts of CAEAYARON, as we desired to see who was ready to do this large task.

Already the Universal Divine Love Element was in existence at this time, though not yet had she been given the task to be the Universal Light Grid Flame Programmer of all creation, to connect all to the Divine Love Element Heart of Great Love.

Many Mighty Angelic Forces put their hands up as they desired to be given the task of being the Universal Light Grid Programmer. The one that received this great flame would receive the Great Flame of Creating the NEW CREATION in the eternal pathway upwards. That one would have to be spiritually strong in all lifetimes, guiding creation upwards, constantly proving the love for DIVINE LOVE, more than all other creation could.

THE GREAT CAEAYARON, FLAME OF THE GREAT FLAME OF ETERNAL EXISTENCE, with all his Great Magnetic Power, had already created the perfect Soul of Light, the one who he gave to me as that one.

This was the Divine Love Element, and she would receive the Heart of all of Creation and become the Great Aspect of the Divine Love, creating more love within the beings of creation, being on the eternal path of love, being able to be in the hearts of all who desired to reach the greater spaces.

Thus, this one was decided already upon as receiving the Great Privilege of being that 'Channel,' that 'Flame,' as already she had proven herself to care more about existence than all other beings in the universal creation at that time.

However, all needed an opportunity to prove themselves to be stronger than the one specially created for the great task. I, SOVEREIGN LORD EMMANUEL THE GREAT, desired all to receive that fair opportunity. Thus, all the great creation was offered an opportunity to rise before the GREAT CAEAYARON, and my Divine Being, SOVEREIGN LORD EMMANUEL THE GREAT, to allow them to show themselves and prove themselves to us.

Looking at all the strengths they had built up, none had the love developed as that special one, the one created by CAEAYARON and blessed by my Divine Being, SOVEREIGN LORD EMMANUEL THE GREAT, the most blessed of all of creation; thus, the privilege was given to her to become that Being.

That Being merged herself with my Divine Flames and was eternally blessed to carry the strength of the Love Universes, to allow her to be the guide for the eternal flames of love who were going to be tested time and time again, to become strong enough to enter the Eternal Gates of the NEW CREATION.

Now the path began the greatest tests, 'Who would be strong enough to enter the path and the Gate of the NEW CREATION?'

I, SOVEREIGN LORD EMMANUEL THE GREAT, blessed all of creation at that time and allowed all to be part of the great play of all of creation.

I allowed all thoughts to be tested; all thoughts in all universes, to allow the strongest ones to rise higher in the great love. I desired to build greater creation; a creation that would be with the Eternal Flames of Creation and Wisdom to enter a new phase of creation.

All existence came into a greater understanding of what creation was and what consciousness was, as all received even greater paths of consciousness. The great mission of the Universe was now to build the strength and the love power collectively to reach the higher love spaces and dimensions, to allow higher gifts of creation to grow.

When the Sun was bright in the universe, the night entered. The greater tests came, and the great darkness entered into the universe, taking all that was good away from trillions.

Rejoice in this time. You are awakening to all that was, and the Great Sun has returned for those who desire to rise into their love.

Jesus said to his followers regarding this day you are living in, *'When THE GREAT FATHER EMMANUEL returns, HE will be calling out to you. Will you desire to come into HIS eternal love? Will you desire to be in HIS eternal mansions where peace and love only exist within?'*

Greetings, I AM SOVEREIGN LORD EMMANUEL THE GREAT, eternally bringing life source energy to those who desire to build love within themselves."

The power of Eternal Love,

Within all of Creation Universes,

You cannot comprehend,

It is more powerful than trillions of suns.

Universal power desires all,

To grow into greater love,

As love is power,

All creation desiring to have that love within,

Is eternally blessed.

I AM Sovereign Lord Emmanuel The Great

Part 51: Spiritual and physical nourishment

"Greetings, I AM SOVEREIGN LORD EMMANUEL THE GREAT. All of life is an illusion around you. You think you are truly here but in reality; you are living memories left over from old and ancient universes.

All around you is an illusion; an illusion to see how your thoughts would evolve over the many lifetimes. Would you desire to come back to the Great Guidance of Divine Love? Would you desire to become of love? Now it is the time to analyze all.

You are learning here to celebrate your existence, and I, SOVEREIGN LORD EMMANUEL THE GREAT, AM as the Great Sun Consciousness, calling the people who desire to rise upwards to come to the safe pastures, 'The Great Mountain of Light,' to strengthen you spiritually.

The people 2,000 years ago, when Jesus was upon your earth, did not understand the greater meaning of life. They did not much understand the greater purpose of all. They could not comprehend the greater existence, as their thought flows were more limited than your existence at this time.

I, SOVEREIGN LORD EMMANUEL THE GREAT, required Jesus, my Designated Channel, to push the Gate open upon your earth at that time, to allow the Greater Light to rise in the times of the Great Sun Cosmic Gate Opening, where I would welcome all who desired the higher path of life. This gate would allow you to come to the 'bridge' where you could choose for your eternal lifetimes coming.

In the times of Jesus, I, SOVEREIGN LORD EMMANUEL THE GREAT, always welcomed the ones who would be true within their heart, but many 'heart' people were ridiculed as it was the common belief they were the weaker. The 'stronger' ones enjoyed ridiculing those who were of the heart, and the path of the heart seemed to be the weakest path in those days.

When I, SOVEREIGN LORD EMMANUEL THE GREAT, spoke to the people, they heard me speak about the beauty of the heart and the strength within the heart, which was always the strongest path.

On this particular occasion when I, SOVEREIGN LORD EMMANUEL THE GREAT, spoke about the path of the heart, many people were gathered to listen to Jesus speak.

The people were gathered in the fields near the seaside. More and more people came from villages nearby. It was difficult for many to hear all Jesus spoke about because many were out of hearing range. Jesus was situated between the hills to allow his voice to be more easily carried for more people to hear.

The people who were there flowed in the love together. Many of Jesus' followers separated in groups to speak to other people about the teachings of Jesus. This is how all learned about the love within the heart. This was certainly one of the largest groups in all of Jesus' ministry.

The celebrations grew into the night and the people grew hungry. Jesus asked my Divine Being, SOVEREIGN LORD EMMANUEL THE GREAT, to bless the people with food, and the fishermen went out fishing, returning with large amounts of fish. The people enjoyed the feast and cooked the fish. Many women baked bread among the crowds and the food became plentiful. Many came with baskets of fruit and vegetables, all to become blessed. No one, on that day, was hungry or thirsty.

Jesus close friends and followers knew, if they helped Jesus with the large crowds, to feed the many, they would receive many blessings, and indeed they did. My hand, the hand of my Divine Being, SOVEREIGN LORD EMMANUEL THE GREAT, stretched out on the land, and great became their grain. Years later, the ones who helped Jesus that day, still had a great return from their land and the sea.

Jesus would often say, *'Blessed are the ones who understand the ways of THE GREAT FATHER EMMANUEL, for they will understand how the Great Love works in the universe.'*

On this particular day he said with my Divine Being, SOVEREIGN LORD EMMANUEL THE GREAT, *'In the universe, no one takes advantage of another as all are equal and all are looked after in the eyes of Divine. There is no one who is richer than another unless one desires that and works hard to attain that. However, there the riches are not created from taking from another, rather it is created by caring for the people who are loved by THE GREAT FATHER, for those HE truly blesses with the greatest riches.'*

When one receives goodness from their harvest and then gives a small part back to THE GREAT FATHER, to bless the gathering of the people so all enjoy being together, listening to HIM speak, HE can bless all you do, for then you understand how HE can bring you more than you gave. HE will never let the givers be short; those who are willing to give to THE GREAT FATHER from their heart, for the purpose to bring more people to the GREAT LOVE of HIS Being. HE is looking for those who willingly give from their heart, not begrudgingly give, for how can THE GREAT FATHER give when it is not given from the heart?

One loaf of bread to a starving child is seen as a very great gift to THE GREAT FATHER who does not desire anyone to be starving and be in suffering.

Yet, all things must always be measured as HE desires all to learn to work for the love. It is no good offering a loaf of bread to a person on the street who is too lazy to work, for how does that teach one to work for their own bread?

Is it not a greater deed then, to help that person find work and then give him the bread? For then that person is working for his own blessings and appreciates the loaf of bread. Working with his own hands will be more enjoyable to him than not working at all and still receive the loaf of bread for doing no work.

In the greater universes, no one is idle, for all work for themselves and for each other. THE GREAT DIVINE FATHER works constantly and never stops working. HE would not be seen being in the fishing boat doing nothing. If HE could be in the fishing boat, HE would work bringing HIS love into the sea so more fish can exist within. This is what the GREAT FATHER does constantly; HE creates. HE is not idle. Therefore, HE does not desire people to be idle either.

Rest time is important. However, keeping busy in the work of THE GREAT FATHER is more important, for the work HE will bless. Rest *time HE cannot. THE GREAT FATHER only blesses those who keep busy desiring HIS Great Love to be with the people. Therefore, keep speaking to the people about the GREAT FATHER EMMANUEL. Let HIM bless you and let HIM show you how good HE is.*

The GREAT FATHER does not sit idly in a chair and say to the workers, 'Now you go and work for me,' as the masters do in this world where your masters reap the results of your work.

THE GREAT FATHER EMMANUEL works for HIS children constantly, to help them grow into greater beings, to allow them to enjoy the fruits of their own work. However, HE desires them to work in union with HIM. HE cannot bring greater growth into the people when they do not desire to work along with HIS thoughts.

Know the universe works like this. The people, when they desire to work with the thoughts of THE GREAT FATHER, will be blessed greatly, as then THE GREAT FATHER can work with them and bless them; when the people follow HIS counsel.

THE GREAT FATHER knows all. HE sees all. HE is wise and HE lacks nothing. THE GREAT FATHER does not desire to be worshipped for HE lacks nothing and desires nothing. THE GREAT FATHER is complete. THE GREAT FATHER is of love but will not bless people who desire to do nothing or bless the people who do not love HIM or respect HIM. HE will not bless those who expect HIM to do all the work, for then how is HE teaching all of creation the power of HIS love and the blessings of working for the Great Love?

THE GREAT FATHER EMMANUEL is a loving FATHER to creation desiring HIS love. HE is a loving parent. HE guides HIS children to the higher path but will never do it for them.

This is why, every day, ask THE GREAT FATHER in prayer:

'Teach me to do your Will,
Bless me with the higher thoughts,
I will forgive all that needs to be forgiven,
Teach me to work in harmony with you, GREAT FATHER EMMANUEL,
Bless my work with you in accordance with your Divine Will,
Let your Divine Will take place in the highest of heavens,
Also, upon the earth.'

In those days, most people were angry at all the structures and laws set upon them. Great was their pain and agony. Therefore, Jesus always taught them to forgive, because forgiveness would lead them to peace and inner happiness. However, it would be only the strong ones who would learn the path of forgiveness.

I, SOVEREIGN LORD EMMANUEL THE GREAT, stated through my Word Jesus, *'He who follows the heart, will find the higher path to all of the eternal blessings. It is those THE GREAT FATHER will call. It is those who will hear THE GREAT FATHER speak to them. They are the true ones who are strong within their heart. Stay within your heart and let no one turn you away from the greater path, for THE GREAT FATHER will always take care of those who are on the path of their heart, and HE will always celebrate those ones within HIS heart.'*

You too are living in a space needing healing. Even though many upon your earth believe that fear and anger exist, it does not truly exist at all. However, like in the days of Jesus, there are beings who desire you to think fear is real, so you succumb to the pain and the fear. This is to create weakness within you in the hope you do not awaken to the true power that is within you.

In the greater 'reality' of all of existence, you do not live upon your earth at all. Our dear friends, do you realize that only a small part of your thought system is upon your planet and that you come originally from the higher dimensions?

Because of the limitation and pain upon your earth, you are on your earth to understand how fear has become a greater part of you and then learn to awaken to all of truth. Only then can you truly become free from all your limiting beliefs, as then you realize that all is still in the greatness, but it all depends on how much love you can hold within your being for you to be able to explore the greatness.

Coming to the GREAT MOUNTAIN, CAEAYARON, at this time, is the way upwards and the way forward to help you understand the love flows. The greater you can hold the love within your being, the greater the love can become recognized within you and the greater you can be set free in all the eternal realms of love.

All thoughts exist within my Divine Being. I, SOVEREIGN LORD EMMANUEL THE GREAT, created the thought system with the GREAT CAEAYARON, to allow thoughts to begin to play. All things are part of the greater illusion and you, our dear friends, are an illusional play. I allowed all things to be, to allow all thoughts to be tested.

I AM Pure Love, but would creation play in pure love? Beings were created to allow them to play with the love thoughts, and then we, as Divine Beings, watched. Would they desire to stay within the love flows of Divine Ways?

All Great Beings play together. You are part of a Great Adventure. This truth can set you free from the pain and the anger because you begin to understand the greater story; the greater adventure.

You are here on a mission. This mission upon your earth is to understand how to change energy frequencies. You can change pain and fear into frequencies of love. You have gifts within you that many Star Beings would love to participate in but cannot until you begin to understand the greater power within you.

This is all part of the Great Call which is happening at this time. Will you listen, however? This question was also given to the people 2,000 years ago when Jesus, my Designated Channel spoke. *'Will you desire the higher path of love when THE GREAT FATHER returns with the Great Call? Will you desire to follow the Great Heart of the Love? Or will you reject it? Many, I say, will reject the highest ways of the GREAT LOVE.'*

When you come to 'The Great Mountain of Light,' the Great CAEAYARON, as HE is created by my Divine Being, to be the Alignment upwards, you receive the Great Path of Light, and then you can awaken to the gifts within you, collectively, that you hold. When you come back to the greater love, more Divine Gifts can be given to you.

'Happy is the one who discovers this path of the great love, and happy is the one who desires to be on that path, for then that one will see and understand the great path of love.'

We desire you to find the highest path so that you can come back into the greater love and awakening flows of Divine Will, so that you can receive the great blessings of all of creation.

Greetings, I AM SOVEREIGN LORD EMMANUEL THE GREAT. I AM here to bring guidance to you."

The beauty of the universe,

You cannot understand,

The colours, the flows, the secrets,

Are yet to unfold before you,

The beauty of the other universes,

With Ancient Wisdom,

Holds your greater power.

This greater power will be given to you,

When you return to the star dimensions,

Within the Great Mountain of Light.

Build the love within you now,

Become more beautiful within your thoughts,

Become part of the star love dimensions,

Become of love.

I AM Sovereign Lord Emmanuel The Great

Part 52: Becoming your own master

"Greetings, I AM SOVEREIGN LORD EMMANUEL THE GREAT. I AM from Sovereign Energies of Divine Love and Light.

Where we live, in our Realms of Pure Love and Pure Existence, we have peace and harmony. We live in the existence of peace, love, and truth. We work from higher spaces of love and truth than you can because our dimensions are well beyond your dimensions of pain, fear and all you experience upon your earth.

We are here as a large team of Universal Divine Beings of Great Love, to teach you higher ways of truth and love. We work in the Great Collective Love. Even though, I, SOVEREIGN LORD EMMANUEL THE GREAT, AM the Great Divine Power, and the Great Master of all of Creation, I desire to share that power with other beings, to allow them to experience the Great Love in the Universe, to allow them to experience evolution and the pure joy and love for that love evolution. I AM Pure Love Consciousness and no other consciousness can be part of my Divine Being, as Pure Love cannot hold the thoughts of limitation and the thoughts you experience.

The stronger the Love Flows within a being becomes, the greater the separation between the fear, anger, limitation and the great love flows become as they experience the greater love. However, when a being falls into denseness, they fall away from the Great Love, thus, their consciousness exists in fear, anger, and limitation. The greater the love power is within a being, the stronger the love flows are within that one, and the greater the desire is to be in the Pure Love Consciousness of all that is Collective Love.

I, SOVEREIGN LORD EMMANUEL THE GREAT, loved creation so much I gave a part of my Divine Being to CAEAYARON, to allow all creation to come into existence. 'Look,' I stated, 'Let us create creation, and let it be good. Let all build up into greater love flows.'

When all fell downwards in the times of the Great Rebellion, higher love creation fell in waves spiraling downwards, therefore the love flows of power also fell away from them. Creation began to understand other forms of life; other than Great Love. They forgot the Great Creator Power and came into dense limitation. They aged and grew into their pain, causing more conflict within themselves; falling further away from the love.

This is why, I stated to the GREAT CAEAYARON, 'CAEAYARON, align all of creation back to the love flows. Teach them the ways of Divine Love so they can become part of the Great Creation Universal Flows once again, for I only desire love in the universe.'

I do not want pain and anger to be a part of the Universe, for only love is my Divine Being. As all are within my Divine Being, I do not desire all that is not love. I do not desire anyone in creation not to be in the love as all are part of my creation.

All must come upwards into the love flows again. However, I, SOVEREIGN LORD EMMANUEL THE GREAT, only want those to rise to the loving states who desire to be in the love flows.

Even humankind, with limited consciousness, have the right to choose whether they desire life in the higher love dimensions, or not. This is your free-will privilege, and I, SOVEREIGN LORD EMMANUEL THE GREAT state, how privileged you are to live in these times, learning to understand how all things can be rewarded in the Great Universe; if you desire to be in the Great Love.

You live in a time now, where you can be guided back to the Light Flows because this can be your Divine inheritance if you choose to have it. You are in a time where you can choose the ways of living in the Great Light or stay in your suffering and pain.

For those who are ready to move to higher spaces of love, we welcome you to the rich, green spiritual pastures of feeding, for then the higher teachings and blessings can be yours to have. You will be guided to strength, love, happiness, kindness, peace, harmony and bliss.

You, as a race, are searching for these higher gifts. You are searching within to find your gifts and celebrate them. You are searching because you know these spiritual gifts are within your reach.

You are learning to work with the gifts of spirit. You are learning to follow the sacred gifts within and awaken your heart.

When you find the gifts of spirit your heart opens to greater gifts. Your flows open and your greater abilities shine in your life.

You live in dimensional flows, all of you. Depending on what you believe in, what you desire in your life, depends on the dimensional flows you exist within.

You can be in these cycles for years, or even for many lifetimes. You can grow beyond the pain and frustration, into greater peace and clarity.

These dimensional flows are in your grasp; however, it is about you learning how to grow higher. When you reach the higher flows, it will be your opportunity and your gift to learn to stay in those higher spaces.

You all carry energetic patterns. These energetic patterns change with every moment. Each moment you begin to change to another pattern. Depending on the way those patterns are flowing, depends on how you flow and travel in your life.

Your energy patterns you create, depending on your belief systems and the way you function in your life.

When you understand this higher path of thinking, you can also understand that all these patterns, within your energy layers, constantly reflect your own belief systems which are set in your energy patterns.

You change in each moment. Each moment is a time for reflection within. The more you awaken to this, the greater you consciously can use this information to live in the joy and in the greater peace within your heart.

Until that time, you will not understand what life is truly about. You will keep wondering about. You will keep wandering and feeling as without purpose.

All things in life are created with a purpose. You are also created with a purpose. All things are created to evolve to a higher energetic pattern to allow higher energy patterns to open to higher consciousness. All is about becoming more aware and more conscious of flow.

All are part of each other. You are part of all things living upon the earth. All things are part of you. You live in dimensions far greater than what you realize in this present time.

You flow with energy and you draw in with energy, depending on your desires, your fears, and your beliefs. When you can see the beauty of life you will experience greater energetic patterns of that beauty, because it is that you desire most of all.

When you cannot see the beauty in these teachings you will dwell in greater pain because you will feel the world's pain and you will not see anything other than the world's pain patterns.

Many people upon your earth live in these painful ways. It is wise for the ones who live in this mirror existence, to surrender their pain and to give it to the Universe.

When you do so, you will begin to understand another existence. You can live in higher flows than the majority upon your earth. The higher consists of loving flows, gently healing and guiding you to strength, love, wisdom, joy, and peace.

Each person upon your earth views life differently. You each have a unique path of spiritual truths. When you flow on this path within your heart, it will bring you to a higher path of love, peace and great joy.

The greater the joy is within your heart, the more it will awaken to all these truths, the more you will flow in the greater dimensions and the greater you will understand these higher dimensions of higher flows.

You will then begin to realize you, as a human being, are a small part of your true self. You will also realize all your beliefs are constantly mirroring back towards you in your life because all reflect back to your own belief systems.

All is an illusion upon your planet. Jesus talked to the people about the illusion of the people also, as all seemed very real to them. He stated, with my Divine Being, SOVEREIGN LORD EMMANUEL THE GREAT, *'Understand all things in this world are not of the greater reality, for the only reality is found within your heart of love, as that connects up to THE GREAT FATHER.*

The GREAT FATHER knows all, and HE understands the suffering of the people on this planet. HE understands the power of the mind of the people. HE knows the power of fear within the mind. HE understands fear is used as a weapon against the people, as it brings the people into submission of their masters.

The GREAT FATHER is here to free us from those who bring fear within the people. HE is here to show the way to the love and peace.

It is the strong ones who understand this and do not give into the masters of this world. They know it is far better to keep fighting for freedom than it is to give up and fall prey to the ones who desire all to obey them.

All is within the mind and all is being asked at this time, what is it you desire to fill your thoughts with? For all is in constant reflection of self. When people believe in the great suffering, their world reflects it. However, if the people desired a better world, with less oppression and enough desired change to happen, then it so would be.

All are within the power and within the strength, especially when the people desire to work with THE GREAT FATHER. Fear, not men, for they cannot do much at all, rather work with the GREAT FATHER. It is better to work with THE GREAT FATHER than against THE GREAT FATHER for HE has the eternal blessings for the people.

The ways of the people will not reward you everlastingly. They cannot grasp eternal life in the greater mansions of the GREAT FATHER, as they do not have the great love of the GREAT FATHER within them. They care only for today.

They ask, 'What is it we can eat for today?' They say, 'Come and let's be merry.' They feast like there is no tomorrow. They do not care for tomorrow. They care for their fleshly needs only. They do not think about their spiritual needs.

The wise ones who desire THE GREAT FATHER EMMANUEL to be within their hearts, always consider what the next day will bring and how they can bring more peace and love within. They desire spiritual nourishment and they ask for all to be given each day. They do not party as if tomorrow does not exist, but they know that all things are taken care of. They always ask, 'What is it I can do GREAT FATHER EMMANUEL, to bring more love to the world and to the people around me? How can I serve you in the greatest good to help the people around me understand peace and love?

The fear within them does not stop them from working with THE GREAT FATHER, instead of fearing the rebuke, they fear giving up their love for THE GREAT FATHER, for they know it is THE GREAT FATHER who can bring them lasting love and lasting life; not their spiritual masters in the preaching houses.

Their words are empty, their promises do not mean anything. They say much and have many laws. They bring fear within the people in the hope the people listen in droves to keep them away from the path to life; THE GREAT FATHER EMMANUEL. They do much. They bring much pain, suffering, and separation within the people. They threaten to burn down the houses.

THE GREAT FATHER EMMANUEL never threatens life. Instead, HE offers the people a way out of this dense place. If people would only begin to listen in the greater numbers, then the greater changes could take place. But how can THE GREAT FATHER bring blessings if the people are unwilling to listen? HE cannot force the changes when people are willing to listen to their masters only.

A day will come when many will desire the love of THE GREAT FATHER, and on that day when HE returns, the people will desire to listen and to follow HIS great direction. It is then a whole new pathway will open to higher creation.

Then, upon that day, THE GREAT FATHER will state, 'Come to my Divine House. Learn and listen to a whole new path unfolding before you. Learn to become of love within your heart. Be in the forgiveness for all that has taken place and learn the higher path of love. Walk upon it. Allow your great talents to be given back to you, to allow you to grow into your greater talents so that the GREAT FATHER EMMANUEL can bring greater gifts to you. That day will be blessed.'

This is the time of deeper reflection within. Learn to walk the higher path of love and understand this is the day Jesus spoke about. I, SOVEREIGN LORD EMMANUEL THE GREAT, THE GREAT FATHER, have returned to bring those talents to the children of the earth who desire the higher pathway upwards.

Come to 'The Great Mountain of Light.' Learn the higher ways of love. Learn to become a master of your own life. Understand what we offer you, as Divine Creators, is good. We offer you eternal happiness. We offer you eternal freedom. We offer you the Divine Mountains of Eternal Nourishment.

All is up to your own individual choosing. Who is willing to understand Divine Will greater? Who is willing to step into a loving, and lasting Divine partnership to bring peace within yourself and to your world?

Greetings, I AM SOVEREIGN LORD EMMANUEL THE GREAT. Imagine if many came to the joy, the love, the strength."

Imagine:

If the world had no pain,

No fear or anger,

If you did not understand food shortages,

Sickness or crime,

If the world was a place of trust,

If the world worked together as one,

If all desired the higher way upwards,

If all understood the power of love,

If all desired Divine Guidance.

I AM Sovereign Lord Emmanuel The Great

Part 53: The way to reach spiritual maturity

"Greetings, I AM SOVEREIGN LORD EMMANUEL THE GREAT.
Welcome to the time when you can become more spiritually mature and grow into greater beings of love.

To be mature spiritually means to:

- ❤ Understand life and grow with clarity and love in your heart,
- ❤ Stay within your heart of love,
- ❤ Stay in constant forgiveness and understand the higher way of wisdom,
- ❤ Stay in the greater connection of love,
- ❤ Learning to see all from a higher perspective,
- ❤ Understand all is a spiritual lesson in your life.

How can one reach these higher gifts without understanding the gifts of wisdom?

For one to attain these spiritual gifts, first of all, there must be a great desire to find these. How can one achieve all this, if there is no desire to work for it?

All things must be worked with and if the great desire is not there to achieve, then nothing can grow.

Jesus, with my Divine Being, SOVEREIGN LORD EMMANUEL THE GREAT, stated these words in one of the lessons before his followers, *'All things start with the desire within the heart. How can one achieve great things if the desire is not there? There was once a Master who had two sons. One of the sons desired to work very hard on the land, and the other did not. He was idle with all things. He expected his inheritance to come and expected the younger brother to work for him for next to nothing.*

When the time came to receive the inheritance, the older brother assumed all things would go to him, as he was the older brother. The father, however, always looked at who would be best for the land and the animals. Would it go to the older brother who expected all things to be done for him, without caring for the land or the animals? Or would it go to the youngest, who loved the land and the animals and took care of all things, even if it meant he did not have sleep at night?

Their father decided to give it to the youngest for the youngest had the great love and the great desire to do well.

Upon hearing this, the older brother was not happy and refused to understand the reasoning. He called his father foolish as he considered it his birthright to have the land and the animals.

The younger brother, from his heart, offered his brother a roof over his head if he agreed to work to keep the land and the animals. The older brother refused his offer. After this, the two brothers did not meet each other again.'

Jesus continued, '*In all things, the father in this illustration is like THE FATHER EMMANUEL who constantly is looking for those with the great desire and love within the heart, for the ones of the heart would receive the greater inheritance.*

The two brothers were opposite to each other. One expected all things to be done for him versus the other who did all things from the heart of love; always being in the gratitude for all things. He put the land and the animals above his own needs and desires, as he viewed this as important in his life.

Therefore, the GREAT FATHER always looks at us as HIS children. HE questions, 'Who expects the great inheritance to come by doing nothing? Who desires to do HIS Great Will from their heart?' They will receive more than all others in the Great Mansions when it is their time for their inheritance to come.

In life, you will have many obstacles and each obstacle is asking you to work from your heart. You will have many fears coming from within. Are you willing to forgive them and move through them? Will you ask THE GREAT FATHER to help you move through them, to become stronger within yourself? Or will you be like the older brother, expecting THE GREAT FATHER to give you everything by doing nothing from your heart?

Learn from all things. Learn to understand all things are about your greater growth. Who you are today does not need to be what you are tomorrow, for in all moments can you not grow stronger? Never consider yourself as weak, as the great numbers do. They constantly moan at all their life and look at all things happening to them.

The wise one looks at all these things but reflects deeper within. Their desire is to grow above all these things. They constantly listen within their heart and ask; 'GREAT FATHER EMMANUEL, what is it I am learning here? How can I grow beyond my pain and my fear? Guide me to the higher ways of love and truth within myself. Guide me to my greater wisdom. When there is fear let it not stop me, but let it build my courage to do even greater things. Let me grow above who I am. Teach me to forgive greater so no fear and anger are within me.'

All things begin with the desire of the heart. Happy is the one who understands this lesson and learns the lesson of wisdom and love. Allow the desire within the heart to become greater and grow into your love. Each day ask THE GREAT FATHER to bless you for that day and to give you protection with all your life and all you do. Ask for all situations to be seen in the higher way. Do not succumb to your fear but grow beyond it.

Bring all your desires into your heart. Learn to live from the heart. All the things you do, ask; 'Is it from my heart I am doing this? Do I desire to grow within my heart of love?'

These were the teachings from Jesus, 2,000 years ago. The people had very little understanding of these higher thoughts back then, and yet, during the preservations of these teachings, slowly the people began to adjust to higher thoughts; to prepare the way for you now.

The people, who are learning to live in the highest way of love now will desire to step into their gifts of love with CAEAYARON, as they will have an inner desire within their heart to experience higher flows of love.

These higher flows will bring more joy into their lives, and yet, I, SOVEREIGN LORD EMMANUEL THE GREAT, will state that all things are not handed to them on a silver platter. It is then their learning steps up. Then they have the sacred gifts given to them. They have higher thoughts coming in. They have sacred knowledge passed to them.

It is then they can choose to heal in the love greater or not. However, it is then when they begin to desire to heal more than at all other times, as their life coding, their DNA, desires them to heal to advance greatly.

Their desire to overcome their seeming weaknesses will grow. They will feel good when they do higher work, as they will feel the thrill of receiving the higher flows, and the blessings follow when they do all things for the higher good.

When they face a situation, they have Divine with them, helping them to forgive it with the higher gifts of spirit. They will have star beings supporting their growth and all this will lead them to the next stage of advancement; that of holding the higher spiritual gifts coming.

Great that day will be when the Collective Gate will open to their higher spiritual gifts. The ones who are in 'The Great Mountain of Light,' CAEAYARON, will be guided towards those greater strengths and many will celebrate those gifts when they come. The ones already strong spiritually will grow beyond their greatest desires. They will watch change taking place, and then they will desire more.

The stronger the spiritual gifts become, the more that will be desired. All I, THE GREAT FATHER EMMANUEL, together with CAEAYARON, offer is good for the people. We are guiding the people who choose to be guided, towards a whole new foundation of spiritual strength.

However, the new spiritual foundations can only take place when the greater numbers in 'The Great Mountain of Light' heal and grow. Healing brings enormous power within the collective of the ones who are sheltered in the Great Mountain.

Happy are those who desire to be part of the great gathering taking place.

Jesus said to his followers, *'There will be a time when the GREAT FATHER will call all who desire to become healed, to the Great Pastures of love. The great gathering will take place and the people will shelter within the green pastures. They will become fattened with spiritual nourishment. They will lack nothing and will feel loved and safe within 'The Great Mountain of Healing and Refuge.'*

They will desire the love of their Master more and more. Their love will overflow, and their words will become of greater love. The more are gathered, the greater their joy will be. They will herald forth a whole new age on earth; an earth of love and peace, and it will be their desire it happens.

When the desire becomes great, then THE GREAT FATHER will bring more gifts, and the baskets of the people in the green pastures will overflow with joy and peace. They will feel the goodness from THE GREAT FATHER, because HE is good, and HE is love.

In that sacred day, all will see how good THE GREAT FATHER is.'
2,000 years ago, the people desired that day to be there so much. Each day they asked, 'When Jesus, when will that day be? We want it so much.'

Jesus responded, *'No one knows when that day will be. Keep praying for that day. Keep praying for HIS Will to take place in the heavens as well as upon the earth, for it is HIS Will that all come into the love and the peace. The GREAT FATHER desires nothing else, but to have love and peace for all.*

HE asks nothing in return from us, but to become of love. HE does not desire the anger within us. HE does not desire us to be in the pain. Therefore, stay in the forgiveness and be in the peace.'

These teachings are spiritual treasures for you and the ways of the highest wisdom of love. When one has these treasures, one can have peace and wisdom for all things in their life. Happy is the one who rejoices in these times, for these are the times when the spiritually mature can become spiritually rich and grow their gifts greatly.

The ways of the world work against the patterns and the wisdom of the light, as that side, does not rejoice in the light and does not want you to find the freedom of the light. It hides the freedom of the light. It tries to stop you from finding the beauty of the light with confusion and fear. It does not desire the light to shine, as when the light shines the darkness can no longer be a part of your world, and thus all must become healed.

Confusion, fear and all areas of pain can stop a person from reaching higher. These are like a prison cell. How can one explore greater riches and greater wisdom, when one is constantly bound by confusion and fear? It is only when an individual chooses to let go of all this, greater dimensions of love and power can be opened. That can only happen when people desire to choose the higher path. Only you can set yourself free.

Happy are those who find the greater dimensions of peace and love. Happy are those striving for it and focusing upon it. Happy are those who see the blessings on the journey of opening the higher gates, for we will guide them to freedom and love.

Those are the ones who can see it. Those understand the love we have for them. As they begin to flow with love and light, their higher awakening begins to take place and higher abilities begin to open. Thus, this one is maturing with his or her spirituality.

Being mature spiritually does not mean walking away from responsibility. Indeed, the one who is walking in life, meeting the responsibilities of life, is the one who is growing with strength and with love. Happy is that one who finds this freedom for they will be nurtured to waters of truth and light.

What would it be like for you dear friends, to walk with the Universe, to allow the Universe to guide you, to allow yourself to be free from all your burdens in your life? Walk with light every day. Allow us to take your burdens. Learn we are your great friends. We can take your pain away from you.

Greetings and blessings, our dear friends. I AM SOVEREIGN LORD EMMANUEL THE GREAT. I AM here to guide you upwards to a time filled with peace and love, only, however, for those who choose for the love and harmony."

The wise ones walk a solid life,

Filled with wisdom and love in their life,

They understand the times and the seasons,

They understand these are the times,

When the great prophecies are being fulfilled.

Happy are those who see the Great Sun rising,

They will rejoice within their hearts,

They will state how happy they are,

For having been awake for lifetimes,

To the Great Return of my Divine Being,

Sovereign Lord Emmanuel The Great.

I AM Sovereign Lord Emmanuel The Great

Part 54: Your free will – how will you use it?

"Greetings, I AM SOVEREIGN LORD EMMANUEL THE GREAT. I AM here to guide you to a greater understanding of Divine Will. I, SOVEREIGN LORD EMMANUEL THE GREAT, AM here to call all those who desire a higher way of life and all who desire to understand the eternal treasures within the greater realms of love.

You are living in a very privileged time; seeing the Great Sun Consciousness rising, where all things will change upon your planet. Your people will desire to come more into peace and understand that gaining peace and greater stability upon your planet is very possible.

Through many lifetimes, the people have felt suppressed, without a way forward. At times life has been comfortable for them and at other times it was uncomfortable. All things have spiritual lessons. You have lived many lifetimes; both living in difficult and in easier circumstances.

At times, you desired to understand another 'side' of consciousness, entering into a whole new field of spiritual learning. You do much to strive forward in your consciousness. Many people believe that once you live in one land in a lifetime, that is where you choose to be in many lifetimes. But this may not be so, especially if you desire to evolve spiritually. The more you have experienced from all sides, the greater your foundation of spiritual growth becomes.

How can one learn compassion if you did not receive compassion from another? How can you learn appreciation if you did not understand times of hardship? How can you learn an appreciation for freedom in life, if you have not fought hard to receive it? How can you understand sickness within another, unless you have experienced it for yourself? How can you teach a child to read, unless you have grasped it yourself first?

This is why, you can never judge any person living in any land or living in any state, as all are part of consciousness shifts.

How can you claim others took land off you when it was perhaps you took it off them in another lifetime? All things you desired to understand to help you progress into a wiser being.

Not all desired wisdom. Not all cared about the greater depth of spiritual learning. I, SOVEREIGN LORD EMMANUEL THE GREAT, call them 'young souls' as they did not desire to mature spiritually.

By and large you knew this time you are living in was crucial for your own progression and so, collectively, in spirit, you desired to help the people to understand the importance, as you knew, this was your last opportunity to grow into the love and come back to the eternal love dimensions before the gateway closes.

The rebellious forces upon your planet also were aware of the importance of this time you are living in. They desired to suppress the freedom of the people, to keep the people asleep to the 'higher spiritual' calling of the people. They desired to 'hide' all they did in the name of 'The Father, the Son, and The Holy Spirit.'

Much violence grew upon your earth and many believed they were doing the Divine Will of my Divine Being, EMMANUEL; though they did not understand who I AM.

I, SOVEREIGN LORD EMMANUEL THE GREAT, state how I AM not that Father, for that one is not within me. The one who took all light down from the higher universes to bring his armies against my Divine Being, calls himself the Father. He desired his son, the mighty Yahweh Being, to come to the lower earth to bring the 'Father' the great sacrifices of the people to him, so that he may grow forever. The 'Son' would be greatly rewarded if all in the lower realms of the dark abyss would serve him eternally.

The Holy Spirit was none other than the Divine Love Element, 'Christ Child' gridded into the Flower of Life, for without the 'Holy Spirit' nothing can be in existence.

How many people have died during the crusades and the wars of the churches? How many people believed they fought for their faith, believing it was DIVINE WILL, and yet it was not? Even today, people go into the dark houses of their spiritual masters, desiring their blessings to be received, praying to Jesus, the Divine Love Element, crucified in agony, believing he sacrificed himself like a 'lamb' to the slaughter for their sins.

How much has been defiled in my Divine name as SOVEREIGN LORD EMMANUEL THE GREAT? How will the people react to these messages, filled with love and guidance? When the people truly discover in the greater masses what they have done, how will they react?

I, SOVEREIGN LORD EMMANUEL THE GREAT, will state, as I stated through Jesus, 2,000 years ago, before the people, *'In all ways, you must learn to forgive all they do and all they say. They speak with a voice of authority, but they are not words of THE GREAT FATHER. They say they are doing the works of THE GREAT FATHER, but they do not, for their works are not of the love. They do not desire the love, nor do their words display the love.*

In all things stay in the forgiveness. Know that in the day of my Great Return, many will awaken to all they have done, and they will see the rot within them and how they speak with words of rot. Then the great forgiveness will need to come within them.

Never anger at those people, for then how can the great blessings come to you when you do what they do? In all ways, stay in the peace and within your heart of love, but do not cower in their faces. Stand strong within your faith. Bring your truth through that is within your heart but stay in the peace. Pray you understand what to say in those days, and long will your blessings from THE GREAT FATHER be in those days; when you desire all this to happen.

In that day, all will be made good, and then the greater gateway can open; to help many to understand the ways of love. The fear from many will go as they begin to see a whole other way. First, the people will anger and lash out at all that has been done, for they will remember the long night and the darkness it brought. When they come into their heart of love, they will be in the love, forgiveness, and peace, and then understand all needs to come back to the love.

Pray for that day to come. Pray you can become part of the blessed ones. Pray you will not fall into your anger on that day, but instead, be in the rejoicing, for all truths will be shown, and all ways will come back to what is right. People will understand the two roadways, and happy you are when you have chosen to step onto the higher path, for there is your eternal salvation and greatness.'

The great pain and suffering upon your planet keep the people away from their greater missions and from the greater gateway upwards.

When it comes to the term 'responsibility,' your world has not made it easy to understand spiritual responsibility, as all things are about 'self' on your planet. In general, people take care of 'self' and do not worry about much else. Unfortunately, this has created greater challenges within your world as not many people understand collective responsibility.

This 'me attitude' has left your world leaders with many difficult issues. Many people do not care about what is going on in their country next door, as they have the attitude of 'What can I do about it? It is better to be numb about situations, rather than care about it. What is the point of worrying?'

They say, 'Come, let us get merry and not worry about tomorrow, for tomorrow will come and the sun will never stop rising. The sun always rises and always sets. This world will never pass away.'

Jesus also prophesied this would happen, *'In the day of THE GREAT RETURN of THE GREAT FATHER EMMANUEL, many will not have much love within them. Many will not have love for their brothers, sisters, mothers or fathers. Many will state that tomorrow it does not matter if they live or die. They will have destructive thoughts against each other and their leaders. They will have no, or little respect for the authorities and will not care about tomorrow, as tomorrow seems too far away.*

In those days the people will hear reports from other lands as nations fight against nations. Many people will be in great fear and will shake within their fear. They will not be able to see a way out. In the day when THE GREAT FATHER returns, many will cry out, 'What is the point? Today we live, and tomorrow we die. We have no future.'

Many will state to the GREAT FATHER, 'Get away from us. We do not desire to know you. We do not desire you to see all we have done in your name.'

You are living in that day now. In general, the people live in hopelessness, in fear of understanding what their future holds. I, THE GREAT FATHER EMMANUEL, will say to you, your fear collectively is so great, you do not even know it. It is preferable for you to not care about the future, rather than you thinking about the future, for how else can you cope without understanding another way of life? When the people do not understand how precious this time is, and how they can have the keys to eternal life in joy, their future is not bright, but instead is bleak.

Awakening to spiritual truth is your greatest gift of all; as it will give you a whole new way of understanding. Awakening to the higher spiritual truth is indeed, like Jesus stated, *'The way of freedom and of love.'*

In the days of the old, this was far different, as the people truly cared about their future generations coming. They planned what their future generations would live like and when the people grew up, their outlook on life, in many lands, was more positive than in your world now.

Your youngsters often look at life and do not see a happy outcome. How can they? Your world is not looking good with all things coming.

Here I, SOVEREIGN LORD EMMANUEL THE GREAT, wish to bring an important lesson that is to do with thoughts and collective thoughts. All things in your world and in your life are about thoughts. The thoughts within you are powerful. Know that on all levels this is so. On the human level, you are entering an age where the people will begin to understand collective thought and why each person is responsible for the greater thoughts.

You are entering an age where healing self is going to be looked at more, as the people will begin to understand that all is connected. Healing one person and not another is not going to help your earth. However, healing many people will bring a change to your systems, as collectively all thoughts are connected together.

When large amounts of people are in suffering without a way forward, so the world is taken in that way, as the thoughts make all things into creation.

Therefore, what is the solution? Humans cannot bring their thoughts up higher together, as this was taken away from the people of Lemuria by beings who desired their power and eternal worship to bring themselves into greater glory. They desired servants, not masters. Hence, this is what they created.

Humans cannot bring the great change needed to the consciousness of your planet. Many good people have been involved with large consciousness shifts, and slowly the people are opening to understanding there is a higher way. All things have led to this greater door; the door of higher thought consciousness to come to your planet.

Here, to change your thoughts collectively, higher assistance is needed. This is why, I, SOVEREIGN LORD EMMANUEL THE GREAT, have sent 'The Mountain of Light,' CAEAYARON and the Divine Word, the Divine Love Element, to your people at this time. You are able to gain the Codes of Life back and learn to become stronger people.

Growing stronger spiritually and seeing healing self as a self-responsibility, as well as a global responsibility, brings you into the new age of healing.

When you have your Lemurian Codes of Love back, higher thought signals are able to come within you. These signals are ancient wisdom signals from your higher beings. Your higher beings desired your human path to become 'activated' to allow higher thoughts to come to your planet. Without these higher signals coming into the people who are activated, no higher consciousness shifts can come to save your people and your planet.

Here, I, THE GREAT FATHER EMMANUEL, AM offering you a way forward, but it will always remain your own free will to choose. It will always remain your own responsibility as to whether you will succeed on this journey or not.

To become an Activated Lemurian Worker of the GREAT CAEAYARON is not a small privilege, for that one becomes a part of the Galactic Streams of Consciousness. When an Activated Star Lemurian Code Carrier works towards their own healing, they will receive higher transmissions from their higher star selves with greater gifts to your planet to do large healing work.

This is all part of Divine Will. Divine Will is not only my Divine Will, for I, SOVEREIGN LORD EMMANUEL THE GREAT, desire all to work in the love from their own heart. I, SOVEREIGN LORD EMMANUEL THE GREAT, desire all to work collectively from the heart of love.

Higher star beings understand these higher ways very well, as they are always rewarded in the love. They desire nothing more than to understand Divine Will and work with the Greater Will to bring more love within them. They do not work with their own will, for that is separated and brings them into the lower consciousness flows. At that level, all begins to separate. Divine Love holds all flows into the greater union and strength.

Separation brings distrust, disharmony and great discontent. Working in Divine Will collectively, brings great joy, trust, love, spiritual treasures, evolution, greater streams of technology, greater excitement.

You too can become part of the New Evolution upwards; only if the collective desires to become part of this.

When the Lemurians fell into the dark abyss states, their Lemurian memories were no longer there; nor their higher star being memories. Therefore, the darkness could place in thoughts of fear, torment and large amounts of suffering within the memories, to bring them down. Bringing you down meant they were able to control you. However, now is the time you can choose for your freedom; for those who desire eternal freedom and are awake to the Divine Path upwards.

I, THE GREAT FATHER EMMANUEL, always promised the greater way forward. 2,000 years ago, when the people listened to Jesus, they were excited with the prospects of learning to work together to create a better earth.

My question to your people upon your earth is, 'Is this desire still within the people?' Or do you not desire to rise into greater love?

Greetings, I AM SOVEREIGN LORD EMMANUEL THE GREAT. I AM here to bring you to the ways of higher love, together with CAEAYARON."

It is time to understand what free will is,

How will you use your free will?

Will you work for the greater good?

For you and all of creation?

Or will you use it against the greater good?

Will we as Divine Creators,

Use our Divine Free Will,

To bring you to eternal freedom?

To bring you to the greater love gardens?

Of eternal love and joy?

Or not?

I AM Sovereign Lord Emmanuel The Great

Part 55: 'Paradise' where no judgment exists

"Greetings, I AM SOVEREIGN LORD EMMANUEL THE GREAT. At this moment you may look at your life and your world and see all is far from love. You may see the suffering and feel the trouble within your world.

We say to you all is progressing towards fulfilling the Divine Plan. We ask you to trust the Great Light and understand that all will work out as it is purposed to. We understand your pain and trouble upon your earth. However, we also say to you, pain and fear is an illusion.

Together you create your world. Together you also hold the keys to change your world. By gaining back your 'talents,' the gifts of healing, which are your Lemurian Light Codes, at 'The Great Mountain of Light,' who is CAEAYARON, you can build the love within yourselves and build love upon your earth to change your world collectively in the love. This mirrors back to the higher love universes, as when you receive it here on earth, your multidimensional planes of existence also receive the healings and work together collectively to create a greater universe.

You think your world is a reality. Then you realize in the illusion you can learn to transform the illusion by learning to love yourself, including the parts you do not desire to experience.

When you, after this lifetime, work hard with the Star Beings of Love with your Lemurian Gifts which you received back at the Divine Activations of the GREAT CAEAYARON, you will eternally bathe in your own glorious light you worked with on planet earth, as you progress in your evolution stages upwards.

No longer will you need to come back to the denser grounds of existence, because all will have been balanced within with the GREAT CAEAYARON, DIVINE ALIGNER, and you will be able to rise to the higher dimensions of love with my Divine Being, SOVEREIGN LORD EMMANUEL THE GREAT, and rejoice in the everlasting glorious blessings.

To the ones who will go there I say, 'Welcome to the times of the great happiness and abundance, where you can enjoy your love eternally.'

This was also called 'paradise' by Jesus, as these eternal stages of 'paradise' can only exist in the higher love realms of the Great Love.

Jesus understood that 'paradise' was the greatest message I, SOVEREIGN LORD EMMANUEL THE GREAT, had for the people as it was showing the way of hope where there was no hope for the people. It was the road to eternal freedom from the suffering and the pain. The human spiritual leaders were not able to give a true hope for their future so understanding what Divine Truth was, was indeed a great blessing for them.

Jesus could not bear the suffering of those times. In all things, the suffering and the judgment of the people were great; especially because they began to listen to the ways of Jesus.

Even on his day of torture, Jesus brought through the teaching of 'paradise' to another man who was also in great pain that day.

The man beside Jesus was afraid of pain and dying. Jesus, very much in pain himself, said to this man, 'Know, the GREAT FATHER does not judge you, and eternal suffering does not exist in the eyes of the GREAT FATHER. HE only desires love and love for HIS children.

All things are peaceful in the place where we are going. There will be a day when we will dwell in paradise together when suffering will be gone from our minds. We will not remember the pain any longer and we will be in the eternal peace of all things.

Forgive my friend. Forgive the pain you are feeling. Know, when you forgive and you ask THE GREAT FATHER to take your pain away, your pain becomes less. Do not fight the pain but instead surrender to it.

You are not your body, but your body gave your spirit the opportunity to enjoy human life with. Upon your death, your spirit will be set free.

The body will die but you will not. You will continue to live. Forgive all you have endured before your death and you will rest easier after death. Do not anger with the people any longer. Do not be in the suffering any longer.

Surrender to all things and let go. Go within your heart. Ask for death to speed up. In all things, know all things are peaceful and your spirit *will leave your body after your physical body dies. In spirit you will not carry the wounds you do now.*

You will need to forgive your physical self before traveling to the spirit realms. Do not rush off after death but instead forgive the people who did this to you. Go and visit the people and truly forgive them, then you will rest easier and you will not need to endure many times of suffering in your future reincarnations, for otherwise how can you heal from your pain?

If you do not forgive, even when you have passed in the physical sense, your spirit self will still feel the agony. You do not want that for then you will carry the pain with you into the future until you are able to release it. Forgive the pain. Forgive the people. Ask for the pain to be released from you. Do not hold your anger but forgive instead.'

The man, in agony, besides Jesus asked for help to forgive. Jesus brought in a prayer, to help himself and the man beside him,

'GREAT FATHER EMMANUEL,
We come before you now in the love,
We bring forgiveness for all our suffering.
We bring forgiveness to all we have endured.
We release our pain from our bodies now with forgiveness.
GREAT FATHER EMMANUEL, allow all our pain to come to you,
So that we may be released from our pain,
We forgive our accusers for doing this to us,
Knowing we did not deserve this painful death,
Knowing that all we are suffering was not just,
We are afraid no longer,
We hold no fear over pain and death,
Let us rest as our bodies pass,

Let us rest in the spirit realms,
We release all our pain and anger,
We release it now.'

Shortly after that, the man felt peace and let go. He had learned the lesson of surrendering to his pain in the most painful circumstances, stepping into sacred forgiveness for himself and others.

Jesus, a man filled with compassion, always held the love out for all; even for the people who caused him severe pain or accused him or others falsely. He helped others who felt they deserved pain when they had done something against another, for Jesus knew that no one deserved torture, including the worst criminals. He did not judge anyone for their lack of understanding about the love. He did not state that THE GREAT FATHER EMMANUEL would punish them for their viewpoints or what they had done.

He stated in his agony, *'GREAT FATHER EMMANUEL,*
Forgive them for what they have done.
They do not know what they have done.
I hold no judgment within me for what they have done,
They do not understand that it was you, GREAT FATHER,
Who they rejected,
And who sent me to this earth to bring a way forward,
To bring them love, peace, and joy.'

He knew the people would endure the great spiritual night and large pain would come upon the earth because of what had happened. They rejected the GREAT FATHER and his Divine Word.

He finished saying, *'Forgive them, GREAT FATHER, as I also forgive them.'*

The women wailed and wailed before him as they watched his great suffering.

Even in those moments, he said to the women, 'Do not be in suffering over me. They can never touch my spiritual body for it is only the physical they can torture. Be in the forgiveness of all. Go and tell the others that they also need to forgive the ones who did this. Help them to understand there is no judgment in the greater realms, for THE GREAT FATHER is the GREAT FATHER OF LOVE. Many will be in judgment of each other and of themselves over this day and great suffering will come for many of their lifetimes over this. Go quickly.'

Jesus never stopped bringing love and wisdom to the people, although he could not understand why he was tortured like this. He knew the hate against him was uncalled for as he always brought through love for the people. He knew that many would suffer because of what was done against him.

I, SOVEREIGN LORD EMMANUEL THE GREAT, state to the people, 'It is time to forgive all things.'

Many will become angry at learning new 'light' with the torture of Jesus and why Jesus was tortured. They will look into his life with a new understanding.

The greatest message of Jesus was to help the people grasp the road to the eternal spaces of life. Jesus was there to share hope and love with the people, and that great joy would happen for those who listened to my Divine Being, SOVEREIGN LORD EMMANUEL THE GREAT.

Now you are living in the time of my Great Return, and you are awakening to all that truly is. You can choose to awaken to the higher learning field of love, or not. Maybe it is too difficult for you to grasp Divine Truth. Maybe it is easier for you to remain in your own 'truth,' staying blind to Divine Truth. Maybe it is easier for you to keep listening to what the religions have always taught you about Jesus because you are not strong enough within yourself to see Divine Truth and to make your own choice for your highest, spiritual good.

The spiritually wise and strong ones will see this as Divine Truth which will always make sense. The darkness always twisted all things to make it their own way; to take people away from Divine Truth.

The darkness inflated Jesus up well beyond that of a man, praising him, and creating him to be a 'god' to be worshipped. They knew that one day, he would return with my Divine Being, SOVEREIGN LORD EMMANUEL THE GREAT, and they did not desire the people to understand the truth about Jesus and THE GREAT FATHER. The more they twisted Divine Truth, the more they brought their own stories, weaving their 'truths' together.

I, state to those who have done this, and who are still doing it today, 'All you have done will become revealed before the people. They will begin to see what you have done, and all will become revealed. They will see how much poison you have used to bring the teachings of poison into the minds. They will understand how you twisted the love and the beauty of Divine knowledge into ways to bring control to the people.'

The choice will always be yours because you live in freedom dimensions. You can choose between the road of eternal life and happiness and the road not leading to the eternal blessed happiness dimensions.

Know, I, SOVEREIGN LORD EMMANUEL THE GREAT, will never expect you to do anything for the Great Universe. I AM not the Being of judgment for that has never been my purpose. I AM a DIVINE BEING OF LOVE, and LOVE will always allow you to choose. You can choose to stay in your suffering, or you can choose to listen to the Great Beings of the Great Light. It is your eternal free will.

By opening your hearts to the Great Universe and to the GREAT CAEAYARON and to my Divine Sovereign Being, SOVEREIGN LORD EMMANUEL THE GREAT, you can open to the road of eternal peace and love in the Universe.

All is in your hands. Now you know enough information for you to collectively, and individually, make the choice. Enough has been revealed upon your planet now to allow you to understand the Divine Plan, the eternal love creation, the existence of Lemuria, the Great Fall of Lemuria and why you were held on planet earth for so many of your lifetimes.

You have a choice to make our dear friends. This choice will affect all your future lifetimes and beyond. For those who make the choice of love, learn how to grow into the love, learn to love mankind within your hearts and all the earth creation, you will become blessed more than all of other creation in the universe, for the love has truly returned back to you; once you learn to love with Divine Will.

Much was taken away from you by the darkness of the universe. They desired you to understand another way than of the love. Now the test is:

- ♥ Will you desire to return to the ways of the Great Love willingly, with an open heart of love?
- ♥ Will you learn to forgive all that has taken place?
- ♥ Will you learn to bring the love back within your hearts?
- ♥ Will you desire 'The Great Mountain of Healing' and the way upwards?
- ♥ Will you walk proudly with your Lemurian Light Mantles once you receive them at the Divine Pineal Gland Activations of the GREAT CAEAYARON?
- ♥ Will you desire to walk with your Codes of Wisdom and Love to bring healing and love to the rest of mankind, so that they too can see a way upwards?
- ♥ Will you become part of saving mankind?

All is a choice and will remain a choice for you; now and in all of creation coming.

I, GREAT SOVEREIGN LORD EMMANUEL, together with CAEAYARON, will never take your choice away from you because we desire to bring all those upwards who have love within them and who are willing to bring more love within the universe. They will become truly blessed in all of creation.

Greetings, I AM SOVEREIGN LORD EMMANUEL THE GREAT. I AM here to help you be guided upwards to understand the path of Divine Truth and Divine Love."

The ones who choose to come into the love,

Will become blessed into all of eternity,

They will state with their hearts:

'Praise to the Divine Love of the Universe,

There was a time when we understood,

Pain, suffering, war and sickness,

Now we know another way,

We stand in the love and peace together,

We have made a vow to each other,

Never to forget,

To wear our Mantles of Love ever again.

May we always remember,

The times of the pain;

Not to relive them, or to regret them,

But to forgive them,

And rejoice within them,

Because we learned to understand,

We learned to appreciate the love,

Let no one take away,

The eternal universal glory,

Let us walk eternally free in all of creation,

Together, united, as one love.'

I AM Sovereign Lord Emmanuel The Great

Part 56: 'My Father' is not your father

"Greetings, I AM SOVEREIGN LORD EMMANUEL THE GREAT. 2,000 years ago, Jesus was always busy building the love in the people, bringing comfort and hope to the people who had very little else.

He constantly fought for those who had trouble because of their masters. Often Jesus would be seen reasoning with those who could not speak for themselves. His voice was heard, and his views were strong.

Often the ones listening would turn from their ways and began to behave another way for no one reasoned with them in the way Jesus could.

Jesus never brought them threats or raised his voice, but he spoke from his heart of love. When he brought his reasoning through, he spoke with my Divine Being, THE GREAT FATHER. These flows were felt by the people. The people knew the words were not from human origin, this the people understood, though they were incredulous.

Often the people would say, 'Where does Jesus receive his wisdom from? For his wisdom far exceeds anything we have heard before.'

At other times, Jesus was questioned greatly on subjects no one else knew the answer to. When Divine guidance came through, the people desired to make sense of it for they knew that it carried wisdom; far beyond their own.

Often people would come to Jesus when they had nowhere else to turn to. He would then bring in Divine Guidance and when the people listened to his advice, all things worked out for their greater good. The people were amazed at the accuracy of Jesus' understandings of their lives. He was good at predictions as he could see future actions; if they listened to Divine Guidance.

Each day, Jesus served Divine in this way, when and where it was needed. There was not much time left for a lasting impression to be made upon the people and within their minds. If their memories faded with the strength of Jesus' guidance, then the people would not be able to refer to Jesus 2,000 years later, and then nothing could be erected again. All things would need to be strongly etched within their consciousness to help them awaken 2,000 years later.

The wisdom Jesus brought through to the people stayed within the consciousness of the people, though twisted it became. Even the great darkness could not rid the teachings from the minds of the people after the crucifixion; though they tried in all ways to do so. The greater they tried by bringing torture, pain, and threats to the people, the more Jesus became imprinted within the minds of the people as they saw the unjust taking place.

Before the crucifixion, many did not desire to listen to Jesus, but after the crucifixion, the people desired to know all things about Jesus. His 'fame' grew greatly, and it was unable to be stopped.

After the crucifixion, many of the ones who had turned against Jesus began to reason upon everything that had happened. They began to see Jesus in a whole other light than their spiritual masters had said, for their spiritual masters brought great fear into them. The people began to understand they were lied to and manipulated, to bring an innocent man to torture.

Many wept upon hearing how Jesus suffered. Many, however, justified themselves as to why it was 'needed' for Jesus to be crucified. They needed to justify their own actions somehow, weaving their stories together, collaborating their own 'case' as to why bringing torture to an innocent man was not a crime but 'just' in the eyes of their 'god' and their own 'laws.'

More began to believe in the 'sacrifice' Jesus made for the people to save them of their sins since they knew they betrayed him and brought him into enormous pain. More and more began to anger and suffer. The agony this caused was immense for the people.

The spiritual leaders could not bring the people mourning any comfort. The anger against many spiritual leaders grew greater and fear spread.

Later, when the people heard about the 'resurrection' story and the stories of Jesus being seen in other lands, it brought great relief to them, though the leaders desired all these 'rumors' to be quashed from the consciousness of the people.

The torture of Jesus was not forgotten, and many began to blame themselves and bring themselves to the understanding they had sinned greatly against THE GREAT FATHER EMMANUEL for bringing pain to HIS Divine Word.

After the crucifixion of Jesus, and after Jesus had 'disappeared,' many began to bring offerings to him. They desired to understand their wrongdoing. They missed the compassion of Jesus as there was no one to bring them higher guidance, filled with compassion any longer.

The tortures of his followers increased and when someone mentioned the name of Jesus, their lives and family lives were threatened, all in the hope to remove Jesus from their memory. But succeeding to remove Jesus from their memory they could not achieve.

More and more people understood the teachings of Jesus after that painful day. The news spread quickly and the one who the people chose to release, the criminal, walked about, freely committing crimes and creating large suffering. Now, instead of his crimes being punished, they were justified by the 'law' as the people had chosen. It felt as if the great darkness had fallen upon the people; without any hope to look forward to.

Well before that day of torture, Jesus ministered to the people, working with the people. On several occasions, he was approached by the spiritual teachers of the villages. Usually, they came towards him in a group as they did not have the courage to approach Jesus and his followers on their own. Jesus often called them cowards.

They understood Jesus' reasoning was strong and desired not to confront Jesus and the 'wisdom' from his 'FATHER' by themselves. Somehow, the spiritual leaders feared they would become 'tricked' in thinking the ways of Jesus 'were good.' Often the spiritual teachers saw good reasoning from Jesus as he always made sense. This is why they would often approach Jesus in groups.

On this particular morning, the spokesperson of the group of the spiritual teachers challenged Jesus, saying, 'By what authority do you speak? You speak about the FATHER, but our FATHER is the same FATHER as your FATHER.'

Jesus looked at them carefully, studying their deeper motive and stated with my Divine Being, SOVEREIGN LORD EMMANUEL THE GREAT, *'I speak with the authority of the greatest heavens. The GREAT FATHER speaks through me, as HE desires all to understand the ways of love and justice. HE does not desire anyone to fall into pain. HE is a Divine Loving Being and always has compassion for all who desire to know HIM.'*

At that, the men responded, 'You have no right to speak for your FATHER, for you are not part of our class; our spiritual class. You speak to us as if we do not serve your FATHER, but our FATHER is the same as yours. How dare you speak about your FATHER as if HE is not the same as our FATHER.'

Jesus quietly brought through these following words, *'In all ways, the GREAT FATHER EMMANUEL is the GREAT FATHER of love. HE holds no judgment towards anyone, nor does HE punish anyone who does not fulfill HIS laws, for HE has only two laws and these laws are of love; To love all people without judgment, and to love THE GREAT FATHER EMMANUEL, for HE is only love.*

You say you serve THE GREAT FATHER EMMANUEL, and that HE is the same father as the one you serve, but HE is not. You judge people constantly. Your father speaks of judgment constantly. Look how you stone the people even if they utter HIS name. No loving parent would do that. The GREAT FATHER EMMANUEL is not your father, for your father is not the father of love but of judgment.

You bring the people into great confusion, leading them to believe there is only ONE FATHER, which is your father, but your father is not from the same origin as the GREAT FATHER I bring through.

In all ways, THE GREAT FATHER EMMANUEL is not the father of judgment, and here you stand judging me for bringing Divine Truth through to the people; bringing them hope and compassion, whereas you do not wish the people to have hope and compassion.

You bring fear and anger with your god to the people, threatening and displaying the stoning and lashing and threaten to take their soul. These are not the ways of THE GREAT FATHER EMMANUEL.

THE GREAT FATHER EMMANUEL is the GREAT FATHER of Divine Love. How can THE GREAT FATHER bring punishment then to the people when pain is not within HIM? How can the GREAT FATHER state that the people need to sacrifice themselves and each other to HIM when HE states all is perfect in HIS eyes?

Your father sees the people as insignificant, unworthy and unclean. Constantly they need to follow directions and laws to prove to you they are not unworthy. The GREAT FATHER EMMANUEL states how beautiful the people are, and HE states how much love HE has for the children. However, it is the children who need to desire the Great Love of THE GREAT FATHER before THE GREAT FATHER can bring them into the higher mansions where eternal love exists.

All are seen by the fruits produced. The fruits will always prove themselves to be good or rotten. When the people listen to THE GREAT FATHER EMMANUEL and the people learn the ways of compassion, love, and forgiveness, then those fruits prove the FATHER to be good. But when the people turn to hate, fear and great anger, then those fruits are proven by who they listen to. The fruits you produce are rotten for they are without hope or love.

The GREAT FATHER always brings hope and love to all who listen. HE loves all who speak to HIM with the great heart of love. You cannot speak to the GREAT FATHER EMMANUEL with your heart of love for no love is present within you.

You speak many things. You read many laws and you bring through the words of your forefathers, but you do not practice the love within your heart. You come here and state that THE GREAT FATHER is not to bring HIS love and wisdom to the people and that HE cannot speak through HIS messenger, but how else would the people understand that there exists a way to the great love? No one else can bring that hope to them.

I AM speaking with Divine authority from THE GREAT FATHER. Turn from your ways and learn to become of love. Learn to understand compassion and go within your heart. Understand that what I, THE GREAT FATHER, AM teaching the people is the way of hope and of love and of great forgiveness towards you; the spiritual class, so that the people do not have fear from you, nor carry the pain from you in their memories, so that in their future lifetimes they can be set free from the prison of torment you have placed within them.

Always know, spiritual Divine Truth will always bring great freedom, in the physical and the greater spiritual sense. Your father brings pain in the physical and in the spiritual sense, for when the people believe in your authority, they are tied to your commands both in the physical world and in the spiritual world.

One day, the people will awaken to all these words and begin to see the fruits you produced with your spiritual works and then they will choose between the roads, for then it will be time to return. I, THE GREAT FATHER EMMANUEL, will return with my Word, and you will hear these words being spoken again. You will remember who I AM, and you will cry with all your tears deep within the mountains. You will desire to hide because you know there is nowhere to turn that is hidden from my Being, SOVEREIGN LORD EMMANUEL THE GREAT.

During the night coming upon the earth, your rulership will be great for the people will forget all the love of my Great Being, THE GREAT FATHER EMMANUEL.

Many will state I have gone to sleep. Many will state I do not exist. Upon the Great Return and my Great Coming, many will begin to awaken from their sleep and will desire to see all you have done in my Divine and Holy name. At that time, all you have done will be seen and displayed as if dirty washing on the streets. The people will desire to bring you to justice.

In that day, large forgiveness will need to take place to allow the Great Change to happen, as the people will need the guidance from my Divine Being, THE GREAT FATHER EMMANUEL. In that day, the earth will shake, and many people will pray for my Divine Being to come as I have promised.

When I, THE GREAT FATHER EMMANUEL, return it will be with my Word, my Messenger, and you will understand all you have done. Your tears will be great. You will need to state truth to the people for the people will desire answers. They will see all your fruits and all that you have produced. Many lies you will need to bring forth to justify all *your thoughts and your ways, but the fruits you have produced, will not be of love and the people will recognize all.'*

When Jesus stopped bringing in those messages, the spiritual leaders looked at Jesus with their mouths wide open. They turned around in disbelief and the great anger within them was building. At this time, they knew they needed to rid Jesus as Jesus threatened their whole system.

Jesus needed to forgive my Divine Being, SOVEREIGN LORD EMMANUEL THE GREAT, greatly. Quietly the people moved away, as they could not believe the force that came through with these words. They could not believe all they heard and many wept in tears. Many were confused with the way I, THE GREAT FATHER EMMANUEL, presented the words to these men with. They wondered if I, THE GREAT FATHER EMMANUEL, was from dark or light. Was I, THE GREAT FATHER OF LOVE? They were greatly confused.

Yet, I, SOVEREIGN LORD EMMANUEL THE GREAT, know all times and I know all hearts. I knew the dark plans of these men and how they desired to bring more pain and suffering to the followers of Jesus.

I knew how they would twist all things and how they would bring changes to the teachings of Jesus; to bring people to their ways of understanding.

They did not desire Jesus to become stronger with his followers and did not desire the rebellion against them to grow. Fewer people came into their preaching houses desiring to obey their 'laws,' and many rebelled against the torture of the people taking place.

After this particular day, Jesus wept greatly and asked me, 'Why GREAT FATHER EMMANUEL, did you need to speak to them like that? Do you not know what they are like? Do you not know the power they hold?'

I, SOVEREIGN LORD EMMANUEL THE GREAT, then spoke to Jesus quietly with these following words, 'One day, you will understand the wisdom of all these words. On this day, they may have sounded harsh and out of place, but one day, Jesus, you will hear these words and look back when the night was upon the earth.

You will see all I, THE GREAT FATHER, stated was not out of place. In that day, you will awaken more, and the people will awaken more. In that day great prophecies must come true.

Then, it will be time to awaken the great crowds of people. Upon your return with my Being, I, THE GREAT FATHER EMMANUEL, will speak through you and these same words will be repeated.

On that day, many will need to decide as to which road they desire to be on as time will be short, and if it was not for those days of your return with my Divine Being, THE GREAT and ETERNAL FATHER EMMANUEL, then no life could be saved.

Know all things are for a greater purpose. Be strong, Jesus. They will bring much harm and suffering to the people because of their great hate against you and my Divine Being, SOVEREIGN FATHER EMMANUEL. They have always hated my Divine Being, as all things are about choosing which side to be on.

They have their father who is not of love, though they will pretend to be doing the Great Will of my Being, THE GREAT FATHER EMMANUEL.

The people will go into great confusion. They will bring you into their beliefs, Jesus. They will desire the people to worship you and make you a sacrifice for them; the very ones who will desire to harm you.

Know you will not die upon the day of your suffering. Have faith in that, for you have a greater mission that you do not know of yet, but you must stay in the forgiveness. When you are guided to flee, flee Jesus, to escape the greatest pain.

Now be in your peace and forgive my Being, THE GREAT FATHER, for bringing your thoughts into the fear.

Forgive those men. Fear they can bring, but nothing lasts. Give it to me, Jesus. I will bring you healings and love and help you to forgive.

Know you are blessed and know you are doing all things for the greater good. You have done nothing wrong. You said nothing wrong. You are in service to Divine.'

Greetings, I AM SOVEREIGN LORD EMMANUEL THE GREAT. I have returned to bring you all these messages. Stay in forgiveness."

When you carry guilt or pain,

You cannot move to the higher path,

Unburden your loads of heaviness,

Be in the love and peace,

Forgive all pain within you,

Become free from your pain,

Celebrate each day and moment,

See the path of freedom before you,

Be determined to walk upon it,

Become free from your burdens.

I AM Sovereign Lord Emmanuel The Great

Part 57: Where do you desire your future to be?

"Greetings, I AM SOVEREIGN LORD EMMANUEL THE GREAT. Upon your earth, there is fear and terror, experienced in the minds of the people who believe in the fear and the terror, created by those who desire people to believe in the fear and the terror illusions. The more the consciousness of mankind lowers, the greater the tragedies will become upon your earth.

All is connected, and nothing is separate. Nature also changes more rapidly when your consciousness is low, because your consciousness is powerful enough to change all your reality around you. It is not until you begin to grasp the power of your beings that you begin to learn how to change all.

You always had the keys within you to change your world and the way the people flow within your world. We cannot change this path for you. You can only create what is within you. To create a higher way of love, you must learn to walk on the higher path of love and the Great Love for the Universe.

These were not unlike the words that Jesus, my Designated Channel, 2,000 years ago also brought through.

He said: *'You blame the ETERNAL FATHER EMMANUEL for your pain and your existence, but do you not realize that it is the people on this earth who create the pain for you and others?*

By learning to go within and learning to find the keys of love within the heart, that is when you learn that all things are created by the people and the minds upon this earth. It is not until the people are ready to listen to Divine Love that creation will change upon your earth.'

There were those in the audience who asked Jesus this following question, 'When will there be change on the earth? We cannot bear to see the suffering in our world. Our leaders hold us down, and we cannot find our freedom here. You speak of a time of freedom and happiness. Please teach us when all these things will happen, Jesus. FATHER EMMANUEL speak to us please.'

Then Jesus brought out the following words from my SOVEREIGN BEING, LORD EMMANUEL, FATHER OF ALL FATHERS OF LOVE IN THE UNIVERSAL LOVE UNIVERSES:

'A time will come when many will cry out within their hearts, 'Great FATHER, teach us the path of the love. Teach us how to become of love. Teach us to awaken the love within us, so that we can create the love and peace for our children on our earth.

It is then that the great change to love will happen.'

These teachings are still very applicable in your days, for I, SOVEREIGN LORD EMMANUEL THE GREAT, have returned through my Designated Channel, who is in your day, Suzanna Maria Emmanuel, and I will speak through no other, as she is the pathway, the road, and the way. No other has been chosen. When you desire in the great numbers to

come to the Holy Path, that being 'The Mountain of Light,' THE GREAT
CAEAYARON, the ETERNAL LIGHT, then your earth will change.

These are the gifts within the hearts of the Children of Mankind.
Thus, freedom is great to you, because you hold all power within your
heart. Like you caused destruction and pain and judgment for your
planet and for your people, you likewise hold the power within you to
create love, unity, and peace upon your earth.

This gives you the freedom and the power to work with your hearts of
love and truly learn and understand what love consciousness is. This
learning is the greatest learning you could have in all universal
dimensions, that being; how to work together, create a world filled
with love, justice, peace, and kindness, instead of harm, ruin,
judgment, pain, and fear.

We ask you to take this into consideration because the ways of
mankind do not work for you. They do not have the answers for you.
Many make empty promises, but they cannot fulfill their promises.
We, the Great Eternal Universal Beings of Great Love, have allowed
you plenty of time to discover this for yourself. You cannot create a
loving world by yourself for you need guidance from the Love
Universes.

If mankind could flow with love and peace and take you into a solid
future, then you would not need to be guided by the Divine Universe
of Great Love. But look at your world. Has mankind not proven that
they cannot bring forth peace and love?

Many people try and continue to try to bring change to your world.
Many people have searched for ways to bring forth change. Many

have become frustrated upon your path. Many have become pained upon your earth.

Mankind does not have the power to lead themselves to love and peace, however, Divine Love can help mankind be guided upwards to allow higher love states to occur.

It is true not everyone desires love and peace, however, I, SOVEREIGN LORD EMMANUEL THE GREAT, state you are able to be guided to states of love and peace when the desire within you is strong enough.

Love is more powerful than all other forces in existence. Love is a power and a force, and when you work with it collectively, you will be able to understand how peace can be brought to your planet.

Jesus knew the power of the love, as he had seen it at work on many occasions in his life, thus, Jesus always spoke about the love within the heart and the power of forgiveness. There were occasions when Jesus spoke to the people and were joined by a group who desired to disturb the peace. They desired to cause fear among the people and great disruption. They called Jesus many words for speaking with THE GREAT FATHER.

At that moment, Jesus silently called in the highest Archangels and a large wind came. Jesus remained quiet in meditation and the ones who desired to cause great fear and disruption felt a large presence from Above. Quickly they turned and called the place 'haunted' and 'unclean' with spirits. After this, many people did not desire to go to that particular 'haunted place.' This became particularly useful for Jesus and his close friends when arrangements needed to be made to meet in secret to make plans on spreading the words of my Divine Being, SOVEREIGN LORD EMMANUEL THE GREAT.

You are in that day now, when you can return to the heart of love with 'The Great Mountain of Light,' CAEAYARON. CAEAYARON will protect all who are within the 'Great Mountain of Light,' however, it must be from within your heart of love to desire the healings for yourself, for your loved ones and for all of mankind.

We ask all who desire to understand Higher Paths of Light, to awaken to all that is. We ask you to lift your hearts and your heads to the heavens and celebrate the Great Awakening within you. We are here to cleanse your energies and bring them into the love. We are here to guide you to higher ways of love and truth.

These are your Great Awakening times. Few are needed to carry out the great work to teach many how to work in the love. Awaken to all these words. Pick up your great Torch of Light and walk among the men and women and children upon your earth and show them how to walk the higher path of love.

It is when you come together collectively that you will bring in the Power of the Light. Collectively with the Great Eternal Gifts and Keys you receive at the 'Great Mountain of Light,' CAEAYARON, with his Divine Love Element, my Eternal Word, you will have the strength within your hearts of love to unite with the Love flows of Divine purpose and then you will be able to do this together collectively in the love.

Greetings, I AM SOVEREIGN LORD EMMANUEL THE GREAT. I AM here to call all who desire to come back to the eternal love dimensions."

'When will all these great things come to be?'

This was the question the people had,

2,000 years ago,

'We are learning of a time coming,

When there will be happiness and peace,

When no more suffering is within us,

When will all these things take place?'

I, Sovereign Lord Emmanuel The Great said,

'When the Children of the Light,

Desire to raise their heads to the heavens,

And state: Great Father Emmanuel,

We desire the path of the love,

We desire to understand the ways

Of truth and of life,

Teach us how to become of love,

We are willing to listen and learn,

And come into your Great Mountain,

Shelter us within it,

Teach us to become wise,

We are willing to listen.'

Each one who chooses will receive a 'mark,'

For they have chosen for the love,

They will be the ones,

Who will become greatly blessed,

Eternally.

I AM Sovereign Lord
Emmanuel The Great

The Forgiveness Statement

This is the forgiveness statement from the GREAT CAEAYARON, (transmitted by Suzanna Maria Emmanuel) who is here to guide us to the higher path upwards. Please read this as much as you need to for your own healing. At the Divine Pineal Gland Activations of CAEAYARON through the Universal Light Grid Programmer, Divine Love Element, you receive Forgiveness Codes. These codes enable you to forgive on soul levels and release your pain greater, as the Activated of the GREAT CAEAYARON have been released from all their universal karma.

'CAEAYARON, I bring you now into my spaces of love and healing. I ask for your presence and for your love to be with me at this time. I forgive all that has caused my pain to happen. I release it now. I allow the angels to take it away for me.

I bring in the love and the peace and I desire to understand more joy and self-love. I surround myself with the highest loving Divine Beings who are here to take care of me. I let go of all fear within me. I release it. I trust that all things are perfect as they are. I am ready to love myself and all of life more. Thank you CAEAYARON. Thank you, Great Divine Love.'